DATE		

© THE BAKER & TAYLOR CO.

A publication in
The Adult Education Association
Handbook Series in Adult Education

Comparing
Adult Education
Worldwide

Alexander N. Charters
and Associates

Comparing
Adult Education
Worldwide

Jossey-Bass Publishers
San Francisco • Washington • London • 1981

COMPARING ADULT EDUCATION WORLDWIDE
by Alexander N. Charters and Associates

Copyright © 1981 by: Adult Education Association
of the United States of America
810 Eighteenth Street, N.W.
Washington, D.C. 20006

Jossey-Bass Inc., Publishers
433 California Street
San Francisco, California 94104

Jossey-Bass Limited
28 Banner Street
London EC1Y 8QE

Library of Congress Cataloging in Publication Data

Charters, Alexander N
  Comparing adult education worldwide.

  Bibliography: p. 245
  Includes index.
  1. Adult education. 2. Comparative education.
I. Title.
LC5215.C5   374   80-8911
ISBN 0-87589-494-1

Manufactured in the United States of America

JACKET DESIGN BY WILLI BAUM

FIRST EDITION

Code 8107

THE JOSSEY-BASS SERIES IN HIGHER EDUCATION

The AEA Handbook Series in Adult Education

WILLIAM S. GRIFFITH
University of British Columbia

HOWARD Y. MCCLUSKY
University of Michigan

General Editors

Edgar J. Boone
Ronald W. Shearon
Estelle E. White
and Associates
Serving Personal and
Community Needs Through
Adult Education

April 1980

Huey B. Long
Roger Hiemstra
and Associates
Changing Approaches
to Studying Adult
Education

April 1980

John M. Peters
and Associates
Building an Effective
Adult Education
Enterprise

April 1980

Alan B. Knox
and Associates
Developing, Administering,
and Evaluating
Adult Education

October 1980

Robert D. Boyd
Jerold W. Apps
and Associates
Redefining
the Discipline
of Adult Education
October 1980

Burton W. Kreitlow
and Associates
Examining Controversies
in Adult Education
March 1981

Alexander N. Charters
and Associates
Comparing
Adult Education
Worldwide
March 1981

Foreword

Adult education as a field of study and of practice is not well understood by many literate and intelligent American adults whose exposure to the field has been limited to one or a few aspects of its apparently bewildering mosaic. Since 1926, when the American Association for Adult Education (AAAE) was founded, the leaders of that organization and its successor, the Adult Education Association of the U.S.A. (AEA), have striven to communicate both to the neophytes in the field and to the adult public an understanding of its diverse and complex enterprises. A major vehicle for accomplishing this communication has been a sequence of handbooks of adult education, issued periodically to convey a broad view of the mosaic. In 1934, 1936, and 1948 the AAAE published the first three handbooks. Although the Association had intended to issue a handbook every two years, that plan was not carried out for a number of reasons, including the outbreak of World War II and the termination of support by the Carnegie Corporation. Within three years of the publication of the 1948 handbook the Association dissolved itself in order to establish the AEA, which included the former members of both the AAAE and the Department of Adult Education of the National Education Association. It was nine years before the AEA was able to publish its first handbook, the fourth in the sequence, followed a decade later by the fifth version.

In the early 1970s both the Publications Committee of AEA and the Commission of the Professors of Adult Education (an affiliated organization of the AEA) explored the kinds of handbooks that could be designed to serve the changing nature and needs of the field. They found that different parts of the field were developing at different rates—in some areas information was becoming outdated rapidly, whereas in others a decennial handbook would be adequate to maintain currency. Moreover, the growing literature and the many developments in policies and programs led them to conclude that a single volume of traditional size would not be sufficient to treat the expanding knowledge base, the changing policies and practices, and the controversial topics in adult education. Accordingly, the Publications Committee decided that the next handbook would consist of several volumes, allowing the presentation of an increased amount of information on each of eight selected parts of the field and preparing the way for subsequent revisions of each volume independently on a schedule reflecting the pace of change in each area. The result is The AEA Handbook Series in Adult Education, which is being developed by the general editors with the guidance and assistance of the Publications Committee.

In this volume in the series, the authors have sought to demonstrate how adult educators deal with common problems in a wide variety of ways in different cultural, political, economic, and social settings. They explain why the term *comparative international adult education* is required as they distinguish between it and comparative education, an area of scholarship that can be pursued intranationally. This book both surveys the field and points a beacon to the future.

The authors have addressed the task of identifying practices and policies from the developing world that seem to hold promise if duplicated in the industrialized, urbanized nations. Such a perspective is promising, for it acknowledges the strengths of each culture and encourages emulation of the most attractive elements by other nations, rather than assuming modernization is an unmixed blessing that ought to be shared with enlightened Third World countries for their own good. The authors' hypothesis, which is well supported by their arguments and evidence, is that adult educators in each country can profit from studying the institutions and practices of their counterparts in other countries.

Unlike much of the literature available to monolingual Anglophones in the Western world, this volume of the handbook series pierces the iron curtain objectively and presents a sweeping overview of adult education as both a field of study and practice in the Eastern European socialist countries and in the Soviet Union. Students of adult education who are well versed in the history of adult education in the United Kingdom, the United States, and Canada will find it enlightening to learn about parallel historical developments between their nations and these socialist countries in the education of adults in the nineteenth and twentieth centuries. These brief historical sketches should help alleviate the provincialism of those adult educators whose knowledge of both institutions and practices is limited to their own nation.

By focusing on the nature and level of development of comparative international adult education research, this volume presents a frank appraisal of its current shortcomings as well as some visions for the future. Each chapter is valuable not only because of the factual analytical and evaluative information it presents but also because it provides a case study of one of the research approaches that characterizes the field.

In examining the evolution of professionalization cross-nationally and in analyzing the roles all international associations of adult educators have played and are playing, the authors provide a perspective for considering the special opportunities university prepared adult educators have for learning from each other and in using that knowledge for the good of the profession, the field, and the public. By drawing upon experience in other cultures and in unsuccessful international associations, the reader may gain an appreciation of the underlying commonality of practice as well as of the formidable barriers to be overcome in developing a sound, financially self-sustaining international association that can surmount petty provincial nationalistic concerns.

Comparing Adult Education Worldwide brings together many of the most highly respected and well-known authorities in comparative international adult education worldwide. As the first English language volume of its kind, it provides the benchmark against which progress in the field will be measured over the next score of years. It is a landmark publication.

Preparation of the series required the cooperation and dedicated efforts of scores of chapter authors, Publication Committee chairmen and members, and successive executive committees of the AEA. In bringing together the insights and perceptions of adult education scholars, the series is a major contribution of the Association to the advancement of an understanding of adult education as a field of study and of practice.

January 1981   WILLIAM S. GRIFFITH

                                          HOWARD Y. McCLUSKY

                                          General Editors

Preface

Why was this book on comparative international adult education undertaken? Two quotations may answer this question. One is by President Julius Nyerere of Tanzania (used by Kidd in this volume): "Development has a purpose; that purpose is the liberation of Man. But Man can only liberate or develop himself. He cannot be liberated or developed by another. For Man makes himself." Whether people look only at their own country or abroad, they realize that all individuals and groups are compelled to try to control the forces that grip them or else be controlled by them, that the main instrument to achieve a measure of control is education, and that education must now be conceived of and practiced as lifelong. The second quotation is from John Donne: "No man is an island, entire of himself." What was a religious, poetic insight in the seventeenth century is today recognized as a fact. Those who use lifelong education to achieve personal or societal ends can benefit in their planning and execution by some understanding of lifelong education in other countries. The benefits include a better understanding of oneself, of one's own culture, and of others whose ideas and experiences may prove useful. The goal of the emerging discipline of comparative international adult education is to help the educators of adults in all countries learn from each other.

This book is part of the series that constitutes the *Handbook of Adult Education* commissioned by the Adult Education Association of the U.S.A. While the other books of the series are designed primarily for the educators of adults and the scholars of adult education as a field in the United States, this book is intended to have worldwide significance for educators and scholars. The reason for its wider intention lies in the nature of the subject—comparative studies of aspects of adult education in two or more countries or regions—and in the purposes of such studies—to help adult educators and scholars of the field of adult education in all countries to learn from each other. Further, this book will be a valuable contribution to the literature of the field and will advance the field as an emerging discipline. It is the first full-length, original book on the subject.

Two comments may clarify both these claims and some parts of succeeding chapters. The first concerns the distinctive nature of comparative *international* adult education. A comparative study may include two or more aspects of adult education in the same country. For example, within a single country literacy education in a metropolitan area may be compared with literacy education in a rural area, or continuing education for physicians may be compared with continuing education for lawyers. However, a study in comparative international adult education must consider one or more aspects of adult education in two or more countries.

The second comment concerns whether comparative international adult education is a discipline or a subdiscipline, and, if the latter, whether it is a subdiscipline of comparative education or of adult education. Comparative international adult education necessarily draws upon both these disciplines and the distinction, which is not important now, must await future resolution.

The intention that this book have worldwide significance for adult education governed the planning by the senior author in his decisions concerning the audiences, the themes, the countries or regions, and the authors of the chapters.

This book is written for educators of adults, including professors, teachers, trainers, students, researchers, planners, counselors, evaluators, librarians, program and other administrators, business officers, promoters, media experts, communicators, technicians and other support personnel, supervisors, sponsors, board members, legislators, and policy makers. All these persons do not necessarily identify individually or professionally with the term *adult education*. This book nevertheless is intended to be useful to them in their activities concerning the education of adults regardless of the terms they use or the titles they have. It is written so they can understand it and use its findings where appropriate.

Two factors, themes and countries, were considered together. The themes of adult education are as many as the concerns of adult life, and the education of adults occurs in all countries. Therefore a design was chosen to combine selected major themes and selected countries—the themes together covering a broad spectrum and the countries together covering several broad spectra of characteristics, such as population densities, stages of economic development, ideologies, degrees of centralization of control of adult education activities, languages, and geography. The combination of themes and countries provides a variety of comparative studies valuable in their own right and exemplifies the nature and methods of comparative international adult education as an emerging discipline.

Some scholars argue that any system of education must be perceived and assessed as a component of a total cultural system. Therefore any comparison of parts of two or more educational systems must be grounded in deep understanding of the total cultural systems. Ideally, this is undoubtedly the case, but practically, most scholars must settle for less while striving for as much as possible. The minimum requirements for making studies in comparative international adult education seem to be a familiarity with the education of adults in one's own country, a familiarity with the relevant contexts of the aspects in the two or more countries being compared, a sympathy for and even an empathy with the countries being compared, and a vigilance against the intrusion of one's own cultural and personal biases. The scholars who represented several parts of the world and who were familiar with the selected themes and countries were chosen from among the qualified pool. Two gaps in the list of authors are regretted: There are no women and there are no contributors from Latin America or continental Asia. Two women, two Latin Americans, and two Asians were invited to prepare chapters, but they were unable to take on the assignments. Each of the authors who accepted is a distinguished educator and scholar with considerable experience in two or more countries.

During the planning and writing of the chapters, many consultations occurred among the authors. These communications included visits with each of them. The authors, after consulting, themselves selected the aspects of adult education and the countries for their comparative studies. That three of them included aspects of adult education in Iran is not surprising because the Shah's government was supporting adult education on an ambitious scale. The subsequent revolution in Iran, of course, calls the continuation of the described programs there into question, although it does not necessarily invalidate the studies. More than half the authors were studying comparative international adult education for the first time, and they brought fresh insights and gathered new data.

In Chapter One, Charters describes comparative international adult education in terms of its major elements and concerns.

In Chapter Two, Duke gives comparative descriptions of the education of adults in four Asian countries and Australia and suggests some possible effects the comparison may have on the educators of adults in his own country, Australia.

In Chapter Three, Savićević identifies six of the major factors determining the education of adults in any country, gives a historical description of the systems of adult education in the nine European socialist countries, and sketches similarities and differences among these nine systems.

In Chapter Four, Knoll compares one key aspect of adult education—professionalization—in two countries that are culturally similar and ideologically different: the Federal Republic of Germany and the German Democratic Republic.

In Chapter Five, Hutchinson, from his long experience with the National Institute of Adult Education (England and Wales), with most of the national associations of adult education in other countries, and with all international organizations concerned with adult education since before World War II, indicates the contributions such bodies do and could make to comparative international adult education.

In Chapter Six, Titmus and Pardoen, by both general analysis and specific case studies, demonstrate the value of understanding the comparative histories of laws governing the education of adults in Western countries and the roles these laws and the regulations based on them play in the education of adults.

In Chapter Seven, Ely explicates the use of educational technology as a part of total instructional design and examines its application for the education of adults in four countries.

In Chapter Eight, Ampene considers the several types of adults not reached by education and suggests strategies for reaching them. He does so with emphasis upon the developing countries of the world but in a way that has relevance to all countries.

In Chapter Nine, Ryan, focusing on the education of adults for literacy, establishes that literacy education for adults is not always a means rather than an end in itself and illustrates the major principles for designing and developing such programs by analyzing literacy programs in six countries.

In Chapter Ten, Kidd, who in the Ontario Institute for the Study of Education established one of the first university graduate courses in comparative international adult education and who was the first secretary-general of the International Council for Adult Education, publisher of *Convergence*, deals with research in comparative international adult education—its present status and some of the major tasks it can undertake.

Jane Frost, who has been associated with me for many years, has done the typing as well as much editing. Her assistance and excellence are hereby recorded with appreciation.

Throughout the preparation of this book, Robert Blakely, adjunct professor of Adult Education at Syracuse University and international consultant in adult education, made a significant contribution by advising on the concept underlying this volume. His important role in planning and editing is also deeply appreciated.

In her role as friend, colleague, and hostess in our home to many international guests, my wife Margaret Charters has assisted in our learning from each other.

Syracuse, New York ALEXANDER N. CHARTERS
January 1981

Contents

The Authors

KWASI AMPENE, director, Institute of Adult Education, University of Ghana

ALEXANDER N. CHARTERS, professor, Department of Adult Education, Syracuse University

CHRIS DUKE, director, Center for Continuing Education, Australian National University

DONALD P. ELY, professor, Department of Education, Syracuse University

E. M. HUTCHINSON, secretary (retired), National Institute of Adult Education, London, England

J. R. KIDD, professor, Department of Adult Education, Ontario Institute for Studies in Education, Toronto, Canada

JOACHIM H. KNOLL, professor, Institute of Education, Ruhr University, Federal Republic of Germany

ALAN R. PARDOEN, associate dean, Extended Campus/Continuing Education, Mankato State University

JOHN W. RYAN, chief, Training, Research and Evaluation Division of Literacy, Adult Education and Rural Development, UNESCO, Paris, France

DUSAN SAVIĆEVIĆ, docent professor, Department of Adult Education, University of Belgrade, Yugoslavia

COLIN J. TITMUS, senior lecturer, Department of Extra-Mural and Adult Education, University of Glasgow, Scotland

Comparing
Adult Education
Worldwide

Chapter One

Learning from Each Other

Alexander N. Charters

This chapter introduces comparative international adult education by describing the field in terms of its characteristics, its procedures, and some of its major concerns. Because the field is in an early stage of development, the description was arrived at inductively, on the empirical basis of what is, rather than deductively, on the logical basis of what should be. This approach to description is in keeping with previous studies and with the studies reported in the following chapters, which contribute to the development of the field by making comparisons and calling attention to obstacles and needs.

Characteristics

The nature of comparative international adult education can be distinguished by considering relevant definitions, its purposes, its content, the people who use it, the limitations of the field, and the resources, including individuals, organizations, and associations, it can draw upon.

Definitions. In this chapter adult education is defined as the education of men and women who have assumed mature responsibilities as citizens, workers, family or group members, and social beings and who are learning purposefully to achieve their individual and societal goals. They may be learning on a part-time or full-time basis for short periods of time. They may be self-motivated or they may have external compelling reasons to participate. Adult education is viewed in the context of lifelong education. It is that aspect of learning beginning with the attainment of adulthood (however that word may be defined) and extending until death. Adult education is comprehensive in that it occurs in all countries and many agencies, it includes all formats, methods, and other elements involved in the purposeful learning by adults, and it concerns all subjects in which adults are interested and all objectives they have.

A clear definition of adult education provides a set of terms that helps the educators of adults learn from each other in a worldwide context. But making a clear definition is difficult: Different educators of adults may use the term *adult education* with different meanings and other terms may have the same meaning to some educators. Several authors of the following chapters deal with the problem of defining terms. Duke provides a variety of terms for adult education in Asia and Australia. Saviĉeviĉ gives many terms used in the socialist countries of Europe. Titmus and Pardoen not only define adult education for their own usage but also document the various terms used in the legislation of some Western countries. Knoll presents the various terms used for the education of adults in the Federal Republic of Germany and the German Democratic Republic. And Ryan charts the changing concept and definitions of literacy education. Nevertheless, with care there can be sufficient agreement on, or at least understanding of, terms to enable educators of adults to communicate at both theoretical and operational levels. Beyond this point quibbling about terms is not important and may even divert energies from the task at hand.

A study in comparative international adult education as it was defined in the preface must include one or more aspects of adult education in two or more countries or regions. Comparative study is not the mere placing side by side of data concerning one or more aspects of adult education in two or more countries. Such juxtaposition is only a prerequisite for comparison. At the next stage one attempts to identify the similarities and differences between the aspects under study and to assess the degree of similarity or difference. Even at this point the work of comparison is not complete. The real value of comparative study emerges only from stage three—the attempt to understand why the differences and similarities occur and what their significance is for adult education in the countries under examination and in other countries where the findings of the study may have relevance.

Purposes. Comparative international adult education has the same basic purposes as adult education and comparative education, fields with which it overlaps. They are, immediately or eventually, to improve the lots and lives of individuals by improving the performance of the educators who help them. Improvement of the educators' performance can come about in two ways. One is by giving them knowledge and skills they can apply directly. The other is by increasing understanding of and information about adult education for its own sake. The debate about the relative values of these two ways is not fruitful because knowledge for its own sake is often translatable into empirically useful knowledge and empirically useful knowledge can increase knowledge for its own sake.

Hutchinson demonstrates in this book the importance to adult educators of knowing about the resources available through national, regional, and international associations. Titmus and Pardoen point out the importance of understanding the evolution of laws concerning adult education. Several other authors (Duke, Saviċeviċ, Knoll, Ampene, and Ryan) show the direct use of adult education by governments for national development.

Subjects. No list could exhaust the aspects of adult education that can be compared in two or more countries. Some of the main ones can be grouped into three categories—the adult learners, the learning opportunities available to them, and the operational environment of the available learning opportunities.

The results of studies of people in any stage of the life span may be generalizable to all stages, or the results of a study of one stage may be adaptable to another.

The study of the adult as a learner may be approached from various points of view. The characteristics of adults, including their attitudes, values, and appreciations, might be studied. Another approach would be to consider adults' abilities to assume responsibility for their continuing learning. Similarly, adults' competencies in their roles or functions in life may be viewed to see which factors are common to all adults and which may characterize a particular segment or culture. Another factor to be considered is adult needs, to identify which are generic and which may be peculiarly related to ethnic origin or background.

Political, social, physical, educational, and religious environments always have a significant impact on learning. Factors affecting interest and motivation also are important. Moreover, it is necessary to pay attention to how the various factors fit together as a cultural matrix within which an adult lives. Chapter Eight, on reaching the unreached, is a significant illustration of this point. Certainly, alternative styles related to adult learners and learning can be usefully studied in various international contexts.

Another set of aspects of adult education for comparative international studies concerns learning opportunities, which concerns the whole format of program design and program development and the context in which learning takes place. Ryan examines design and development in detail and in relationship. Learning is an individual phenomenon; only the individual learns. But the task of the educator of adults is to provide favorable and alternative opportunities to learn. Essentially, learners are self-directed, but it is useful and appropriate for them to have suggestions and guidance from other persons, such as teachers and counselors. The aspects of learning opportunities encompass the assessment of needs; the setting of objectives; the delivery systems with their varied types of formats, instruction methods, locations, and teachers or tutors and a range of other support personnel; and evaluation. Duke's observations, Ely's study of the uses of educational technology, and Ryan's discussion of functional literacy relate directly to the provision of learning opportunities viewed on a comparative basis internationally.

As adult education becomes a mature field of study and as the movement expands, concern for considering it in its totality grows, whether within a nation or worldwide. The concern for considering it all simultaneously is variously referred to by such terms as *structure, systemization,* or, more generally, the *operational environment.* Adult education as a worldwide movement may be considered to involve policy making, organization and management, and the systematic implementation of learning opportunities for adults. Concern for all these elements together assists adults to gain access to learning opportunities. Most of the chapter authors refer to the question of the degree of centralization of power over adult education activities. Centralization can be in the form of either direct administration or coordination. In the case of direct administration, priorities can be set at a high level and funds allocated and procedures developed for widespread implementation. In the case of coordination, the system often has a minimum of centralized direction and involves a mixture of governmental, private, and other nonpublic initiatives. In this flexible, decentralized system, responsiveness to need may be immediate but gaps in meeting needs may be evident.

One observation made in several of the following chapters is that adult education is generally considered outside the mainstream of discussions on education. Adult education is certainly not yet accepted as an integral part of education in all countries. The explanation may simply be that adult education has not yet matured to a level comparable to that of education for children and youth. If the philosophy and concept of lifelong education is accepted and acted upon, then adult education will be included as an integral part of the educational system, regardless of how that system may be structured. As Duke points out, perhaps adult education should not follow the public school system model. As he and others state, if the nontraditional aspects of adult education are linked with the traditional ones, there could be a transformation of the traditional. But there is little evidence that adult education will be strengthened by imitating the preschool, school, and higher educational systems in most countries. It seems that whether the general policy toward adult education in a country is a strong governmental one or a volunteer one, the governmental and volunteer components complement and supplement each other. This relationship varies according to the intent of the major sponsors, governmental or nongovernmental.

The operational environment includes the factors of the nature of the economic and political system, policy making, and financing. Saviĉeviĉ reviews laws concerning adult education in the nine socialist countries of Europe. Titmus and Pardoen give a comparative study of legislation in three Western countries.

Users. Comparative international adult education is designed to help several types of users. First, it is to assist educators of adults in their role as continuing learners. It seems reasonable to expect that adults can benefit from each other's experiences, irrespective of the particular contexts in which they live, provided they are communicating. The educators of adults cannot be classified into categories such as developing and developed or those who know and those who do not. Rather, their abilities may be viewed as a continuum extending from the least to the most qualified. Individuals in any country can be found at any point in the continuum and so can the educators of adults. Perhaps the educators of adults in any one country can "on the average" be placed at a different point in the continuum from those in another country. But all educators of adults can learn from each other only if the information and knowledge are made available in forms they can understand and adapt to their particular situation. Learning from each other should not be by chance but by design. Kidd and Knoll are much concerned with the designs of learning developed by the educators of adults.

A second group of users of comparative international adult education is in the institutions, organizations, and agencies that provide programs for adults. In a broad sense these include any group of individuals who in some way relate to the education of adults. The institutions, organizations, and agencies in which they work may be separately established for the education of adults; they may be designed for some other level of education of which adult education is a component; they may have been previously unrelated to adult education in mission and objective but have subsequently assumed an adult education role; or they may be international agencies such as UNESCO, the World Bank, and the International Labor Organization (ILO).

A third group of users of comparative international adult education is the sponsors of adult education programs. The sponsors, of course, may be the individuals or the institutions, organizations, or agencies previously referred to. The sponsors may also be government agencies or private foundations. These may take the initiative and give leadership to provide resources so a given agency or individual can provide programs. In such cases the sponsors are one step removed from the actual conduct of the programs offered to adults.

In recent decades governments have increasingly intervened in adult education to encourage, facilitate, or directly provide adult education programs, using incentives or coercion in varying degrees and operating with varying degrees of centralized control. At the same time even those governments with the most coercion and centralization often rely upon the voluntary efforts of individuals and organizations. Duke, Sa\v{c}ićević, Hutchinson, Titmus and Pardoen, Ely, Knoll, Ampene, and Ryan all describe this tendency.

In brief, comparative international adult education may be useful in meeting needs if it helps individual educators of adults to improve their competencies; helps institutions, organizations, and agencies to achieve their objectives more effectively; and helps the sponsors, including governments, to accomplish their missions.

Resources. A basic factor involved in the study of comparative international adult education is the identification and accessibility of resources. The main steps in using resources are identifying, processing, disseminating, and evaluating. At Syracuse University, for example, four basic library documents related to resources and their use are available as aids to access. They are titled Category of Resources for Educators of Adults, Descriptive Subject Headings, Alpha-Numeric Code, and Bibliographical and Annotation Forms. One descriptive subject heading is Comparative-International, which may be taken as the basic heading or topic. Items under each of the other descriptive subject headings may also be used for further breakdowns. The resources at Syracuse University include print and nonprint materials as well as human expertise.

The authors of this book have used various resources as a basis for their contributions and each clearly cites them. For example, Duke refers to personal notes from recent visits; Titmus and

Pardoen refer to legal documents; Ely refers to case studies; and Ryan refers to research findings regarding literacy education. I did a computer search of Educational Resources Information Clearinghouses (ERIC). In time other educators of adults will be able to utilize these contributions as resources for further studies.

The researcher's first task is to identify the materials for the study and to determine the nature and extent of their availability. Closely linked to availability is accessibility, which means more than the availability of the physical resources or items. Many educators involved in the international area have had emotional, psychological, or political experiences that in effect preclude them from obtaining or using resources objectively. In other cases resources are likewise available but tools for access may not be. These tools for access might include having proper catalogues, acquisition lists, bibliographies, or computer printouts. Materials and other resources may or may not be accessible to educators of adults in terms of location, time (such as hours of the day), proximity to transportation, mail service, and other factors. An important aspect of accessibility is the learner's ability to use the resources after they have been selected and made available.

Another factor involved is the dissemination of the information about the resources or the resources themselves. This element is particularly acute in comparative international adult education because more than one country is involved.

The language of the resources is a crucial issue. Ryan discusses the importance of selecting languages in education for literacy, and this point may be generalized to include studies in comparative international adult education.

As reflected in the chapters of this book, individuals are also important resources for comparative studies. Many of them can give information and data that have not yet been published or might not be written otherwise.

Organizations and Associations. As with all aspects of adult education, the most crucial factor in the development of comparative international adult education is individuals who are committed to the field. An individual makes a contribution when he initiates an activity or project that will identify, analyze, describe, and interpret an area of comparative international study. Such studies are usually conceived by individuals, but they are often designed and conducted by a group or team. These groups include organizations and associations. They may be local, national, regional, or international. This book is an example of a project implemented by a team under the auspices of a national sponsor, the Adult Education Association of the U.S.A. International organizations such as the International Congress of University Adult Education, the International Council for Adult Education, and the United Nations Educational, Scientific, and Cultural Organization (UNESCO) are particularly useful resources for comparative international adult education studies.

To be effective, such organizations and associations need continuity. They should have links with or at least knowledge of the past. National and international leaders should neither be ignorant of nor ignore previous achievements but should, rather, build on them to give a base and stability to the field.

Moreover, there are resources for adult education in the organizations and associations of other disciplines and fields. One is the field of formal education, with which adult education overlaps. The relationship between education and adult education varies from society to society, according to their theories and practices. In the United States the situation is mixed. Although most adult education is conducted separately from formal educational institutions, much is conducted by educational institutions. The most important links between adult education and formal educational institutions are with the public schools; community colleges; and universities through classes, correspondence courses, nontraditional programs, special degree programs, university extension, and continuing education programs for professionals and other specialized clientele. A pervasive influence of higher education upon adult education in the United States is through the graduate departments of adult education in many universities, which provide instruction and conduct research. The relationship between the formal educational systems and adult education is also mixed in many other countries. For example, Saviçević and Knoll recount the debate in European socialist countries between the philosophers of "pedagogy" and "andragogy."

Resources for comparative international adult education are

also in the organizations and associations of other disciplines and
fields, such as instructional technology (see Ely), the humanities
and arts, information science, anthropology, and sociology. Additional resources are in the organizations and associations related
to these disciplines and fields. For example, at a 1975 conference
of the Comparative and International Education Society in Montreal, there was a section meeting on comparative international
adult education.

The influence of the individuals, organizations, and associations, of course, depends on their purposes or missions. The international organizations and associations are important for all
aspects of adult education but particularly so for the field of comparative international adult education because they give a person
from one country access to other persons with similar interests and
goals in other countries. Hutchinson cites the important role of
certain national, regional, and international organizations and associations of adult educators as communication and information
channels.

The crucial influence and impact of a relatively few individuals are recognized as they lead the development of their
fields and employment of the resources of organizations and
associations.

Limitations. Comparative education has only recently become
of serious interest to the educators of adults, and comparative international adult education as a field of study is in the beginning
stages. Even so, the study of comparative international adult education has been a useful resource to educators of adults. It should
become increasingly significant as a resource for improving the
understanding and knowledge on which educators of adults can
base both their theoretical studies and their practices.

Because it is an emerging field of study, the extent of the
studies and literature in comparative international adult education
is sharply limited and the quality is uneven.

One problem is that in studying comparative international
adult education, it is difficult to identify topics on which there is a
substantial data base from which to make a comparison. The problem is twofold. First, in many countries there is a lack of well-based
research and other data on any topic in the field of adult education.

Second, even in cases where detailed information may be available on some part of the field in one country, there is rarely sufficient evidence in a second country on the same topic to make sound comparisons. In their preliminary discussions contributors had to identify and search out the available data in two or more countries to select the topics for comparison.

The authors of this book usually were not able to base their comparisons on existing data from two or more countries. In nearly every case the available evidence was far less than had been anticipated, and in some cases it was so incomplete that the authors had to identify and collect the data in each country as a basis for their comparisons. The strengths and particularly the weaknesses of local or national studies are compounded when they are used in turn as the basis for comparative studies. To a large extent the quality of comparative studies is only as good as the local and national studies on which the comparison is made. As some of the chapter authors had to do, the researcher must often strengthen or add to the basic evidence before making a comparative study.

These comments about the data bases for this book reflect the general state of comparative international adult education. The researchers are limited both by the secondary analyses they judge dependable or can supplement and by the primary study they can make. They must examine these limitations in each problem they undertake to research.

Procedures

The procedures of comparative international adult education can be illustrated by discussions of relationships with other fields, methodology, research, and evaluation.

Relationships with Other Fields. A comparative international adult education study properly has its base in the broader area of comparative international education because the same elements are involved in both. The only difference is in the specific application made to the narrower field of adult education and the narrower implications inherent in it. Kidd relates how comparative international adult education grew out of comparative international education.

Comparative international adult education has ties also with other comparative international fields, such as sociology and anthropology. Such fields of study provide a useful foundation for the study of comparative international adult education. There are relations also with other fields of study through organizations such as the ILO and the International Bureau of Education, which have extensive resources for the comparative study of topics in two or more countries. In order to use the results of research in other fields effectively, the problem attacked must be stated in terms that make evident the specific relevance to adult education.

Methodology. In the literature of comparative international adult education, considerable attention is given to the methodology used in conducting research. It sometimes appears there is something unique about adult education that requires a unique type of methodology. Knoll comments that comparative international adult education may have given itself a distinctive methodological profile but that studies along the line of this profile are in fact relatively sparse.

This book reflects the premise that the methodology to be used is the one most appropriate to the particular hypothesis or question and to the context and design of the study. In effect there is no one method for comparative international adult education, but there may be a most appropriate method for a given study, in a given situation, and at a given time. The research methods used might be borrowed or modified from education in general or even from other fields, but, as Knoll advises, the perspective should always focus on adult education. Indeed, a combination of methods might be used if a combination is appropriate to a particular study. Some categorization of methods might be useful to the individual conducting comparative adult education studies, in each case distinguishing between characteristics common to two or more methods and characteristics unique to a particular method. Comparative international adult education from a methodological standpoint is complex. No matter which method or combination is chosen, it should be used with rigor and flexibility within its inherent limits.

Research. In preparing this book a search was made of the literature, bibliographies, and other sources to identify relevant research. After extended investigation, including an ERIC search, it became evident that a large body of research conducted in comparative international adult education is now available to the educators of adults.

In reviewing the research and studies, it was also important to review the status of the information available to identify trends and the needs for further research and study. Kidd directly addresses this topic.

Evaluation. Evaluation is a significant aspect of comparative international adult education. The fundamental purpose of evaluation is to provide a basis for decision making by educators of adults, who in this book are identified as those individuals, institutions, organizations, and agencies that directly offer educational opportunities for adults and those that sponsor such offerings. Evaluation assists each educator of adults to make decisions in his or her area of responsibility.

As one views the field of adult education worldwide, one must surely be amazed at the extent and nature of the adult education programs reaching into the lives of hundreds of millions of adults. Many valuable programs are being conducted, but there are few substantiated, documented reports of their results.

The specific function of evaluation is to determine whether the selected and stated objectives of educational programs have been achieved. The difficulty is, first, the objectives are frequently not stated in terms that can be evaluated and, second, there is often no plan for evaluation. Unless objectives are stated in measurable terms and a plan for evaluation is made before the educational experience is begun, it is impossible to determine whether the financial and other resources are being used effectively and efficiently. The great mass of programs has had only cursory evaluation in terms of objectives and other standards. Little evidence is available to show how well the vast funds and other resources expended in the education of adults have been invested.

With or without evaluation the adult education effort may be important and productive. Without some form of evaluation, however, there is little evidence to determine whether the programs being offered are necessary or acceptably effective. Evaluation is necessary to guide decision making at every step of the

educational process. Without evaluation it is not known whether
the "reached" are being reached in terms of their felt needs and
objectives (not to mention the "unreached," to whom Ampene
refers).

Major Concerns

In reading the chapters in this book, you will recognize pervasive common threads and convergences of views. The usual caution about generalization is in order—how far can one take the
findings of some selected studies involving two or more countries
and then generalize worldwide? The authors have been careful in
stating the specific contexts and limitations of their studies. Nevertheless, after recognizing the limits to the conclusions of each and
considering them all together (thus further limiting the general-
izability), a few statements can be offered about major concerns
reflected in the chapters.

Criteria for Studies. Two complementary comments are justified: First, researchers and sponsors should select topics that are
significant and vital not only to themselves but also to other educators of adults—that is to say, topics that are both urgent and
important. Second, a high priority should be given to studies that
will have maximum adaptation and translatability to other countries. To facilitate the selection of such topics, better channels of
communication are needed to inform researchers about completed
studies and projects under way in comparative international adult
education so their studies can be viewed in context and with
priority.

Attention to Context. All the chapter authors stress that comparative international adult education must take into account the
context of adult education, such as the social, political, economic,
ideological, and cultural factors. Each author has done so in his
own study. It is important to identify which factors are relevant to
the particular topic being studied. Accordingly, the researcher
should identify and isolate the one or ones that do influence the
specific study. In this way generalizations can be made from the
studies so the relevant factors may be more precisely identified and
the results of the studies more easily adapted to other situations.

Design and Conduct of Methodology. If comparative international adult education is to be in the mainstream of comparative education and significant in adult education, it must become increasingly rigorous in the design and conduct of the studies. The chapters in this book are examples of carefully designed and conducted studies. The reporting of studies of various topics in various countries is of use, but it should not be confused with rigorous comparative study. The consensus of the authors in this book is that no methodology is unique to comparative international adult education. The method or combination of methods and the design must be appropriate to the subject, focused on adult education, and rigorously followed.

Financing. Concern with the financing of adult education pervades this book and indeed the whole field of adult education. The approach to financing is based in the philosophy and attitude of individuals and society. If the education of adults is considered an investment in people for national development or individual self-fulfillment, then it may be viewed as a national concern and serious consideration given to funding it. If the education of adults is viewed as a low-priority activity, then the funding is likely to be piecemeal and inadequate. Adult education in most countries began as a charitable cause or voluntary activity and in general a fringe activity. While voluntarism or nonpublic support still exists in most countries, there is a growing move toward government intervention through legislation. In other cases, where adult education is highly centralized and responsibility is assumed by government, legislation provides for both policy and implementation. Even there volunteer and nonpublic support make a substantial impact in areas of education to which government policy gives low priority. Support of adult education, whether by public policy or voluntary effort or both, rests upon the conviction that adults' learning and teaching potentials should not be wasted but rather used as assets to both the individual and society.

At least some kind of adult education in most countries is viewed as an investment, and it usually has elements of both governmental and nonpublic voluntary support. The degree to which adult education is viewed as an investment varies in the several countries, and that degree is reflected in the status assigned to it and in the amount of support it receives. Studies of financing on a comparative basis would suggest alternative patterns of funding and the implications of each one.

Voluntary Support. The voluntary, nongovernmental support individuals and organizations give to the education of adults is often considerable. These contributions of talent, time, effort, services, and other resources can be translated into the equivalence of financial support. Often they are not so translated. Only if they are can an accurate appraisal be made of the total investment in the education of adults. The most advantageous arrangement is that in which public support and nongovernmental support, including voluntary equivalences, are given in such a way that each stimulates the increase of the other.

Voluntary, nongovernmental support contributions have an intangible value far beyond their equivalence in terms of money. They are the most convincing evidence that the contributors esteem the education of adults. Moreover, by voluntarily providing adults opportunities to continue their education, the contributors are engaging in both self-directed learning and the management of their affairs.

Adult Education and Development. The chapters that follow include many statements about and illustrations of the relation of adult education to individual and national development in terms of both material and human resources. As previously mentioned, there is a place for the study of comparative international adult education for its own sake, but this book gives it a secondary priority. As a field of activity, adult education exists within the social, political, economic, and cultural environment of a society. The chapters by Duke, Saⅴićević, Titmus and Pardoen, Ely, Ampene, and Ryan are all accounts of the use of adult education as a tool to bring about desired changes in societies and individuals. Clearly, if adult education is to serve its purpose, it must relate closely to personal and national aspirations. It should be an integral part of the lives of the illiterates, the neo-literates, the professionals, the leaders, and the citizens. The extent that education should be preparatory for action, or even be action itself, is a decision to be made by each adult education sponsor, agency, and educator. But it is clear from the authors in this book that adult education is not just for the ivory towers but is also for the marketplace. Studies in comparative adult education that transcend national boundaries should enable educators of adults to use adult education to facilitate people's control of the quality of their lives.

Applicability of Findings. I stated earlier that increased rigor in the design and conduct of studies in comparative international adult education is needed to provide a valid base for adoption or adaptation in other situations. Several of the authors of these chapters refer to the pragmatic purposes of comparative international adult education studies. It follows that the educators of adults who are to benefit most from the reports of the comparative studies will be those capable of analyzing them so they can identify the studies of possible use to them, understand the background factors of the study and compare them with the factors in their own situations, and adapt the findings of the study where possible to their own specific tasks. Reports of the findings of studies in comparative international adult education should be presented in ways that assist the readers to make their own analysis and thereby use the findings.

Opportunities for Adults to Learn. The illustrations given in this book support what is known from other sources: that the opportunities for adults to begin or continue learning are increasing in almost every country. Clarification of the purposes of adult education, its financing, its relation to individual and national development, and its methods is needed to expand adult education. There is an urgent need for more as well as alternative learning opportunities offered at times and in environments conducive to learning. In this way the mass of the educationally unreached and barely touched adults may be steadily reduced, and those who are reached may be helped to take charge of their own lifelong education. The comparative study of alternative ways of providing opportunities may suggest ways to increase, improve, and enrich the learning opportunities for adults everywhere.

Chapter Two

Australia in Asia— Comparison as Learning

Chris Duke

This chapter suggests uses of comparative studies in adult educa-tion by reference to recent experience. Its main source of informa-tion is the author's field notes from recent visits to countries in Asia as officer in a regional nongovernmental organization, the Asian–South Pacific Bureau of Adult Education (ASPBAE), which is the regional arm of the International Council of Adult Educa-tion. The chapter is restricted to an examination of what the approach to adult education of four countries in the region—Bangladesh, Burma, Indonesia, and Iran—might suggest for a fifth country, Australia. (This chapter was written before the over-throw of the Shah in Iran.)

This chapter will explain why these four countries were chosen by means of a brief note on each and by a longer note on

Australia, discuss the use of various terms for adult education in these countries and their significance for the various purposes for which adult education (however named) is conceived, examine in each of these countries six aspects of adult education, describe Australia in greater detail, and speculate on what Australians might learn by comparing adult education in these four countries with their own.

These countries were chosen because they differ on such important dimensions as their socioeconomic circumstances and their political philosophies and systems. Bangladesh, a recently independent country with a large population compressed in a small land area, has few natural resources other than the diligence and ingenuity of its people. It is struggling to recover from the ravages of a bitter war. Its per-capita income is exceedingly low. Poverty is an ever present, often overriding, consideration. Many people are reportedly so poor they have no energy and motivation to learn, which constitutes a severe obstacle to adult education.

The Socialist Republic of the Union of Burma, adjoining Bangladesh, has succeeded since achieving its independence in maintaining a nonaligned stance that has largely excluded external influence. It is little known to the Western world. Socialist, non-Communist, in internal politics anti-Communist, and centralized and firmly Buddhist, its approach to literacy is markedly at variance with the functional approach favored by the United Nations Educational, Scientific, and Cultural Organization (UNESCO) and adopted, with variations, in most Third World countries. This approach proved so successful, however, that in 1971 Burma won the annual Shah M. Reza Pahlavi Prize awarded by UNESCO.

Indonesia, the largest in population of the countries considered here, is also predominantly rural. Literacy and rural development loom large as preoccupations for adult, social, or nonformal education. Indonesia is more visible internationally than the two countries mentioned so far, aspiring to leadership in Southeast Asia through such regional associations as the Association of South East Asian Nations and the South-East Asian Ministers of Education Organization (SEAMEO).

More economically fortunate is Iran, with its recent wealth from oil. Like Burma, prerevolutionary Iran had a massive literacy campaign, different in form and style and very recent in origin. The Iranian literacy crusade was planned and financed on a scale unthinkable to Bangladesh. Tehran was becoming a regional center for the south and west Asian region; at the same time the city displayed the problems and tensions inherent in rapid growth and the transposition of village dwellers to a confusing city environment. Adult education was planned from a national development perspective, but here finance was not really a problem.

By contrast with each of these countries, Australia is highly urbanized and industrialized. It is generously endowed with natural resources, has a high per-capita income, and is not overpopulated. National development planning is not a familiar concept. The virtual absence of such planning makes Australia an interesting contrast with most Asian countries, and comparison is instructive for reflecting on the future of Australia generally and of its adult education in particular.

Before considering various aspects of adult education in these countries, it is useful to consider the various terms for adult education used in the several countries because they reflect the purposes adult education is conceived to serve.

Terms for Adult Education

Although the term *adult education* is widely used in the region, its meaning varies and it is a source of some confusion. It is commonly equated with adult literacy—frequently nowadays functional literacy—even though a rider may be added to the effect that its scope is wider. Burma and Iran concentrate almost entirely on literacy. In Burma the Central Literacy Committee is strong politically and administratively, with secretariat resources in the Ministry of Education. The National Center for Adult Education and Training, established with United Nations Development Program (UNDP) and UNESCO assistance in Iran in 1974, has been given formal autonomy within the ambit of the National Committee for World Literacy Program. The center supported, by planning, organizing, evaluating, and conducting research studies, the national literacy crusade that aimed to eliminate illiteracy in the seven to fifty age group by 1988. At the same time the center's charter and functions refer to permanent and lifelong education and to technical, civic, social, and cultural elements and dimensions of adult education. The Burmese Central Committee is responsible for planning the national campaign and providing such support services as literacy materials, publicity, and transport. The campaign takes the form of mass mobilization and "saturation" of different regions and towns, a few at a time, sweeping them to almost complete literacy within a few months before shifting attention to other places. Those who service the work of the committee speak of other forms of adult education in Burma, including workers' education and part-time and correspondence study options; however, the main work at present is the campaign.

The term *nonformal education* is used through much of Asia and tends to be preferred on several grounds: because of the narrow connotation of adult education—basic remedial education, mainly literacy, and for some in the British tradition, nonvocational, noncredit, nonfunctional education—and because it is not age restricted and may encompass education for out-of-school youth even of a very young age. Whereas in Burma and Iran literacy training is equated with adult education, Bangladesh and Indonesia tend to use nonformal education. The committee appointed by the Planning Commission of the government of the People's Republic of Bangladesh in 1974 was a committee on nonformal education. Its 1975 report is subtitled "A Strategy for Development." The Indonesian World Bank project for the period to 1981 also takes the term *nonformal education*, as do the case studies prepared as documentation for the project. At the same time in both Bangladesh and Indonesia, the term *adult education* is used quite freely for administrative purposes, although the preferred translation from Indonesian tends to be social or community education.

While nonformal education has appeal under some circumstances, its use is also a source of confusion. The view is expressed in India, Malaysia, and the Philippines that some definition of terms must be agreed upon to distinguish formal from nonformal education. In Malaysia adult education refers to work with adults in the evening arranged by the same ministry with the same teachers in the same schools for the same courses leading to the same examinations by the same methods. It is argued that this, while being adult education, is clearly not nonformal education. One cannot therefore assume nonformal education automatically subsumes all adult education. Possibly because of confusion such as this, there is some resentment over the term on the ground that energies have been diverted into semantics and away from the important work of educating adults.

Lifelong education is another term that attracts both interest and irritation. As an overarching philosophy, it has appeal, as was demonstrated at the UNESCO Asian Project for Educational Innovation and Development workshop on lifelong education and the curriculum in Thailand in 1976. At the same time, as discussion there revealed, there is a feeling that the concept is too vague and too ambitious, that it too diverts energy and interest into abstract speculation and away from practical tasks. The terms *recurrent* and *continuing education*, which are employed in Australia, are seldom used in the four Asian countries. Continuing education, if used at all, refers to high-level refresher education for the already well educated—a tendency, as with nonformal education, to follow North American usage.

Six Aspects of Adult Education

The aspects I shall discuss include the role of adult education in national development, its relation to the formal educational system, the scale of governmental support of adult education and the nature of governmental direction, the role played by the nongovernmental sector and by professionals and nonprofessionals, and a particular approach, "conscientization," advocated by Paulo Freire.

Role and Centrality of Adult Education in Development Planning. While there are differences among the four Asian countries compared here, they all cluster well along a spectrum on which Australia, like most other Western industrial and postindustrial societies, would be located toward the far end. Australia lacks a development plan and is ambivalent over the very concept of national planning, but each of the other four countries works with such a system. The significance attached to literacy in Burma is attested by the membership of the Central Literacy Committee, the chairman and vice-chairman of which are the vice-chairman of the Lanzin Youth Central Organizing Committee of the Burmese Socialist Program party and the vice-chairman of the Central People's Peasants' Council. There are other representatives from the party and the Central People's Workers' Council and, at deputy minister and managing director levels, from all relevant ministries and public corporations. But education tends to attract less investment than such sectors as agriculture, industry, and transport.

The 1975 Report on Nonformal Education in Bangladesh sees nonformal education as central to development planning. It recommends a national coordinating council, probably serviced from the Ministry of Education. Despite the lack of visible progress since 1975, nonformal education may yet become a prominent feature in the five-year plan that began in mid 1978. In Iran the literacy crusade was planned over a twelve-year period; the sixth five-year plan (1978–1983) was expected to include support for nonformal education within a lifelong education framework. The Indonesian situation is similar to the situation in Bangladesh except it is less constrained financially. In the Indonesian government sector the directorate of community education (Penmas) has a staff approaching nine thousand, and many kinds of nongovernmental endeavors are recognized. The World Bank Project is intended to strengthen this structure, mainly through resource centers, materials production, and personnel training. While nonformal education has a longer history and is more firmly rooted in the community in Indonesia than, for instance, in prerevolutionary Iran, its development may for this very reason be less heavily directed within a national plan than in some other countries in the region. At the same time Indonesian government-sponsored research and development in nonformal education provides an example that might be emulated elsewhere, and not only in the Third World.

Relation to the Formal Education System. How far, if at all, does adult and nonformal education interact with and influence the formal system? In Iran the Ministry of Education, unable fully to meet the need for primary schooling, reportedly welcomed any initiative the national center took to develop alternatives to the formal school system for the six to eleven age group in the "nonscholarized" rural areas. The crusade itself had a cadre of some twenty-five thousand trainers and instructors, mostly taken from the formal system and given a crash course in adult literacy methods in an effort to modify their heavily didactic style. The question of its influence, and of relations with the formal provision of the Ministry of Education, was a matter of live and positive interest prior to the revolution.

In Burma, where the campaign has been running for over a decade following pilot projects in 1964–1965, the influence on the formal system is indirect: Parental involvement has resulted in more children being sent to school and staying longer, but there has been no evident effect on the rigid instruction methods employed in elementary schools. At the tertiary level, however, part-time and correspondence education are seen as legitimate alternatives to full-time study on campus. The new regional colleges, opened in 1977 as an obligatory step between secondary school and university, are to provide one year of fairly conventional academic study and one year of guided work experience. This could represent one form of merger between formal and nonformal education within the formal system.

No evidence was found regarding adult education's influence on the school system in Bangladesh. An impression is that, with the emphasis on local initiative and nongovernmental effort and the lack of central planning of nonformal education, any influence would be intangible. In Indonesia and the Philippines, where the SEAMEO Associated Center, Innotech, has been fostering alternatives to conventional elementary education, nonformal approaches and methods clearly influence thinking about formal schooling, and there are future possibilities for wide practical influence on the formal system. There is recognition here that nonformal approaches offer ways of enhancing the capacity, efficiency, and utility of the formal system and that nonformal education might become an attractive option for all groups at all levels. But there is fear that moving in this direction will formalize and bureaucratize the nonformal approach so much its distinctive contributions may be lost.

Scale of Resource Allocation to Adult Education. Precise data about resource allocation are not available even in terms of public expenditure, but some impression may be gained as to whether adult, nonformal, and literacy education are well or poorly supported. The literacy crusade in Iran had a well-staffed national center in Tehran and a very large field operation with paid staff and local committees taking the crusade to many parts of the country and seeking to match central resource allocation with local effort. Experienced personnel were at a premium, and more such persons were needed, but money as such was not a serious problem.

By contrast Bangladesh has not yet been able to extend the Comilla Institute of Adult Education model to other parts of the country. Eight pilot projects started in 1964 and 1967 have yet to be replicated elsewhere; most of the work in these projects is unpaid. Not surprisingly, there is more emphasis on nongovernment effort here than in Iran, and the work of the Bangladesh Rural Advancement Committee (BRAC), where it is not voluntary and unpaid, is financed from overseas aid. The contrast between these two countries is highlighted by the observation in Dacca that the estimated $45 per-capita cost of the Iranian crusade pays for five years of education in Bangladesh. Indonesia is somewhat less impoverished, but the amount of resources allocated to adult education is still very modest—only 0.5 percent of the Department of Education and Culture's budget in 1975–1976 according to the World Bank report for the four-year project, to be increased by about 200 percent by 1982.

Central Coordination, Planning, and Direction. Central coordination, planning, and direction are linked with but distinct from the relationship of adult education to development planning: The adult education component in a five-year development plan could be decentralized while adult education, though excluded from the framework of national planning, could be highly centralized. And unplanned, uncoordinated provision could be generously funded, while provision as part of a national plan integrated with other components could yet be starved of resources within plan allocations. Also, professed purpose may differ from practice. Participation and decentralization are widely acclaimed in all five countries. Yet there was criticism of centralized provision in Indonesia and prerevolutionary Iran as well as, increasingly, in Australia, with the emergence of the Technical and Further Education

(TAFE) sector. Burma appears to balance an ordered and centralized approach to the literacy campaign, directed by a powerful central committee using strong subcommittees, with a high level of local and voluntary effort for implementation following the initial intensive and public intervention for mass mobilization of effort in the locality. If central control is exerted during implementation, it is more through the expectations and requirements of a socialist, Buddhist country than by close central supervision. At the same time a "saturation" approach that is employed in each successive local effort has evolved in Burma; literacy remains the central objective, with functional applications a distinct second stage. Group pressure in the township or locality is used to take the people rapidly to literacy, which is sustained both for the community and for a high proportion of individuals in the area.

Iran placed a comparably high value on mobilizing local effort through literacy committees; the six thousand local committees were seen as a key. Committees had yet to be established and become self-directing in many areas. The campaign may have been so highly planned and orchestrated from the center that local participation and commitment could be sacrificed to the blueprint requirements as to what is to be taught and how. Instructors were trained to use set texts in specific ways, though the schedule for class timing was varied to fit the circumstances of different groups of younger and older men and women and of urban and rural groups. In addition to the problems presented by seasonal rhythms, there were complications posed by regional diversity. The Iranian adult education planner confronting a massive task in a large country with a sense of urgency had to foster local initiative from the center. Yet the minimally trained elementary teachers followed a routine and were regimented in their approach, and the provinces were subservient to and dependent upon the national prerevolutionary government. The approach included "programming" instructors to teach in a partly responsive and participative way rather than exclusively authoritarian-didactic and encouraging provinces to seek skills through workshop training in locally produced literacy materials relevant to the circumstances of that region.

Indonesian adult education and community development workers also value local community effort. They emphasize the need to identify and support local resources and initiatives, whether within or outside the government sector. The research and development arm of the Department of Education and Culture is exploring, in cooperation with Penmas, means whereby the local Penmas officer may head up a task force (Satgas) to facilitate community-based learning opportunities however these manifest themselves in the subdistrict. The diversity of learning opportunities and resources, including voluntary agencies, available throughout the society is recognized. The attempt to resolve the tension between central planning and direction and local initiative and diversity is seen in the province-based administration of Penmas itself and the project province approach to the World Bank exercise. This, like the large UNDP UNESCO program that helped launch the crusade in Iran, raises a question about the relation between external aid and expertise and internal styles of management and development: Does reliance on outside help correlate with greater central control and direction? In other words, is the dependency-autonomy dimension matched externally and within a country? If not, how is this mismatch to be avoided?

Nongovernmental Sector and Professional Versus Part-Time and Voluntary Teachers and Workers. These two aspects, though distinct, may be considered together. Bangladesh, which like Australia inherited a colonial British administrative tradition, places value both on local effort and initiative and on nongovernmental provision. In part this sharing of responsibility reflects economic circumstance, but the cause is deeper, to judge by the strength with which the view is held. BRAC, which started in 1972 as a postwar reconstruction agency, is highly regarded by senior personnel in education and some other relevant ministries and looked to as a model in a way that would be surprising in many (Western) countries. (BRAC is taken as an illustration, not as the only effective nongovernment agency.) Growth and experimentation have been shared with and legitimated in the voluntary sector in Bangladesh. BRAC is a highly professional operation, judged by its conceptual clarity, sense of purpose, and program execution. It also hires doctors for its programs where relevant and pays its own staff of approximately 250 persons. At the same time it places requirements on its clientele (in three different project areas at present) for unpaid time and effort, so much that most of the work BRAC generates is unpaid. Small seed monies are made available for economic development only where there are local contributions and where the need is undeniable; even then such aid is short-term and quickly phased out to foster rather than weaken self-sufficiency. BRAC distinguishes professional competence, for instance in the careful training of its own workers, from debilitating professionalization. Workers are prevented from fostering dependency and staying in a project region while encouraged to value local initiative through deliberate diversity of approach and avoidance of any one "model."

Bangladesh somewhat resembles Australia on this dimension of voluntary and nongovernmental effort inasmuch as two countries in such different economic circumstances can be compared. Iran presented an interesting contrast to both. Its massive twelve-year strategy was almost as far removed from the Australian style as it would be unthinkable in Bangladesh. Nongovernmental provision of adult education in Iran, whether modern or traditional in form, attracted little official attention. The emphasis was on training and using special crusade instructors.

The director of Penmas identifies some nine thousand private adult education agencies in Indonesia, including over a thousand in Jakarta alone. This may reflect both Dutch traditions and more recent U.S. influence without denying its contemporary endogenous character.

More obviously endogenous, and challenging for Australian comparison, is the approach in Burma. A centralized state with very limited resources for capital investment or recurrent expenditure relies on voluntary community effort drawing both on Buddhist tradition and on the expectations of a Socialist party and state. It is tempting for Australian observers to dispute the appropriateness of the term *voluntary*; it is precisely in confronting rather than dismissing unsettling comparisons that the value of comparative studies lies.

Conscientization. It might seem surprising to introduce the philosophy and methodology of Paulo Freire, the Brazilian philosopher and educator, into this discussion. (See the discussion of his goals and methods in Chapter Nine.) Freire visited Australia and was acclaimed by critics of the Australian educational and social system in the early seventies, but the impact of his work in that affluent society has been minimal, though its applicability, especially for aborigines, seems clear. One might not expect the approach and its underlying values to find favor in the other countries referred to here. The facts prove to be somewhat different. The main Iranian Crusade appeared to owe nothing to Freire, but the small Lorestan project was firmly rooted in his philosophy and methodology, its patron Majid Rahnema, member of the former Faure Commission and sometime minister for higher education in Iran, being a personal friend of Freire. In Bangladesh BRAC adopted a quite explicit Freire approach, both in its general philosophy and in the particular methodology for teaching literacy, duly adapted to the language of Bangladesh. This means a heavy emphasis on exploration and discussion in BRAC's literacy classes guided by a *shebok* (one who serves). Such an approach might be thought impossible where a military dictatorship is attempting ordered development; yet BRAC's programs are approved and supported by the government. Discussion in classes may highlight unsatisfactory social, economic, or legal arrangements, but *sheboks* steer toward nonrevolutionary outcomes that avoid directly confronting authority while fostering active citizenship rather than merely specific functional skills.

The research and development arm of the Indonesian Department of Education and Culture, BPPPK, has made a study of nonformal education, started in 1976, that draws explicitly on Freire's method of literacy teaching in a context of attempted community mobilization. Possible tensions with other preoccupations of government are obvious, given the problems (common to many countries in the region) over ethnic and cultural minority groups that aspire to independence. A Malaysian at a recent Australian seminar on education for a plural society emphasized Australia's advantage in that its cultural pluralism did not threaten national survival. Australia could therefore lead in exploring models of education for cultural diversity that did not represent a threat to unity. Functional literacy tends to mean preparation for and adjustment to economic roles required by the present politically approved socioeconomic system. Conscientization represents a fundamental questioning of these roles and relationships—an end to the culture of poverty, silence, and oppression. While Freire attracts more attention among adult education planners and administrators in some Asian countries than in politically stable Australia, the view is also expressed (specifically in India) that adult education has failed throughout the region because it has so far been for adjustment rather than liberation.

What value have such comparative reflections for the student or administrator of Australia? Before answering this question, I shall give a more detailed picture of adult education in Australia.

More About Australia

The historical origins of nonaboriginal Australia still loom large. Its history, from the beginning through to recent times, has sustained an orientation toward Britain as a source of ideas, models, and personnel and toward similar formerly colonial, substantially Anglo-Saxon societies, notably the United States, Canada, and New Zealand. Different European ethnic groups within Australia, such as the Italians, Greeks, Dutch, Germans, and Serbo-Croats, retain some ties with their countries of origin, but at an official level Australia's interest in these countries as reference points or models is slight. Even aboriginal Australians, for all their disenchantment with white domination and exploitation, tend to look mainly to these countries (especially North America) for comparison and support. Individuals and small groups of aborigines have visited and derived inspiration from countries like Papua New Guinea, Sri Lanka, and the Philippines, but there seems to be more antipathy toward Asia than interest among some aboriginal leaders.

The reality of Australia's geographical location has, however, registered with politicians and businessmen, especially since the creation of the European Economic Community and the American withdrawal from Vietnam. These developments are likely to make Australians and their administrations more concerned with Asia than they have been in the past. In 1974, Australia became a member of the UNESCO Asian region for program purposes, and it is an associate member of SEAMEO. ASPBAE, established at a regional seminar in Australia in 1964, may in a sense have been before its time for Australia: Certain individuals apart, Australian adult educators have shown little interest in adult education in neighboring Asian countries. However, beginning in 1976, the *Australian Journal of Adult Education* began enhanced coverage of Third World matters.

A profile of Australian adult education would include the following. There is a plurality of purposes: Adult education as its own end (liberal education) is contrasted with adult education for social and community change and with adult education for individual advancement or for raising the skill levels and adaptability of the labor force. The last is considered somewhat beyond the traditional bounds of adult education if it is either vocationally oriented or for accreditation. The term *further education*, also of British origin, has acquired currency in recent years. Sometimes it subsumes technical education; more commonly, reference is to both technical and further education (TAFE). Nonvocational adult education for recreation or personal development is included within further education. While there is adherence to a traditional specific meaning of adult education, there is also increasing acceptance of the wider understanding employed by the Organization for Economic Cooperation and Development (OECD) and by UNESCO in its 1976 Recommendation for the Development of Adult Education. This wider understanding has won acceptance with the Australian Association of Adult Education. The association's membership and span of activities have greatly widened of late, although its main interests tend to be in community and leisure-oriented education and only to a modest extent in the vocational education of adults. Some organizations prefer the term *continuing* to *adult education*, in an effort to avoid the rather narrow connotations of the earlier term. Another term attracting interest among adult educators as a strategy for educational reform is *recurrent education*. The main source of ideas and inspiration for this strategy has been OECD.

Adult education is quite marginal in terms of the interest and commitment of government. Training related to manpower needs is administratively separated from education, and the administration of TAFE, which is a state rather than a federal government responsibility, finds adult education in an uncertain position. There is hesitancy as to its scope, purpose, and utility, a tendency to see it essentially for leisure, while acknowledging that a philosophy of lifelong or a strategy of recurrent education would require fundamental reconsideration of educational planning and resource allocation. There is no government commitment to develop adult education or any plan for national development, of which adult education, and education itself in turn, could be a part.

Association of adult education with the formal education system is tenuous, and adult educators are not involved, as they are in many Asian countries, with nonformal educational opportunities for school-age children. School premises are used for adult evening classes, schoolteachers teach adults part-time in the evening, and many postschool institutions have significant proportions of postexperience, mature-age students studying full- or part-time for a qualification. Many such institutions also have quite substantial noncredit extension or outreach programs for adults. These activities have little influence upon the work of the formal system at either school or postschool level. There is increasing awareness of deficiencies of the formal system and some acknowledgment of "alternative education" through community-based learning exchanges and neighborhood centers. However, the impact of the formal system is negligible.

In terms of resource allocation, adult educators in Australia tend to feel underprovided and, in very recent times, because of the general economic depression and the cutback in public expenditure, under particular threat. There is some evidence that funds for adult education are being channeled increasingly into vocational training rather than to programs intended for social or individual enhancement and growth.

There is no federal coordination, planning, or direction of adult education in Australia, partly because of the division of responsibilities with the states. In the states, despite variety and flux, there is a recent trend toward coordination and rationalization through new state TAFE structures. These have begun to provide machinery that enables adult education to be centrally identified and funded, but traditional adult educators tend to consider this more of a threat than a promise, the prospect being that adult education will be subsumed within technical training, which is seen as overly rigid, bureaucratic, and subservient to the needs of employers.

There is in Australia a strong voluntary tradition. Although workers' educational associations survive only in New South Wales and South Australia, other nongovernmental agencies, such as YMCA, country women's associations, and the churches, continue the tradition, along with such community-based movements as the learning exchanges. The view that more public funds should be allocated to support nongovernmental agencies and activities is tempered by the concern that government interference, even in the benevolent form of financial aid, will reduce autonomy and frustrate voluntary endeavor.

There is a similar tension over the question of professional versus voluntary workers. Adult educators' demand for professionalization of the service has had little success so far, although professional preparation of adult educators, mostly part-time, has achieved a more or less tenuous foothold in a few tertiary institutions. Australia is underdeveloped in this respect compared with North America and much of Europe. There is concern that professionalization might further widen the gap between providers and learners, thus reducing rapport and contact with groups in particular need of adult education services. There is a hesitancy approaching schizophrenia among adult educators, which is comprehensible in the light of the Australian tradition in adult education and the contradictory contemporary thrusts toward formalization, systematization, and professionalization, on the one hand, and participation, decentralization, and debureaucratization, on the other. Australian adult education mirrors a society in postindustrial transition exacerbated by persisting economic difficulties and uncertainty over national identity and future direction.

Consequences of Comparison

The difficulties in Australia over the use of the un-Australian term *nonformal education* is illuminated by comparison of the sometimes bitter exchanges about the terms *adult, continuing, recurrent,* and *lifelong education.* Rejection of *adult education* in some Asian countries because of its narrow literacy connotation is similar to the reaction in Australia against a tradition that excludes activities attracting certification or having vocational relevance. The quest for new terms is at times transparently political: Adult education may be abandoned in favor of some other term with currency and (con)temporary appeal not necessarily well founded in social theory and values. The *adult* versus *continuing-recurrent-lifelong* controversies in Australia become more comprehensible when these political factors are considered and the prescriptive functions disentangled from the descriptive. The difficulties presented by *nonformal* in many Asian settings may make it easier to understand similar matters in Australia. The way Freire's *conscientization*—education for liberation in contrast to education for conformity—is introduced and possible difficulties handled tends to throw new light on ideological purposes and differences in Australia and to provide insight into the role of adult education in Australia in terms of social change and liberation versus adjustment. The comparison is unflattering, and it challenges adult educators in Australia to look more seriously at their social role and responsibilities.

An obvious difficulty about this comparative sketch concerns national development planning, conspicuous by its absence in Australian peacetime tradition and practice. The end of the recent period of remarkable prosperity, immigration, and economic expansion under a laissez-faire government, however, is forcing even an antisocialist administration toward some measure of planning, at least at sector level. In 1977, a new Tertiary Education Commission subsumed three separate federal education commissions, and a major Committee of Inquiry into Education and Training was examining linkages between education and the economic system. TAFE, now a council of the new Tertiary Education Commission, is acquiring salience as the (albeit modest) growth sector of Australian education, with the prospect of greater centrality for planning purposes; on a wide definition TAFE can be largely equated with adult education. Adult education in the traditional sense of liberal education, however, is marginal and largely irrelevant to Australian national development; this is highlighted by Asian compari-

sons. The content of adult education is different in a largely urban
society where literacy is the norm rather than the exception; but
the comparison still has validity in terms of skill education for each
particular society.

Resource allocation to adult education in Australia takes on
a different hue when compared with that in other countries. It is
not just the obvious relative affluence in Australia that is striking,
since, also relatively speaking, adult education may be deprived of
resources compared with other sectors of public and private spending. The scale of the Iranian campaign in its second year of operation made public expenditure on Australian adult education appear meager. The overall poverty of Bangladesh suggests how
fortunate are Australian adult educators, for all their criticism of
the concentration of public revenues into the formal system. Comparison may thus induce reappraisal of the fortunes of adult education in Australia, realizing how relative any judgment is.

The habit of bewailing the marginality of adult education in
Australia, judged by both the resources and the educational and
social significance accorded it, is now tempered by unease over the
rationalization of postschool education. Although adult education
has little interest for educators generally—unlike recurrent education, which is widely discussed at the postcompulsory level—it is
feared that rationalization and planning may sacrifice such qualities as local initiative and responsiveness, client participation, and
a sense of social purpose. The concern is strong among organizations that have sought to sustain this voluntary tradition. Considering these issues in the light of Asian comparisons is not easy:
Perhaps there are no necessary correlations between official recognition and support, strength of the voluntary sector, degree of
centralization, and commitment to liberation and community development. Comparison suggests caution rather than any specific
change of definition or policy. Particularly teasing are the instances
of Burma, where central planning depends on a high level of voluntary community participation, and Bangladesh, where extreme
poverty goes hand in hand with change-oriented programs in the
nongovernment sector.

Considering aspects of adult education systems in general
through the situation in various Asian countries thus encourages

reexamination of some aspects of the Australian system. New perspectives emerge; some of them make one cautious about unanticipated consequences of certain lines of action; some assumed correlations are discredited, as they do not occur in other settings. Such are among the practical benefits of adopting a comparative perspective.

The countries chosen for this sketch are less easy to compare with Australia than are more similar countries like Canada and New Zealand. The absence in Australia of an overall development philosophy and plan within which both educational and adult education planning can be located is particularly serious. At a time when Australian education is under critical pressure to demonstrate its utility and education budgets appear more likely to contract than to expand, it may, however, be useful to look to very different societies, especially those where problems are more acute and resources more scarce, for new models and approaches.

Several Asian countries have exercised imagination and ingenuity in mobilizing human resources and enhancing the use of scarce capital facilities. Some have made significant progress in integrating adult education planning into national development goals and strategies. Some have made significant progress toward mobilizing voluntary community effort through government assistance that does not disable. Several have taken steps toward exploring the liberation of *conscientization* through adult education of Paulo Freire, which steps make Australian adult education appear shamefully complacent. Each of these areas of experience has importance for the future of adult education in Australia.

Apart from the consideration that Australia's future cannot but be more Asian than its past, the conclusion to which this chapter points is that Australian adult educators would be well advised to take seriously the experience of neighboring countries, to reorient themselves to become colleagues rather than mainly donors or tourists to the exotic, and at least to temper their reliance upon North American and European experience with the less reassuring learning that may flow from comparisons with Asia. The same may be true, if less immediately, for all countries in the rich industrialized world.

Chapter Three

Adult Education Systems in European Socialist Countries: Similarities and Differences

Dusan M. Savićević

This chapter compares and contrasts the systems of adult education in the European socialist countries. Its thesis is that the characteristics of adult education in any country are determined by a number of factors, of which six major ones are identified. Also it deals with nine countries. All nine must be included; no one or no sampling of a few is representative; yet all share many characteristics. Their common characteristics have been formed by history, particularly the years since the establishment of socialist systems, beginning with the October Revolution of 1917 and continuing to the present day. This chapter discusses six of the major determinants of the characteristics of adult education and then examines the characteristics determined by these factors in nine countries, giving the historical background and contemporary situation in each. The chapter concludes with a comparison of the nine countries.

The European socialist countries form one region, but from the standpoint of adult education, they are not unified. Multidimensional aspects of the systems of adult education make comparative research particularly complicated. European socialist countries are not identical in their socioeconomic development. The Soviet Union has been a socialist country for sixty years. The other countries included in this chapter adopted socialism after World War II. The differences among the countries are further magnified as the history of development of each country is examined. Some of them were under foreign occupation for several centuries. The European socialist countries did not have a unified economic development, and they have not achieved the same level of economic development today. Until World War II, Czechoslovakia belonged to the highly developed industrial countries, while Hungary, Bulgaria, Rumania, Yugoslavia, and Poland were predominantly agricultural countries with a tendency toward developing industry. Albania is still an agricultural country with remains of feudalist and patriarchic elements in its social relations. Today the Soviet Union, the German Democratic Republic (GDR), and Czechoslovakia have achieved a high level of scientific and technological development; the other countries are entering the circle of medium-developed countries.

These differences are even more pronounced with regard to literacy and education. In the period between the two world wars, Hungary had an adult literacy rate of 93.1 percent (1941); Poland, 77.0 percent (1931); Bulgaria, 72.2 percent (1934); Rumania, 61.1 percent (1930); Yugoslavia, 55.4 percent (1931); and Albania had only 17.0 percent (Kuzmina, 1976, p. 23). Czechoslovakia had introduced eight-year primary education in the nineteenth century; GDR has reported for a long time that there is no problem of illiteracy; and the Soviet Union virtually eliminated illiteracy in the period between the two world wars.

The systems of adult education have only recently become a subject of scientific research, conducted within the UNESCO Center for Leisure and Education in Prague. These are the reasons why any comparison of the systems of adult education in European socialist countries must be of a general character and must emphasize significant points in their economic, educational, and cultural development. There are also great language differences, both among these countries and within them, further complicating the comparison of the systems of adult education.

Determinants of the System of Adult Education

Despite such complexities, certain factors enable us to discern and define common characteristics in the system of adult education in these countries. The best method in comparative research of the systems of adult education leads from generalities toward particulars and individualities, searching for common elements in general determinants. Six of the general determinants of common characteristics in the systems of adult education in European socialist countries are the following:

1. The nature of social organization
2. The development of science and technology
3. The demonstration of education in general and adult education in particular
4. Acceptance of the philosophy of lifelong education
5. Linking labor and education as factors and ways of the all-round development of a personality
6. A professionalization of adult education based on social needs and scientific research

A consideration of these general determinants of adult education in the European socialist countries complements and is complemented by several other chapters of this book: Chapters Eight and Nine, which show that the drive to reach the unreached is powered by a concern for adult education as an instrument to achieve various social ends, particularly the linking of education and labor; Chapters Five and Six, which document that governments regulate adult education in order to achieve changes they consider desirable; Chapter Ten on research; Chapter Two, which surveys adult education in several countries, among them Burma— a socialist state that is not in Eastern Europe; and Chapter Four, which compares the development of professionalism in adult education in the GDR and the Federal Republic of Germany (FRG).

Nature of Social Organization. Apart from the Soviet Union, only since World War II have the other European socialist countries changed their basic social structure. The transition of means of production from private to social ownership has affected the democratization of education in general and the organization and structure of the system of adult education in particular. The aims of education common for children, youth, and adults have stemmed from the nature of the organization of society and the Marxist philosophy and ideology. The basic aim is an all-round creative development of the personality. Naturally, the efforts to realize these aims take on somewhat different forms in each country.

Socialist ideas in adult education date back to the second half of the nineteenth century and the strengthening of the working class. Subsequently, in the first decades of the twentieth century, the working class began to exert a significant influence in the field of education. The workers' movement of these countries is mainly responsible for the socialist orientation, and within this movement the education of the working class is conceived as a function of the revolution and social changes and exhibits distinct class dimensions.

Development of Science and Technology. During the last ten years there has been an accelerated development of science and technology in most of the European socialist countries. Naturally, the intensity of the development of science and technology in each of these countries in this part of Europe is not identical, since the economical potentials and degrees of development are different, but science and technology seem to influence the entire educational system, and adult education in particular, in all countries. The development of science and technology has created material and social conditions for the development of the system of adult education, for broadening forms and content, for a selective choice of contents, and for the flexible formation of curricula, facilitating adaptation of the educational programs to changing conditions. Under the influence of the scientific-technological revolution in all fields of human labor, intellectual labor increases. That is why in the countries included in this chapter a demand for a higher level of knowledge and qualifications is shown. This fact imposes new demands for people to acquire knowledge and for educators to strive continuously to adapt their programs accordingly. The scientific-technological revolution in European socialist countries has brought about the problem of choosing a "nucleus" of knowledge and modeling it into curricula. In most of these countries, the dialectical unity of education, science, and material production as an instrument for bringing about an increase in labor productivity is emphasized. However, education is regarded in a much broader sense, and it goes far beyond the framework of labor productivity and economic utility. Raising the average level of education of the public generates new needs, raises the necessity of their fulfillment, and contributes qualitatively to new changes of contents in human life and to the enrichening of the personality. From the standpoint of adult education, the scientific-technological revolution and the changes it brings about are always viewed through social frameworks.

Democratization of Education. Access to education has greatly increased in the postwar period. This increased access relates also to adults and their greater participation in various educational activities. Adult education appears as an important factor in the development of society and the individual. It offers possibilities for acquiring qualifications and skills, for requalifying, and for educating people to participate in the social and political life of a country. In the 1950s and 1960s, major progress was made in the reform of the system of education in nearly all the countries included in this chapter. Through these reforms adult education acquired a significant position and is now equal in status to the other parts of the educational system. In most of these countries, adult education is regarded in a new way. The rights of adults to further education and specialization are determined by law. Adults receive special social, moral, and material stimulus: shorter working hours during the day or week, paid leave for examinations, compulsory exercises and other forms of instruction, paid material expenses for education, and faster job promotion for individuals who work and study at the same time. These kinds of stimuli have brought about increased adult participation in certain forms of education. That is why the system of extramural studies has developed in most of these countries. In fact, in most countries an entire system of adult education has been constituted. This is the so-called second educational path, which greatly contributes to the democratization of education as a whole. The democratization of the system of education of the youth has greatly contributed to the democratization of adult education. Apart from the various forms of adult education in schools, there has been a great increase of out-of-school forms of educational and cultural activities organized by cultural institutions, mass media, and social and political organizations. In all these countries a developed network of forms for specialization and the lifelong education of adults contributes to the fuller democratization and accessibility of education.

Acceptance of the Philosophy of Lifelong Education. In at least one of the countries included in this chapter (Czechoslovakia), the idea of lifelong studying has deep roots in the history of education. It would be sufficient to mention J. A. Comenius, who as far back as the seventeenth century considered that one should learn throughout one's entire lifetime. The last twenty years have been marked not only by theoretical explanations of the concept of lifelong education but also by attempts to find the most suitable ways of realizing this concept. Theoretical research on lifelong education has been carried out, particularly in Poland and Yugoslavia. In all the countries included in this chapter, the educational system is being transformed and constituted within the framework of the philosophy of lifelong education. This fact has contributed to the closer linking of the systems of education of youth and adult education into a unified system in which education is acquired by children, youth, and adults. In some countries (Czechoslovakia, Hungary, and GDR) adult education is regarded as the "second educational path," but under the influence of the philosophy of lifelong education, there is a closer linkage of the "first" and "second" educational paths in all these countries. Schools of various levels—from primary schools to faculties of universities—are coming to be regarded not as institutions meant for only one age group but as institutions for lifelong learning. This in no way implies elimination of special institutions for adult education.

The acceptance of the philosophy of lifelong education has created fields for theoretical and empirical research in the field of adult education. The problems of adult education appear all the more often in the research plans of universities in some nations (Poland, Hungary, and Yugoslavia), in the research plans determined by the state (Czechoslovakia), or in special research institutes within academies of pedagogical sciences (GDR and the Soviet Union).

Under the influence of the concept of lifelong education, an increasing number of scientists are conducting research in the field of adult education and learning. In most of the countries included in this chapter, adult education is regarded as a complex phenomenon on which it is possible to conduct scientific research only on the basis of an interdisciplinary approach. Such conceptions are particularly noticeable in Czechoslovakia, Poland, and Yugoslavia. These conceptions give adult education new dimensions in the entire concept of lifelong education and give other sciences (psychology, philosophy, law, economics, sociology, and cybernetics) a chance to create—together with andragogy—new syntheses of the possibilities and needs of adult education and studying. Such an acceptance of the concept of lifelong education contributes to a system of adult education and also greatly widens the possibilities of research in this field.

Linking of Labor and Education. A common approach in all of the countries included in this chapter is linking labor and education, not only as a form of studying and learning but also as an important method in the all-round development of a personality. In these countries special significance is attached to work as an element in developing the personality, and therefore the need to link labor and adult education is emphasized. In most of these countries, reforms of the education system are directed toward linking educational institutions, economic organizations, and social services. Economic conditions and social services as a whole appear as significant factors and partners in adult education. Economic factors are really responsible for a large part of the activities in the field of adult education, from the standpoints of both forming curricula and financing. This relates not only to professional adult education but also to a much wider and broader education: sociopolitical, cultural-aesthetic, health education, education concerning family life, and national defense. The economy also appears as an important factor in adult education. Within the economy there are new services for planning, programming, and organizing education. In some countries (Czechoslovakia, Poland, and Yugoslavia) a whole microsystem for educating those who are working is being constituted in which all levels of education are included, starting from elementary level and going up to higher education and occupational specialization. The economy in a wider sense appears as a sphere of study and education encompassing a number of fields of human knowledge. In some countries (especially Yugoslavia) an exchange of labor between the economy and the educational institutions has begun. This process of an exchange of labor brings education into a completely new situation, as it will no longer depend on the will of individuals—factory owners or the state as a collective representative—but various relations will be mutually arranged by those who need education and the institutions that organize and provide it. The process of determining how best to achieve an exchange of labor between education and the economy and social services is one of the major problems all the countries of the modern world will have in moving toward the twenty-first century.

In some of the countries included in this research (Hungary, Rumania, and Yugoslavia), the governments adopt decrees or laws on the integration of education and the economy directed toward the full integration of science, production, and education. The importance of such an integration is particularly emphasized in the Soviet Union. This trend, noticeable in nearly all countries included in this chapter, has a strong influence on the development of education and contributes to the appearance of new forms and differentiated contents directed not always toward the efficiency of performing the functions of labor alone but also toward the management of labor and the enrichment of one's inner life.

Professionalization in Adult Education. Traditionally in most of the countries included in this chapter, adult education has been equated with "enlightenment of the people," the activities of which were performed on an amateur basis. Such ideas were abandoned after the second half of the twentieth century. Today in nearly all European socialist countries there is a noticeable tendency of greater professionalization in adult education, of creating on a scientific basis professional cadres capable of organizing and accomplishing complex tasks in this field. These ideas were conceived on the basis of scientific research conducted in the field of adult education and on the basis of social needs. Institutions of higher education made a great contribution in preparing cadres for adult education.

The approach in preparing cadres for the field of adult education in countries included in this chapter is not uniform. It depends on the theoretical conceptions of adult education, on the conception of the position of andragogy in the system of educational sciences, and on its position in study plans and programs of universities. In some countries (USSR, Bulgaria, Rumania, and Albania) theoretical research in adult education was greatly neglected until the 1960s. There was rich and varied practical experience, but there was no theoretical basis to this. In other countries (Czechoslovakia, Poland, and Yugoslavia) during the 1950s and particularly during the first part of the 1960s, there was a development of serious theoretical research on adult education and learning. Such research was later undertaken in the other countries as well, and impressive results were achieved, especially in the Soviet Union. However, apart from the results achieved, there are two conceptions of the theoretical dimensions of adult education in the European socialist countries. The first conception, noticeable in the GDR, Czechoslovakia, the Soviet Union, Rumania, and Bulgaria, classifies all problems of adult education within the framework of adult pedagogy, and adult pedagogy is regarded as one of the pedagogical disciplines. The second conception, noticeable in Hungary, Poland, and Yugoslavia, classifies all problems of adult education within andragogy as a relatively independent science dealing with the research of adult teaching and learning. From these various theoretical attitudes to adult education there resulted various solutions in training professional cadres for this field. In some countries (Czechoslovakia and Hungary) cadres are trained at special faculties after secondary school. In other countries (Poland and Yugoslavia) there is advanced training streaming after the second or third year of studying pedagogic sciences, and in the Soviet Union this training mainly takes place during postgraduate studies. In most countries cadres are trained both for the field of education and for that of culture. In some countries, such as Hungary, there are combined studies of adult education and library science.

In spite of the existing differences, there is a general belief that adult education should be professionally based, since this is one of the factors not only of constituting but also of scientifically founding a system of adult education.

Emphasizing what is common in the field of adult education in the European socialist countries by no means implies neglecting the specific aspects that derive from social, historical, economic, and cultural characteristics and give a special characteristic to the system of adult education in each country. I shall later outline some of these characteristics.

The operations of the six determinants identified cannot be examined mechanically, country by country, or selectively in one country after another because they all work together and work also with others not previously identified. One of the other determinants is the peculiar history of each of the countries. Therefore I consider in alphabetical order the historical background for each of the countries (except for the GDR) and then describe the contemporary situation.

People's Republic of Albania

The history of Albania, both before and after the end of World War II, has been varied. Now it is clearly counted among the European socialist countries.

Historical Background. The five-hundred-year-long Turkish occupation of Albania left a distinctive mark on the development of its education and culture. In spite of the occupier's attempts to achieve cultural and political assimilation, the Albanians conducted a persistent struggle to retain their identity and develop a network of schools that used their mother tongue. The first schools were founded in 1887. When Albania became independent (1912), it had a very dark heritage in the cultural and educational sense. Between the two world wars 83 percent of the inhabitants of Albania were illiterate. In 1938, Albania had eight hundred thousand inhabitants, and yet it had no theaters or houses of culture. In 1938, there were 2,374 churches and mosques, 5 museums, and 2 libraries.

The ideological base for adult education in Albania was laid during the People's Liberation War of 1941–1945. After World War II, the main task was to root out illiteracy and to raise the level of general and professional education of adults. Work was done simultaneously on sociopolitical education with great emphasis on the role of the Communist party of Albania and other sociopolitical organizations. In the postwar period the struggle against illiteracy underwent two stages: from 1945 to 1948 and from 1949 to 1955. Albania is one of the rare countries included in this chapter that passed a law in 1949 requiring all inhabitants between the ages of ten and forty to learn to read and write. A central committee for the struggle against illiteracy was formed and attached to the government of Albania. According to some reports, by 1955 illiteracy had been eradicated among people between ten and forty. During the 1950s and 1960s, the number of people included in various forms of education had greatly increased; in 1960, every fourth adult was engaged in some form of education.

Contemporary Situation. The system of adult education in Albania after World War II, and the entire educational system as well, developed under the influence of Soviet experiences until the breach of cooperation between Albania and the USSR and other European socialist countries in the early 1960s. As in the other European socialist countries, a system of adult education closely linked to the system of education of youth was constituted, and together they form a unified education system. Apart from the forms of adult education at schools, there are various forms of nonprofessional cultural activities for adults. The system of adult education in Albania is organized on the following basis: schools for elementary adult education, lower technical schools, secondary schools of general education for adults, secondary vocational schools for adults, and—on the level of higher education—institutes and the University of Tirana (Kolići, 1976, p. 2), with twenty-two branch centers in other towns in which most adults study.

Apart from the school forms of adult education, the system of adult education includes various out-of-school forms of education: libraries, theaters, cultural centers, workers' clubs, and mass media. One can conclude that the system of adult education has a varied and dynamic organizational basis. Albania has achieved significant results in the field of education and culture under very difficult conditions. The system of adult education that enables individuals to gain knowledge on various levels without leaving the sphere of labor has greatly contributed to the democratization of education. The workers can educate themselves not only in schools but also in certain forms for education in business, industries, and factories. One of the main characteristics of the system of adult education in Albania is its close connection to labor. After 1963, when Albania cut off relations with the Soviet Union, the link between labor and education became even more prominent. In the field of education, Albanians started following the Chinese example of "depending on one's own forces." The school year was of the following structure: six and a half months lectures, two and a half months productive labor, one month military training, and two months holidays (Kuzmina, 1976, p. 290).

After 1969, even more emphasis was laid on linking labor and education and on the role of adult education. Parallel to the day schools, the system of correspondence adult education and evening schools has also been developed, which is characteristic of most European socialist countries. In Albania the number of forms of adult education and of people engaged in it grew much more rapidly than was the case with education for the youth. This growth can be seen from the following data: The number of pupils in primary schools grew from 374,900 to 465,900 between 1966–1967 and 1969–1970 and in secondary schools from 12,600 to 14,900. In the same period the attendance at evening schools for elementary adult education increased from 5,900 to 40,800, and in the evening and correspondence secondary schools the number increased from 4,300 to 7,500. According to statistical data from 1973, there were 103,000 adults engaged in the system of correspondence and evening education (Kuzmina, 1976, p. 293).

Significant progress was made in Albania in the field of education of women. Not only has the number of female youth in schools increased (45 percent of the total number of pupils), but also this percentage has grown (to about 30) in adult education. The percentage is even more impressive when it is remembered that religious and conservative traditions in Albania excluded women from social life and education.

Adults who are working and acquiring education at the same time get special consideration and facilities: The workday is shortened by two hours; there is twenty days leave for taking annual examinations; and there is twenty-five days leave for taking diploma examinations. There are also various other kinds of stimuli: financial, moral, and political. Those who are working may study in the twenty-two centers belonging to the University of Tirana. Local businesses assist in the financing of extramural studies. There are firms that organize education for all those working—ranging from elementary education to university education. Part-time students' studies last a year longer. The approach to education—whether daily, evening, or correspondence—is determined by the firm for which the individual works. Workers who receive recognition for the quality of their labor are responsible to the social and work institutions that provide the opportunity for their education.

The cultural centers, workers' clubs, and people's libraries have a special role in the system of adult education. The cultural centers organize various forms of education in towns and villages. The workers' clubs are active within firms and factories and are directed toward developing amateurism among the workers. The workers' clubs organize various forms of educational work, especially in the field of sociopolitical education.

Libraries in the towns and villages, firms, and workers' clubs are an important factor in adult education. There are about thirty large libraries in Albania and many smaller ones. The libraries organize various educational activities: literary evenings, discussions with writers, seminars, and other forms of work (Kulich, 1977, pp. 1–5).

The system of adult education in Albania was constituted and developed mainly under the influence of Soviet experiences. It is closely linked to the system of education of the youth. Through the system of adult education, the Albanian Labor party and the state are striving to achieve their proclaimed goals in the field of education. The basic characteristics in the development of the system are centralized planning and the active role of the state in its directing.

No theoretical basis for the system of adult education in Albania has been developed to date.

People's Republic of Bulgaria

Like Albania, Bulgaria emerged from Turkish rule and after World War II became associated with the European socialist countries.

Historical Background. Adult education in Bulgaria has a long tradition. Bulgaria's historical development has left noticeable marks on the development of adult education. Bulgaria was under the Turkish feudal system from 865 to 1908, and this was a period of minimal activities in the development of adult education. Between the fifteenth and eighteenth centuries the churches and monasteries were the most significant educational centers. Libraries were there, and literacy and education spread from them. In the nineteenth century the movement of national awakening was felt strongly, and under this influence many people's libraries and reading rooms were founded. The first reading room was opened in 1856 in the town of Shumen (Chilingirov). The libraries and reading rooms were the organizational framework within which literacy was spread and schools and courses were organized. In the second half of the nineteenth century, they not only gathered books, newspapers, and magazines but also issued publications, including instructions for basic education. After liberation from the Turks, the reading rooms became "real schools for adults," as contemporary Bulgarian writers call them (Chakarov and Atanasov, 1962). Great effort was put into teaching illiterates how to read and write. At the end of the nineteenth and the beginning of the twentieth century, new reading rooms and evening and Sunday schools were opened in both urban and rural areas. At that time the working class appeared not only as a political force but also as an important factor in education. The echoes of the October (1917) socialist revolution were such that this influence increased even further. Education organized by the working class was directed toward awakening a class consciousness and preparing to conduct revolutionary changes. Between the two world wars the number of reading rooms, evening and Sunday schools, professional schools, and readers' circles increased. This was a period when people's universities were opened in Bulgaria, not as independent institutions but within the framework of reading rooms in which courses in foreign languages, agriculture, and domestic science were given. It was also a period during which the idea of university extension was strongly felt in the Balkans. University professors gave lectures for adults, and faculties made extramural studying possible and established consultation centers, which assisted adults in preparing for examinations. In the same period training of adult educators began at the faculties of social sciences, and this was realized through lectures, consultations, discussions, short courses, and seminars. In 1921, the Free University was founded with an aim to educate people employed in the state institutions. It was called the Free University because there were no restrictions on enrollment, but the criteria during the course of studies were so low that it soon lost its reputation and after some time closed down altogether (Minovski, 1974).

Between the two world wars the museums, cultural centers, theaters, and cultural and sports organizations developed activities among the adults on a nonprofessional basis. In spite of all these efforts, the educational and cultural level of the population remained quite low.

After September 9, 1944, great changes that had considerable effect on the organization of education as a whole and the organization of adult education in particular took place in the organizational structure of society. The working class and the Communist party of Bulgaria came to power and began organizing the society on a socialist basis. Particular attention was paid to education and adult education especially.

In 1944, 23.4 percent of Bulgaria's population was illiterate (Chakarov, 1954). The main task was to eradicate illiteracy. During the first few years after World War II, the results were minimal.

Dissatisfied with such a situation, the Bulgarian government set a task of priority significance—that illiteracy be rooted out by 1953. The Ministry of Education was given the task of carrying this out. The result of these efforts was that one-year schools for illiterates and two-year schools for semiliterates were opened and courses in reading and writing were organized within firms and social organizations. Classes were established wherever there were at least five illiterate people. Parallel to these extensive activities, efforts to raise the general educational level of adults were made. To achieve this, two-year and four-year schools of general education were opened for working adults. The data concerning the percentage of illiteracy in Bulgaria do not coincide with the official statements of the Communist party of Bulgaria. At the Fifth Congress of the Communist party of Bulgaria in 1948, it was stated that illiteracy had been eradicated, but in 1951, the government set the task of eradicating illiteracy. In 1950, 16.4 percent of the population of Bulgaria was illiterate (Chakarov, 1954).

Contemporary Situation. After World War II, the Bulgarian system of adult education developed mainly under the influence of the Soviet experiences. The basic characteristic is a strong link between the system of youth education and centralized state management. The first law on people's education, passed in the new state in 1948, formed a unified educational system in which adult education was given an equal position with other parts of the system. Various functional tasks were set before the system of adult education, among which were the training of cadres for a faster scientific and technical development and the building of socialism in Bulgaria. In order to achieve this, various forms of adult education were established in Bulgaria: evening schools, factory schools, people's and workers' universities, and school centers for professional (vocational) education. The contents were diverse: primary general, professional-technical, ideological-political, and cultural-aesthetic education. The goals of adult education were determined by the Communist party and the state, and the goals were defined by certain legal regulations. The Ministry of Education directs the development of adult education, determines curricula, and gives instruction for teaching. In this whole process the importance of linking labor and education is stressed. On entering the world of labor, individuals assume an obligation to continue their education. The state institutions and economic organizations pay special attention to the working people younger than thirty-five.

There are various ways of acquiring education in Bulgaria: at one's work place, by correspondence, in shifts, individually, or by the "brigade" method, which is realized under the instruction of a highly skilled worker or within a "work brigade," where experiments are also included. Cultural-aesthetic and ideological-political contents are transmitted through lessons, the essence of which is a diffusion of knowledge in various fields of science, politics, and ideology. The Patriotic Front in Bulgaria, as a sociopolitical organization, has great influence in achieving this kind of education. Adult education is also organized by sociopolitical organizations, cultural-art societies, and professional associations.

The system of adult education in Bulgaria has a varied organizational basis consisting of evening secondary schools of a general educational character, evening technical schools, school centers for vocational education, people's universities, cultural centers, agricultural-rural winter schools, libraries and reading rooms, museums, theaters, galleries, and mass media. Apart from these forms of education, schools for educating youth from the primary level to the university level are also engaged in adult education. The institutions of higher education, which have a long tradition in the field of adult education, have a significant role as well. Two-year schools of higher education and faculties organize extramural studies through a network of correspondence-consultation centers. Working people who are acquiring education are provided with certain advantages: shorter working hours or weeks, leave for examinations, and compulsory practical work, as well as moral and sociopolitical stimulus.

The dynamic activities in adult education in Bulgaria are not followed by a systematic development of theory, scientific research, and personnel training. Work in adult education is performed by teachers who have been trained to educate children or by other specialists who are not academically qualified for work with adults. As a result of the insufficient training of teachers to work with adults, many adult students withdraw from education, and in certain fields of education, this amounts to over 50 percent of the students (Minovski, 1974).

There is no theoretical basis for the study of adult education in Bulgaria.

Socialist Republic of Czechoslovakia

Unlike Albania and Bulgaria, Czechoslovakia has been a European country. After World War II, it became associated with the European group of socialist countries.

Historical Background. Czechoslovakia has made a significant contribution to the sociophilosophical ideas on adult education. It is sufficient to mention the implications of J. A. Comenius's conception of education lasting through a person's lifetime. If his *Pampaedia* had been accessible to the public, it might have had much greater influence on the scientific ideas of adult education than his *Great Didactic* had on the theory and practice of youth education. In the provinces of Czechoslovakia, a positive attitude toward adult education has been traditional. Germany and Hungary had an influence on the practical activities of adult education and the organizational structure of these forms of education, but toward the end of the nineteenth century, the influence of the British experiences in adult education began to be felt, especially concerning the organization of university extension. With the strengthening of the workers' movement and the Social-Democrat party as a political expression of the movement, much more attention was paid to adult education, particularly when the Workers' Academy was founded in Prague (1896) and later the Central Workers' School. The organization *Sokol,* founded in 1862, contributed greatly to the physical, intellectual, and moral education of children, youth, and adults (Kulich, 1967). Libraries and reading rooms, educational societies, the People's Enlightenment League forms of the university extension of Charles's (Karlov's) University in Prague, and the *Matica Slovenska*—a cultural literary society—all greatly contributed to the expansion of adult education at the end of the nineteenth and the beginning of the twentieth century.

Between the two world wars work in the field of adult education acquired new dimensions. The law on adult education and libraries, which the parliament passed in 1919, greatly contributed to this (UNESCO, n.d.). On the basis of this law, boards of adult education were formed throughout the country. Between the two world wars Czechoslovakia was one of the leading countries in the worldwide movement of adult education. The activities of the Masarik Institute for Adult Education (founded 1925) contributed by helping organize new forms of adult education, expanding the existing ones, and initiating research in this field.

During the 1930s, the Czech Socialist Academy was founded, and it took over the positive traditions of educational and cultural work that were present in the workers' movement at the end of the nineteenth and beginning of the twentieth century. The Socialist Academy mostly gathered the leftist intelligentsia.

After World War II, the conception and system of adult education changed under the influence of social forces. After 1948, adult education developed under the ideological influence of the Communist party and state centralized management, which had as a basic aim to construct a socialist society in Czechoslovakia. In 1959, the law on adult education, libraries, museums, and art galleries was passed. In this period the system of education was reorganized, and new forms, such as cultural centers, centers for adult education, and societies for propagating political and scientific knowledge, were founded.

Contemporary Situation. On the basis of the constitution, two relatively independent but functionally unified systems of adult education were founded in Czechoslovakia: the school system and the system of adult education. The law passed in 1948 formed a basis for a unified system of adult and youth education, founded on the following principles: The system was to be democratized, polytechnical, scientific, free of charge, and unified.

The system of adult education is regarded as an organic part of the unified system of education for children, youth, and adults, but the various specific aspects of adult education in the scientific, teaching, and organizational sense are taken into consideration. As a whole, adult education is regarded as a relatively independent part of education, with three subsystems: the school system of adult education, adult education in firms, and out-of-school adult education.

The Czechoslovakian school system of adult education is called "the second educational path," and it offers adults the possibility of acquiring education and degrees the state recognizes. The essential characteristic of the second educational path is that it makes possible people's educating themselves and acquiring socially recognized qualifications and skills without leaving their jobs.

Adult education within the school system is organized through the nine-year general-educational primary school, general-educational secondary schools, secondary vocational schools, and institutions of higher education. Education provided for individuals employed full-time was particularly intensified after 1952, and the chief aim was to enable members of the working class to educate themselves. The economy and social services were interested in stimulating this path to education financially. Above all, this increased the number of those working and educating themselves simultaneously. All levels of education could be acquired in this way, including an M.A. or a Ph.D. This greatly affected the democratization of education as a whole. The combination of labor and education is very diverse and flexible. It may include education at a distance (correspondence education), returning to education from the world of labor according to the needs of a work organization, participation in research projects, and education at evening schools.

Adult education in businesses and industries is a subsystem of the complex and multidimensional system of adult education. Its contents are diverse, including acquisition of qualifications, education of technical and economic personnel, and education of leading cadres. Such education can be acquired in factory schools, technical schools, and institutes of the firms.

Out-of-school education, also a subsystem, is directed toward acquiring general cultural and sociopolitical knowledge, based on the interest and needs of an individual, and it is realized in leisure time. It takes place in people's academies; in people's universities of science, technology, and art; in cultural institutions; and through mass media. People's art schools and people's conservatories should be added to this list. Czechoslovakia even has a subsystem for the physical education of adults, which is not found in other countries included in this chapter.

Thus the system of adult education in Czechoslovakia is multidimensional, concerning both the structure of its forms and the field of contents. It provides adults with an opportunity for getting in touch with educational and cultural works.

Czechoslovakia may be counted among the first countries engaged in research on scientifically based adult education. Research concerning adult education may be found not only in universities but also in activities approved by the state. Czechoslovakian authors are systematically trying to found a scientific discipline—adult pedagogy—and also to further the concept of andragogy (Skalka and Livecka, 1975).

This research has been followed by the systematic training of professional adult educators. In Czechoslovakia adult educators are given five years training at special faculties. Training begins after secondary school at the universities of Prague, Bratislava, and Preshev. These studies are a combination of philosophical, pedagogical, and andragogical disciplines.

Through systematic research and personnel training, favorable conditions are created for constituting a system of adult education, for its organizational and contents expansion, and for the democratization of education in the widest sense.

German Democratic Republic

The GDR, the youngest state included in this chapter, has a long tradition of adult education in its territory, which I shall not discuss. The creation of two German states of different social orders brought about the creation of two different educational systems, in both the ideological and organizational sense, and correspondingly, two systems of adult education. The GDR, with seventeen million inhabitants, was founded as a state in 1949, aiming to build a socialist society under the leadership of the Unified Socialist party. The GDR is a highly developed industrial country that pays special attention to various forms of education of its citizens. The first step in creating a new system of education was taken in 1946 through a law on the democratization of schools, aiming to free education of the Nazi ideology. During the early postwar years efforts were made to broaden forms of adult education, particularly by opening new schools of people's higher education. Attention was paid to ideological and political education and specialization. Management of education was centralized. In this period and until 1959, the system of adult education was primarily based on the experiences of the Soviet Union. New institutions and organizations for adult education—cultural centers and societies for propagating scientific knowledge—were founded, and the old institutions were reorganized. The folk high schools were reorganized in 1956 into general-educational and vocational schools on a secondary level. Three kinds of institutions emerged as a result of this reorganization: people's schools of higher education, factory academies, and village academies.

During the 1960s, great efforts were made in the GDR to constitute a unified system of education. As a result, a law on the unified socialist system of education, which encompassed all these levels and forms of educational—from preschool institutions to institutions of adult education—was passed in 1965. According to this law, adult education is an indivisible part of a unified system of education. Although various terms are used for adult education in the GDR, this educational activity is conceived in the widest sense and includes general-educational, sociopolitical, vocational, and cultural-aesthetic contents with an aim of contributing to all-round personality development.

In 1970, a law concerning the education of workers was passed. It further emphasizes the conception of lifelong education and the unity of vocational and political adult education. Primary education in the GDR extends over ten years and is conducted in the ten-year general-educational polytechnical school. There are also forms of general education for adults but on a higher level.

The system of adult education in the GDR has a varied organizational basis. A division exists between the school system of adult education and the out-of-school system of adult education. The first includes secondary vocational schools (*Fachschulen*); folk high schools (*Volkshochschule*), which some experts call "people's universities"; academies of businesses and industries (*Betriebsakademien*); village academies (*Dorfakademien*); and institutions of higher education, which organize correspondence education and extramural studying.

The system of out-of-school adult education includes the society for propagating scientific knowledge (*Urania*), cultural centers, clubs, theaters, museums, cinemas, libraries, mass media, and social and professional organizations. Thus there is a very diverse and flexible system of adult education in the GDR offering wide possibilities of acquiring knowledge. Each year about two million people—about every fourth adult—take part in various forms of adult education. In principle every worker has the right to continue his education without having to leave the job (Schmelzer and Pagoda, 1975). In the GDR there are extramural studies and correspondence education, which are equally recognized by society. Those who acquire education in this manner are offered special facilities and encouragement, such as leave from work amounting to seventy-seven days per year while retaining the right to a full income. Apart from this, many secondary schools and institutions of higher education have educational centers in business and industry. Special attention is paid to advanced professional training of all workers with secondary and higher education. There is close cooperation among business enterprises, schools, and scientific institutions in the organization of further education.

The overall plan of adult education in the GDR led to the systematic training of personnel who had to be ideologically educated and professionally and methodically trained. Prior to 1958, various forms of specialization for adult educators had been organized periodically, but from 1958 onward those permanently employed in institutions for adult education were required to complete a one-year supplementary training program at the universities of Leipzig and Dresden. Later an Institute for Adult Education was formed within the Karl Marx University in Leipzig. It had three departments: systematic and historical pedagogy of adults, didactics and special methodics, and pedagogy of adult advanced training (Kulich, 1977). Studies in the field of adult education extend over four years, and during the fifth year students gain practical experience in one of the institutions for adult education. It is possible to enroll for two courses so that adult pedagogy is the major subject, and the other subject can be one of the social or philological sciences.

Permanent specialization of adult educators is also organized in the GDR and there are five-year studies for training personnel to work in cultural institutions. These specialists are trained at the Institution for Aesthetics, but their study plan includes adult pedagogy and psychology. Knoll, in Chapter Four, also treats professionalization of adult education in the GDR, comparing it with that in the FRG.

Research and theoretical work in the field of adult education is being developed in the GDR. Adult pedagogy forms the basic conceptual framework of such research, and it has several specific subdivisions: pedagogy of education in businesses and industries, pedagogy of higher education, and military pedagogy. Thus a whole system of disciplines within adult pedagogy is being developed in the GDR, and the limited conception of adult pedagogy as a single discipline, a branch of pedagogical sciences, is overcome. Moreover, adult pedagogy is also taught at the universities of the GDR within various other specializations, such as the section of professional pedagogy in Dresden, or within general pedagogy at the Humbolt University in Berlin.

Owing to the systematic training of adult educators during the last ten years, a considerable number of works have been written as part of diploma or M.A. examinations on adult education. The main scientific-research institutes that conduct research in the field of adult education are the Academy of Pedagogic Sciences of the GDR (conducting research on people's universities in particular), the Central Institute for Vocational Education (dealing with the problems of vocational education of skilled workers and craftsmen), and the Institute for Higher Education (dealing with the problems of the further education of those who have completed secondary or higher education) (Schmelzer and Pagoda, 1975).

Research conducted in the field of adult education in the GDR has created a firm basis not only for training personnel but also for creating the system scientifically and for linking it to the needs of society and the individual.

People's Republic of Hungary

Hungary, like Czechoslovakia, has a European history. Since the end of World War II, it has been associated with the European socialist countries.

Historical Background. Adult education in Hungary was introduced under the influence of the French philosophers of the Enlightenment in the eighteenth century and was encouraged and organized mostly at the initiative of individuals. It gained importance with the development of capitalism. As in the other countries included in this chapter, capitalist social relations appeared in Hungary later than in Western European countries, but there was some economic motivations in the development of adult education to increase industrial and crafts production, to increase agricultural production, and, parallel to this, to educate the working class in order to gain class positions. Thus by tradition adult education was functionally oriented, directed to labor and political life. The history of adult education in Hungary confirms that this education was intensified due to the limited provision for public education and the inaccessibility of the school system. Its task was to substitute for the school and to establish a connection between general and vocational education. When the workers' movement in Hungary appeared as a political and economic force, there was a great need for teaching illiterates how to read and write and to acquire other basic skills. Courses for teaching illiterates were organized, and various Sunday schools, forms of vocational education, and people's academies were founded.

When the Social-Democrat party emerged from the workers' movement toward the end of the last and the beginning of this century, various forms of political education were organized, of which the most well known are political schools and readers' circles. The Council of the Hungarian Republic founded workers' universities in 1919 as specific institutions of adult education. Parallel to the development of educational forms, various forms for cultural work and physical education of adults developed: amateur theaters, choirs, orchestras, museums, libraries, and gymnastic societies, which sought to link educational, cultural, and physical activities.

A system of educational and cultural work with adults had already been established before World War I. Between the two world wars differentiation and some restrictions of activities in the field of adult education took place. The restrictions applied particularly to sociopolitical education within the workers' party, and this had to be organized in semilegal and illegal forms of work (Csoma, Fekete, and Hercegi, 1967).

After World War II, adult education in Hungary was more widely organized and was based on the aims Hungarian society assigned to education: to build socialist social relations and to foster the all-round development of the society.

Contemporary Situation. After World War II, two subsystems of adult education were developed. The school system of adult education includes primary schools for adults, secondary general-educational schools for adults, three-year vocational-technical schools for training skilled workers for work in the economy and agriculture, and four-year vocational schools—technical schools followed by higher education for adults. A whole system of institutions for providing socially recognized levels of adult education and skill was formed, and special classes for adults were formed at regular schools for youth—evening classes or correspondence courses that enabled adults to acquire education without leaving the world of labor. During the last quarter of a century, the number of participants in these courses increased unexpectedly. Immediately after World War II, 6.8 percent of the population in Hungary was illiterate, and many more had not completed primary school. In the postwar period about one million adults completed primary school education, nearly half a million finished secondary school, and about a hundred thousand received a degree of higher education (*Characteristics of the Hungarian System of Education*, 1976).

Higher education in Hungary has been considerably democratized by enabling adults, primarily those who are working, to study at the same time. Adults who have not completed their secondary education may enroll at a university if they complete a nine-month course beforehand and prove themselves capable of following courses at the higher educational level. During this period of full-time education, those who are working retain their rights from employment—full income and health and social insurance.

There are two forms of adult education in the Hungarian institutions of higher education: evening courses and correspondence courses. The number of people studying in each form has recently increased. In 1974, those who acquired a degree in this manner were 45.2 percent of the total number of people who received a university degree (Klement, 1975). The need for recurrent education is emphasized in Hungary, particularly relating to the working class. The return to education encompasses all levels and fields of education: general, vocational, and political. The government has legislated that all working people have an obligation to return to education after five- to eight-year periods and in this way renew their knowledge and receive advanced training in their vocation. Although this return to education is mostly voluntary, some businesses and industries have been given the option of making recurrent education compulsory.

The subsystem of out-of-school adult education consists of the following: the society for propagating scientific knowledge, workers' academies, the summer university, political schools of various levels organized by sociopolitical organizations, theaters, cinemas, concert halls, museums, art galleries and workshops, libraries, radio and TV, and various kinds of circles (scientific, technical, and local history), as well as various forms of cultural amateurism. To these should be added the forms of education organized by social and professional organizations.

The entire system of adult education in Hungary (both the school system and the out-of-school system) is closely linked to the system of youth education, and together they form an integral system of education managed and directed by the state. A State Council for Adult Education was formed in 1958, and in 1974, the government named a special council for adult education whose president is vice-president of the government (Fucasz and others, 1975).

During the 1960s, parallel to the development of the dynamic practical activities and the creation of the system of adult education, theoretical and empirical research of the phenomenon of adult education in Hungary had begun on a very wide basis. An all-inclusive perspective, which relates not only to primary and secondary adult education but also to forms and contents of higher education, mass cultural work and amateurism, and problems concerning adult self-education, is evident. In the theoretical sense adult education is regarded as a phase of lifelong education. There are two approaches to founding a science dealing with adult education, one that considers pedagogy a general-educational science and regards adult pedagogy as a part of pedagogy and a second that considers pedagogy a science dealing with youth education and andragogy a science dealing with adult education. This second conception is much more widely accepted than the first. At the first National Conference on Adult Education held in Hungary in 1963, the second conception was emphasized. It takes anthropogogy as a science dealing with human education divided into two scientific fields: pedagogy and andragogy. The primary proponent of this conception in Hungary is Matyas Durko of the University of Debrecen (Csoma, Fekete, and Hercegi, 1967).

Research on adult education and the training of adult educators is organized at two well-known universities in Budapest and Debrecen. The training of adult educators starts after secondary school, lasts four years, and leads to a university degree. An interdisciplinary attitude characterizes these studies, since they are combined with the study of library sciences. The studies of andragogy and library science can also be found at two-year pedagogical schools of higher learning in several towns in Hungary. Apart from basic studies, postgraduate studies in the field of adult education are organized, and it is also possible to earn a Ph.D. These systematic studies are followed by advanced training of adult educators. Advanced training is also organized by the Society for Propagating Scientific Knowledge and some schools that train cadres for work in sociopolitical organizations.

The Hungarian system of adult education, diverse in its forms and contents and functionally linked with the system of youth education, has been an important factor in the overall democratization of education and is also instrumental in the develop-

ment of society as a whole and each individual. Although it fulfills
the tasks set by the state and is based on the ideological premises of
the Hungarian society, the system of adult education, through theoretical and empirical research, gains its scientific basis, which is the
foundation of the professional training of personnel.

People's Republic of Poland

World War II was another chapter in Poland's tragic history
as the battleground between Eastern and Western Europe. Since
then, it has been associated with the European socialist countries.

Historical Background. Organized adult education in Poland
has a long tradition, beginning in the eighteenth century when
Sunday schools and other forms of adult education were organized. These schools spread widely in the first half of the nineteenth
century with the aim of enabling adults to acquire basic general
education and vocational training. Evening schools, which contributed to the reduction of illiteracy and enabled people to acquire
basic skills for employment, were later formed. In the first decades
of the nineteenth century, cultural organizations and associations
organized work on adult education, opened reading rooms, and
formed reading room societies. All activities in adult education had
a patriotic dimension directed at retaining a sense of national identity and were a strong wall of defense against Germanization, which
threatened a part of the Polish population.

In the second half of the nineteenth century, the workers'
movement became a significant factor in education. Various forms
of educational and cultural work were organized within the workers' movement: reading rooms, public lectures, different forms of
entertainment, and magazine publishing. In the second half of the
nineteenth century and at the beginning of the twentieth century,
new forms of adult education appeared: the Flying University (so
named because it often changed its location), the University for
Everybody, the Association of People's Universities, and the Polish
School for Mothers. Parallel to these forms of education, a strong
movement of self-education flourished in Poland, and this was also
the time when the first theoretical works on problems concerning
adult self-education were written. Correspondence adult education

and organized forms of consultations also appeared at this time (Pachocinski and Polturzycki, 1975).

The political independence gained by Poland in 1918 was followed by vigorous developments in adult education. A special department for postschool education was formed within the Ministry for Public Education. The Ministry of Education organized a scientific center for adult education, which tried to give a scientific character to the whole system and all activities in this field. Later, in 1929, the Institute for Adult Education was formed. The network of forms for adult education at all levels was broadened—primary, secondary, and higher educational. At the initiative of the Social-Democrat party, workers' universities offering three-year programs were formed within the workers' movement, and they provided people with knowledge of social sciences and vocational training. Between the two world wars various associations and cultural and humanitarian organizations also developed activities on adult education: the Association of People's Schools, the Association of People's Libraries, the Association of Polish Schools for Mothers, the Pedagogic Federation of Social Organizations, the Association of Polish Primary School Teachers, the Cultural Society of Agricultural Circles, and others. The rich and varied activities in adult education between the two world wars in Poland were accompanied by significant publishing activities and the beginning of the systematic training of adult educators at the Polish universities.

World War II not only inflicted a large number of casualties (six million Poles were killed) but also caused great losses in the material and cultural sense by destroying material and cultural goods and delaying and retarding the development of adult education in Poland.

Contemporary Situation. After World War II, Poland faced up to the problem of illiteracy. In 1946, more than 18 percent of the Polish population was estimated to be illiterate. Various forms of teaching illiterates and of primary adult education were organized, since there were more than seven million adults who did not have primary school education. The low level of literacy was not only an educational but also a social problem. That is why the Assembly of the People's Republic of Poland passed a decree in 1949 on the elimination of illiteracy. Polish authors point out that the significance of that decree lay in its "social compulsoriness." All persons between the ages of fourteen and fifty had to learn to read and write. Those who were literate had to "serve society in the struggle against illiteracy" (*Education in People's Poland*, 1969). The campaign for eradicating illiteracy lasted until 1959, when illiteracy as a mass phenomenon was practically stamped out. However, the Polish people did not stop at this but put great effort into raising the level of primary education of adults. In 1956, the Polish government decided to determine the number of adults who did not have a primary school education, particularly among the working people, and to organize schools and school centers within businesses and industries (*Education in People's Poland*, 1969, p. 179). Apart from the schools for primary adult education, which were opened in towns and villages, a network of schools and courses at factories and other firms was also developed. However, the population poll of 1968 showed that 1,400,000 people still did not have primary school education (*Education in People's Poland*, 1969).

Apart from the primary schools, a network of secondary and two-year schools of higher education for adults was developed: secondary general-educational schools (lyceums), technical schools, and vocational lyceums for adults. A large number of adults acquired education at these schools through correspondence courses or evening classes. Secondary schools cooperate closely with factories, in which they conduct classes.

A whole subsystem of adult education on the level of higher education has been developed in Poland. The following forms of education are available to those who wish to study at this level: evening courses, correspondence education, and external courses. Great interest is shown for these forms of studying. About 40 percent of the students at Polish universities are adults. This means the universities and other institutions for higher education are becoming centers for lifelong education. In addition, the universities provide postgraduate courses and specialization and advanced training, all closely linked to various professions.

Apart from the school system of adult education, the systems of out-of-school educational and cultural activities are also developed in Poland, and they include various forms of education in business and industry, forms of education organized by socio-political organizations, and cultural institutions (cultural centers, national libraries and reading rooms, museums, people's universities, theaters, cinemas, mass media, societies for propagating scientific knowledge, education in the armed services, and forms of self-guided education).

There is a long tradition of training adult educators and conducting research on the problems of adult education in Poland. Between the two world wars Polish universities in Warsaw, Krakow, and Poznan had developed departments for training adult educators. During the last ten years, research activities and activities in preparing andragogical cadres broadened greatly. At the universities in Poland, there are eleven departments for adult education in the form of teaching and scientific units. The number of university teachers and research workers in this field has also greatly increased. According to recent data, about two thousand people received an M.A. degree in adult education between 1965 and 1975 (Pachocinski and Polturzycki, 1975).

Studies of andragogy as a subject in Poland do not begin until after secondary school; instead, andragogy is studied together with pedagogy in the second, third, and fourth postsecondary years. Students of other faculties may, if they wish, choose andragogy as an elective subject and study it for two years. It is interesting to note that the universities in Poland, apart from giving specialized adult education degrees, also issue diplomas stating an individual is trained to work in cultural and educational institutions for adults.

Poland is one of the several European socialist countries in which andragogy is developed as a science dealing with adult education. A whole theoretical concept of andragogy and its position in the system of social sciences has been developed (Turos, 1976). Intensive research is also conducted. The approaches to research vary. They can be historical, theoretical, empirical, comparative, or a combination of these. The fields of research are wide and encompass cultural and educational institutions, self-education, vocational education in businesses and industries, the organization of the school system, other forms of adult education, and the philosophy of lifelong education, as well as problems of self-education.

Theoretical problems of adult education are emphasized at the universities of Warsaw and Poznan. Although significant results have been achieved in research work and the training of adult educators, Polish authors who comment on the system are not satisfied with the position of andragogy within the family of university disciplines, and they have pointed out that far greater efforts are needed if it is to become relatively independent.

The contemporary system of adult education is based on historical tradition and is guided by the general goals of education that have been accepted in Polish society. It is multidimensional by structure and its program orientation, and it is closely linked to the system of youth education. In this way a unified system of education of children, youth, and adults based on the philosophy of lifelong education is formed. It has a firm theoretical basis in andragogy of lifelong education and andragogy as a relatively independent science dealing with the problems of adult education. The dynamic activities in adult education and the results of research have created conditions for including andragogy in the curricula of study offered by universities.

Socialist Republic of Rumania

Rumania is another country with a European history. Since the end of World War II, it has been associated with the European socialist countries.

Historical Background. In Rumania the nineteenth century may be marked as a period of intensive organization of various forms of adult education. The expansion of the capitalist way of production, the abandoning of feudal relations, the appearance of the working class, and the struggle to retain the national identity, language, and culture all demanded the spreading of education among the adult population.

Adult education in Rumania in the nineteenth century first appears within cultural-art and educational societies. The oldest cultural and educational society in Rumania is the Association for Rumanian Literature and Popular Education, founded in 1861. It was active in founding libraries and reading rooms, organizing lectures, founding museums, publishing books, and engaging in other educational activities. With the appearance of the working class as a new social force, educational and cultural activities were organized, directed toward forming a class consciousness. Socialist ideas spread among intellectuals, and they took part in adult educational activities. Various forms of education were formed within the workers' movement. Among them the cultural-art activities were particularly noticeable. When the Social-Democrat party was formed from the workers' movement, it became an important factor in education.

In the middle of the nineteenth century, a special society, Athenaeum, with headquarters in Bucharest, was founded. This society organized cultural activities in the field of adult education and culture, opened cultural institutions, published books, and organized courses and lectures.

The societies for propagating scientific knowledge had a specific role in the history of adult education in Rumania. The League for the Cultural Unity of all Rumanians was formed in 1891. This organization later founded libraries and reading rooms, amateur groups, choirs, museums and organized lectures, and other activities (*Adult Education—Scientific Research and Cultural Action,* 1968).

At the beginning of the twentieth century, numerous schools for adult education were founded to teach adults, especially women, to read and write. The Association for the Culture of Agriculturists, formed in 1892, had this aim.

At the beginning of the twentieth century, the activities of the university extension started in Cluj and later spread to other universities, especially in the period after World War I within the Free University in Bucharest.

Between the two world wars activities in adult education developed in two directions: one under the management of the state and another originating in private initiative. In all these activities the most complex problem was that of illiteracy. Before World War I, an estimated 40 percent of the population of Rumania was illiterate (*International Handbook of Adult Education,* 1929, p. 371). Rumania's economy between the two world wars was primarily based on agriculture. In an economic sense Rumania was one of the most backward countries in Europe. Nevertheless, this period has a special significance in the history of adult education in Rumania.

In the period between the two world wars, an idea was put forward that the conception of adult education was limited and that another conception should be accepted that was not limited to a certain period of life and not restricted to the elementary level of knowledge (*International Handbook of Adult Education*, 1929). This was a reaction to the rather limited conception of adult education found in some Western European countries (England and Denmark) at the time that included only general (liberal) education of adults. The need for legislation in the field of adult education was felt in Rumania and a board of experts was formed for drafting such laws (*International Handbook of Adult Education*, 1929). This was a period when expert attention was paid to adult education. The Rumanian Institute for Education had a special department for people's education, which later contributed to the forwarding and broadening of adult education. At the initiative of the Agricultural Council, people's universities, which aimed to spread practical knowledge, particularly in villages, were formed. University professors and other specialists gave lectures at these universities, so this was a form of agricultural extension. People's academies were also active and their work was organized through sections— pedagogical, literary-historical, political-economic, and science. Lectures combined with professionals reading texts were given at these academies. People's universities were also active in this period in Rumania, and they directed their activities toward rural areas.

Education homes were special institutions created between the two world wars to develop culture and education in the villages, particularly by providing libraries, reading rooms, and lecture halls; by opening chemists' shops; and by providing land for agricultural experiments. In this period there were six hundred education homes in Rumania, which formed their own society and published a monthly magazine, *Education Home* (*International Handbook of Adult Education*, 1929, p. 37 I). The workers' university was formed within the workers' movement, and its aim was to promote education among the working class. Educational activities were realized through a series of general and specialized lectures.

Contemporary Situation. After World War II, Rumania started developing as a socialist society. Although it had a tradition of adult education work, the percentage of illiteracy was still high. During the first postwar years, a systematic action to reduce illiteracy was organized. Various forms of education lasting one or two years were established. About a thousand centers for educating people were active, in which about one million people learned to read and write. In spite of this organized activity, according to the population poll of 1948, 23.1 percent of the people in Rumania were illiterate (Kuzmina, 1976). The previous system of education had to be reconstructed, based on new principles in accordance with the direction of social development. That is why the grand national assembly passed a law in 1948 to reform the system of people's education. The reform designated the priority tasks: eliminating illiteracy among the population between the ages of fourteen and fifty, training experts on a secondary and higher educational level, training adult educators needed for people's education, and training research workers for the field of education and culture (Kuzmina, 1976).

The activities to eliminate illiteracy continued after the law was passed. There was a widespread network of forms for teaching people to read and write and to further the primary education of adults. By 1955, illiteracy was eliminated among the population between the ages of eleven and forty. On the basis of a 1956 poll, 10.1 percent of the population was illiterate, mostly among those over the age of forty-four (*History of Rumania*, 1971, p. 552).

After 1948, the system of education as a whole became centralized and the state took over management of adult education. The school and out-of-school systems of adult education in Rumania were also developed on this basis. The school system of adult education includes primary schools for adults and classes attached to regular schools, evening schools of a secondary level of general-educational and vocational education, and forms of higher education. The form of studying at evening schools and through correspondence was also developed. Nearly 30 percent of the students study in this manner. In 1970, the law on the vocational education of workers resulted in the broadening of vocational programs relating to the requalification, advanced training, and education of leading cadres. Following the conception of strengthening the role of the state in the field of education, professional education and advanced training are the responsibility of respective ministries and central organs that control the execution of programs in firms and factories. Vocational education in Rumania is conducted in close connection with labor and research, particularly with regard to higher education. In 1976, the Rumanian government passed a decree on the integration of higher education with production and research, aiming to achieve an efficacious link among labor, education, and science ("Integration of Higher Education," 1976).

The out-of-school system of adult education includes forms of sociopolitical education (party schools, youth political schools, and trade union schools) and forms of cultural and educational activities (people's universities, cultural centers, cultural clubs, museums, libraries and reading rooms, and mass media).

The system of adult education in Rumania is functionally linked with the system of youth education and is based on the conception of lifelong education. During the last ten years there has been a noticeable development in research of a theoretical, empirical, and historical nature. Rumanian researchers are trying to establish a reciprocal relationship between educational and cultural activities with adults, regarding them as two parts of a unified process of adult education. Recent theoretical studies on adult education in Rumania have given this field of research comparative dimensions as well (Popesku, 1974).

Rumania had experience in empirical research, particularly concerning readers' habits between the two world wars. More recent research is much more broadly based, and its main characteristic is an interdisciplinary approach to research on mass cultural-educational activities and their scientific management. This kind of research is an attempt to provide an answer to questions related to problems and principles of scientific management of cultural-educational activities, problems and attributes of scientific management of cultural institutions on a local level, criteria for assessing the efficaciousness of cultural-educational activities, principles and criteria for predicting cultural-educational activities, and training personnel for cultural-educational activities (Jinga, 1975). The theoretical concept of adult education in Rumania is adult pedagogy, which leans greatly on sociology and psychology.

The training of adult educators at universities is a recent development in which the University of Bucharest is most prominent. Apart from the universities, teacher training colleges also have theory of adult education as a compulsory subject in their curricula. It is an elective subject at technical schools (Kulich, 1977).

The contemporary system of adult education is a significant factor in the culture and education of the Rumanian people. It is based on their cultural heritage and the contemporary aims society seeks to achieve through education. It is thus a significant step in the democratization of education, enabling all persons to avail themselves of cultural and educational achievements.

Union of Soviet Socialist Republics

Since the 1917 October Revolution, the USSR has been under socialist philosophy and policies.

Historical Background. The origin of organized adult education in Russia dates back to the seventeenth century. At that time the church was the most important factor in satisfying educational needs. Toward the end of that century, with the beginning of the capitalist way of production, it was realized that education was important and useful, not only for the church but also for the state. The acceptance of this view was a slow process. Nearly a hundred years passed before work was done on separating secular and religious education. In the first half of the eighteenth century, a law on people's education was passed. It emphasized the need of the state for vocational education, which was dictated by economic motives and interests; general education was accepted only in the function of vocational education. Between the reigns of Peter the Great and Catherine II, vocational schools were opened for the need of the state; these were religious, military, naval, medical, and mining schools—all with a strict class orientation and division. However, the needs of vocational education could be satisfied only with previous general education, so the state issued a decree on the founding of primary schools. Under the influence of Western ideas in the middle of the eighteenth century, great progress was made in secondary and higher education, particularly for members of the aristocracy and bourgeoisie. The idea of education for the larger part of the population existed only in the minds of progressive individuals.

The decree on abolishing serfdom (1861), by which twenty-two million peasants were proclaimed free, was very significant for the development of adult education in Russia ("Adult Education in Russia," 1922). Most of the peasants were illiterate. The ideas of progressive intellectuals were directed toward primary adult education. The government, considering itself endangered, persecuted the intelligentsia. The forms of adult education in Russia most characteristic of the time were Sunday schools founded by individuals with local government funds. Teachers worked at schools voluntarily without pay. Through the activities of these schools, a positive andragogic heritage was acquired: Initiative and creativeness were developed in the students, and classes were formed according to age groups. Much attention was paid to opening libraries and reading rooms, giving lectures, and spreading popular literature. In spite of all this, at the end of the nineteenth century, only 18 percent of the population was literate ("Adult Education in Russia," 1922, pp. 1–19). The government strictly controlled all forms of adult education. Special permission was needed for founding libraries and reading rooms or for giving lectures. By the law of 1891, all forms of adult education were subject to strict police control.

The development of industry and, concomitantly, the increasing independence of the working class in the second half of the nineteenth century gave a new impetus to adult education. The Russian revolutionary social democrats—Vissarion Belinskiy, Aleksandr Herzen, and Nicholai Chernyshevsky—contributed greatly to the development of sociopolitical education. In the 1890s, circles were organized within the workers' movement in which the works of Marx and Engels were studied. V. I. Lenin not only organized but also gave lectures in these circles. N. K. Krupskaya was also active in them. From this period up to the October Revolution, Lenin discussed the problems of adult education several times, pointing out the positive experiences of Western countries, especially concerning the work of libraries.

The 1917 October Revolution is one of the most significant

events of the twentieth century. The establishment of a new social order influenced the development of adult education. Soviet authors point out that the basis of today's system of adult education in the Soviet Union was laid down in the first years of the Soviet Republic, with Lenin at its head (Darinski, 1970).

Lenin's historical decree on eliminating illiteracy (1919) is well known. On the basis of this decree, all people between the ages of eight and fifty were obligated to learn to read and write and classes were formed in various places: schools, clubs, reading rooms, factories, military barracks, and even out of doors. In the first ten years of the Soviet Republic, fifty million illiterates and forty million semiliterates were taught to read and write at these courses. The success achieved can be seen by comparing the population polls from 1897, 1926, 1939, and 1959 (*Pedagogic Encyclopedia*, 1964, pp. 612–613). Lenin's concept of functional literacy was realized in international dimensions only after half a century, under the leadership of UNESCO.

After the October Revolution Lenin initiated the creation of a new system of adult education: schools for primary adult education, workers' faculties, workers' universities, party schools, Communist universities for sociopolitical education, libraries and reading rooms, workers' clubs, cultural centers, forms of education in the economy, museums, and mass media. At his initiative a closer link between labor and education was established; education through work was developed; and broad activities in the field of self-education were initiated. Important theoretical activities in the field of adult education were started in the period between the two world wars. N. K. Krupskaya made a special contribution to this activity by writing theoretical treatises and editing professional journals on adult education.

During World War II, all human and economic resources were drafted for the defense of the country. In this period all advancement in the field of adult education stopped. However, even in these war conditions a wide network of evening schools for youth and adults developed, which they could attend without leaving their defense-related jobs.

Contemporary Situation. After World War II, adult education in the Soviet Union was organized in two subsystems: the school system and the out-of-school system. A constant raising of the level of youth education significantly stimulated adult education, which may be taken as a common factor for all countries in this chapter. The development of the Soviet society shows each phase of development is followed by specific educational problems. During the 1920s, the main task was to eliminate illiteracy, and today the main task is to provide every worker, particularly young workers, with secondary education. Recently, a great deal of attention has been paid to adult education, since it is closely linked to the scientific-technological revolution, which conditions lifelong education. Soviet authors emphasize that general and vocational adult education are the most significant components of lifelong education (Darinski, 1972).

The school system of adult education includes the following forms: secondary general-educational schools for adults, which aim to provide adults with complete secondary education in three basic ways—through evening education, correspondence education, and education in shifts; vocational schools for adults, the programs of which can be combined with general education; and adult education in institutions of higher education.

Apart from regular studies, the system of studying without leaving one's job is also widespread in the Soviet Union. The latter is organized through evening faculties and at correspondence faculties. There is a widely developed network of these faculties. Evening and correspondence studies last a year longer than regular studies. Studies at evening and correspondence faculties are regarded as a matter of enormous social interest and significance. Adults who are working and studying at the same time receive social and financial incentives: public recognition, paid leave for consultations and examinations, and improved chances of promotion.

Individuals acquiring education are responsible for the quality of their education and its effectiveness to the institutions of higher education and the work organizations that encourage their studying.

The role of institutions of higher education in lifelong education is constantly growing in the Soviet Union. The forms of vertical and horizontal adult training are being broadened. This situation increases the need for closer cooperation between education and the economy, not only from the standpoint of financial benefits but also from the standpoint of promoting science, the social and cultural life of society, and a creative use of leisure time.

Special significance is attached to the out-of-school system of adult education, which consists of people's universities of various profiles, people's libraries, cultural centers, workers' clubs, parks of culture and rest, theaters, museums, galleries, the federal society "Knowledge," mass media, and a network of forms of directed self-education. All these forms and institutions organize various forms of cultural and educational activities for adults and none has examinations or issues degrees, but this kind of learning is no less significant than that organized through school forms, since it contributes to the satisfaction of intellectual curiosity, the enrichment of inner life, and the creative use of leisure time.

The rich and dynamic experiences of adult education in the Soviet Union for a long period after World War II were not followed by corresponding research (theoretical or empirical) in the field of adult education. The continuity in this field, which had begun between the two world wars, had been interrupted. The reasons may be found in the traditional conception of the subject of pedagogy as a science dealing with the education of youth. For a long period pedagogy did not cross the Rubicon to adult education in the Soviet Union. This limited conception has had and still has an influence on some of the other countries included in this chapter. Essential changes occurred in the Soviet Union during the 1960s, both in the orientation of research and the broadening of the subject of pedagogy. The Scientific-Research Institute was formed within the Academy of Pedagogic Sciences of USSR, and theoretical and empirical research of the phenomenon of adult education was initiated. Although the theoretical basis of adult education is adult pedagogy, the subject of adult education is being broadened in the Soviet Union, and there are several scientific fields that form the system of disciplines of adult pedagogy (military pedagogy, economic pedagogy, legal pedagogy, adult didactics, and others). The latest sources show some Soviet authors also use the term *andragogy* in their works, especially when discussing comparative problems of adult education (Tonkonogoj, 1976).

There is an interdisciplinary approach to the phenomenon of adult education in the Soviet Union. Research in the field of the sociological and psychological dimensions of adult education is particularly important (Ananev and Stepanova, 1972). The results of such research on adult students in evening schools, which include results concerning specific aspects of adult education, the adult as a subject of educational activities, adults' differential acceptance of oral and written statements, and characteristic aspects of the process of problem solving, are quite interesting (Kuljutkin, 1977).

Although the unity of the system of youth and adult education is emphasized in the Soviet Union, there is as yet no systematic training of adult educators. The universities offer possibilities of postgraduate studies of adult pedagogy and of acquiring the M.A. or Ph.D. degree in the field of adult education. However, the cultural institutions provide four-year training for cadres who will work in cultural-educational institutions and who are mainly the organizers of educational and cultural activities (Genkin, 1971).

The number of M.A. and doctoral dissertations in the field of adult education in the Soviet Union is growing, which leads to the accumulation of knowledge needed for constituting a theory of adult education, a process unfortunately deemphasized before the 1960s.

The contemporary system of adult education in the Soviet Union is based on the experiences of the sixty-year-old socialist development of the country and on the goals of education, which include the conception of the all-round development of a personality. The realization of the scientific-technological revolution has brought to light the philosophy of lifelong education, and the school and out-of-school systems of adult education are the most important parts of lifelong education in the Soviet Union.

Socialist Federal Republic of Yugoslavia

Yugoslavia came into existence after World War II. Since then it has been associated with the European socialist countries.

Historical Background. Yugoslavia was founded as a state in 1918. The areas that constitute the country were previously either independent states or part of the Austro-Hungarian Empire. Various influences—political, economic, and cultural—were reflected in the structure of education and the level of literacy as a whole. All these contribute to the great heterogeneity in the field of education and culture in Yugoslavia today.

As in some other countries included in this chapter, the church had been a center of culture and education in the regions of the present country, especially in the Middle Ages. The Yugoslav peoples came into touch with diverse cultural and political influences from the East and West, for example, the Byzantine, Roman, and Central-European civilizations. These influences are noticeable in the architecture, folklore, language, and religion of the country. However, in spite of the strong influences from the outside, the Yugoslav peoples retained their identity throughout their long struggle for freedom and independence. Thanks to education, by which they accepted progressive ideas, they built a civilization and culture that reflects their own unique characteristics. The mural paintings in the churches and monasteries of the Middle Ages are examples well known throughout the world.

Further advancement in education and culture in the territory that is now Yugoslavia was interrupted for several centuries, especially in those areas under Turkish rule. The first systematically organized forms of adult education (schools and libraries) appear in Croatia and Slovenia in the second half of the eighteenth century. However, before the nineteenth century, there was no wider organizing of institutions of adult education. The *Matica Srpska*—a broadly based cultural center—was founded in 1826, and the *Matica Hrvatska*, in 1842. Both in time became the most important educational institutions in Serbia and Croatia. In the first half of the nineteenth century, many libraries and reading rooms were founded, as well as schools and courses for adults and teachers' associations (Samolovčev, 1963).

In the second half of the nineteenth century, a polarization appeared in the field of adult education. There were educational forms organized by church organizations and private initiative and others founded by the workers' movement. During the 1870s, socialist ideas penetrated into the territories of today's Yugoslavia and were accepted by the working class as a new social force. The socialists, especially Svetozar Marković, realized the importance of adult education and worked on spreading knowledge and culture among the people. At the end of the nineteenth century, there were wide activities on forming workers' cultural and educational societies, and the Social-Democrat party, formed at the beginning of the twentieth century, has its origin in them (Savićević, 1962).

In the period prior to World War I, adult education in the territory of today's Yugoslavia was developed under the influence of the state on one side and the workers' movement with the Social-Democrat party on the other. The first decade of this century marked the founding of people's universities (1907), schools and courses, forms of political education within the workers' movement, and cultural-art and educational societies; the network of libraries and reading rooms was broadened; textbooks for adult education were published; the influence of the British university extension could be felt in Zagreb and Belgrade (Bulatović); and on the whole the basis for adult education was greatly broadened. However, the main problem was the low level of literacy of the population.

Apart from the unsolved national and agrarian problems, the newly formed state of Yugoslavia was also faced with a low level of education and a high percentage of illiterate population. According to the population poll of 1921, 50.5 percent of the population was illiterate. In some areas of Yugoslavia, the percentage of illiterates was even higher. In Bosnia and Herzegovina, for example, it was 78.2 percent, and in Kosovo, 95.5 percent. Even later there was no improvement of the level of literacy, which can be seen from data of the 1931 population poll (*Statistical Data* . . . , 1964).

In the period between the two world wars, adult education in Yugoslavia was organized and developed under the influence of the state and bourgeois parties on the one hand and the workers' movement and the Communist party of Yugoslavia on the other. In this period efforts were made to organize courses, seminars, and schools; the network of people's universities, libraries, and reading rooms was broadened; the first forms of adult correspondence were established; and new cultural-art and educational societies were formed. Under the influence of the Communist party, a system of sociopolitical education, which first worked legally, then semilegally, and finally illegally, was formed. The activities of the university in jails is well known, and the most prominent members of the workers' movement in Yugoslavia acquired education there. Through these forms of education, they were educated for taking over crucial tasks in 1941 when Yugoslavia was occupied by German and Italian troops (Savićević, 1968).

The People's Liberation War and the social revolution in Yugoslavia (1941–1945) also had cultural and educational dimensions. Various forms of adult education were organized in liberated territories and in military units: schools and courses, people's universities, military-political schools, cultural-educational societies, theatrical groups, choirs, public lectures, and others. Adult education in this period was a direct function of the revolution and its social orientation. This period witnessed some positive andragogic experiences and the creation of the ideological and organizational basis of the system of adult education (Ogrizović, 1963).

Contemporary Situation. After World War II, a new social structure of Yugoslavia was built on the basis of the social revolution, and its scientific orientation was the construction of a socialist society. The period between 1945 and 1950 was especially significant for adult education. The main problem in adult education at the time was a low level of literacy. In 1946, an estimated 44 percent of the population of Yugoslavia was illiterate. The war years and destruction exacerbated this problem because it produced illiterates in the youngest generation, who had not had the opportunity to attend school.

From 1945 to 1950, the basic organizational framework of adult education consisted of cultural-educational societies in the rural areas and cultural-art societies in the urban areas. Within these societies schools, courses, seminars, people's universities, libraries, and reading rooms was organized.

By 1950, there were three campaigns in operation for teaching people to read and write, which attracted several hundred thousand adults. The percentage of illiterate people decreased noticeably, but illiteracy was not stamped out. According to the population poll in 1971, 15.5 percent of the population was illiterate, these being mostly older people (Savićević, 1975).

Starting from 1950, great social changes occurred in Yugoslavia. Self-management was introduced in factories and later spread to social institutions as well. These changes were of historical significance for the development of adult education. New institutions were formed—the workers' universities—which had as a basic aim to prepare workers for the new self-management functions. The reforms of the system of education from 1954 to 1958 brought about the passing of the general law on education in Yugoslavia (1959), by which adult education is included in the unified system of education and all schools—from primary schools to faculties of universities—were bound to take part in adult education activities. This was a period when the role of the state in adult education diminished and educational centers were formed in factories and businesses and industries. During the 1960s, the constituting of the system of adult education was completed, and it now has a diverse and flexible organizational basis. It consists of the following forms: primary schools for adults, schools and other forms of education at a secondary level, people's universities, educational centers in factories, forms of higher education, political schools (evening and youth political schools, schools of self-guided learners, and trade union schools), cultural centers, theaters, museums, libraries, mass media, forms of education in the army, and sociopolitical and professional organizations. The system of adult education in Yugoslavia is not strictly divided into the school and out-of-school system.

During the 1970s, the philosophy of lifelong education was becoming established in Yugoslavia, and it served as a basis for transforming the education system as a whole and that of adults particularly. In 1970, the federal assembly adopted a resolution on the development of education on the basis of self-guided learners, which is based on the ideal of lifelong education. Constitutional changes from 1974 direct education toward a closer linking with labor and a continual alternation between labor and education during a citizen's working life. The strategy of recurrent education is accepted in Yugoslavia, which is of special significance for adult education on all levels (Saviçeviç, 1971).

Education in Yugoslavia is the responsibility of the republics and autonomous provinces, which pass laws on it. This is particularly noticeable at the secondary and higher levels of education. A process of linking labor and education and of linking educational institutions with the economy and social services has begun in Yugoslavia. The state does not appear as an intermediary in this process, as was the case in the traditional system and conception of education. Organized labor as a whole becomes an important factor in education, not only from the standpoint of financing certain programs but also in forming curricula and providing a place of study.

The system of adult education in Yugoslavia started acquiring its theoretical basis in the 1960s. Yugoslavia was among the first of the countries included in this chapter in which the conception of andragogy as a relatively independent science whose subject is research on adult education was developed. During the last twenty years, a great amount of knowledge has been acquired, through both theoretical and empirical research, which made it possible for andragogy to find its place in the curricula of institutions of higher education. Several universities—those in Belgrade, Zagreb, Rijeka, Ljubljana, Sarajevo, Skopje, Pristina, and Novi Sad—offer opportunities for studying andragogy. Andragogy is studied not only at the liberal arts faculties but also at the faculty of political sciences, the faculty of organizational sciences, the four-year school of higher education for the organization of labor, the pedagogic-technical faculties, the faculty for security measures at work, two-year workers' schools of higher education, two-year medical schools of higher education, and military academies. At the institutions of higher education mentioned, it is possible to study andragogy as a major undergraduate subject or at the postgraduate level (specialization and M.A. studies). It is possible to earn even a doctorate at some. The number M.A. and Ph.D. dissertations in the field of adult education has been increasing over the past decade. The greatest number of these dissertations was written at the Belgrade University. Other university centers have adopted an orientation similar to that of Belgrade: Ljubljana, Rijeka, Zagreb, Skopje, and Sarajevo. During the past few years, a number of theoretical and empirical studies have been written dealing with different aspects of adult education: the concept of lifelong education, adult education, programmed instruction, the theory of military education, recurrent education and associated labor, adult education, and others.

The contemporary system of adult education in Yugoslavia was formed as a result of social needs, and it is a result of the ever-increasing democratization and accessibility of education. The nature of the Yugoslav self-managing society demands lifelong learning that will help people successfully perform functions of labor and management and at the same time enrich their inner lives.

System Similarities and Differences

Apart from the determinants that influenced the constituting of a system of adult education, which I discussed previously, there are important similarities in the historical and contemporary dimensions of adult education in the European socialist countries. Identification of similarities by no means implies an absence of differences among these countries, either in their historical development or in their contemporary framework. I shall mention only some of the similarities and differences.

In the historical development of adult education and the forms in which it appeared, the churches and monasteries appeared as cultural centers in which adults learned to read and write and acquired education (Bulgaria, the Soviet Union, and Yugoslavia). The development of capitalism, and with it the development of science and technology, led to the state's appearing as an important factor in education as a whole and in adult education, too. The churches gradually lost their leadership in providing educational and cultural functions, and these functions were taken over by the state and voluntary associations. The development of capitalism in the nineteenth century in nearly all these countries brought about the appearance of a new social force—the working class—which showed particular interest in education and saw it as a liberating force. In all these countries the working class and its political expression—the Social-Democrat party—organized various forms of education and associations. During the first two decades of the twentieth century, there were constant political and economic stirrings, and new states were formed, a ferment that left noticeable marks on the development of adult education. Of all the various influences, the most forcible and important was that of the October Socialist Revolution in 1917. A new system of adult education was constituted in the Soviet Union, and between the two world wars new forms of adult education were organized in the other countries, either semilegally or illegally.

After World War II, these countries, except for the Soviet Union, which had already done so after the October Revolution, entered on the road of socialist development, producing a marked effect on the development of the system of adult education in all countries. These countries all share the general goals of education, which are determined by society, that is, the class in power and the party of Marxist orientation—the political expression of that class. The realization of these goals acquires certain specific aspects in each country, depending on historical conditions, economic development, and the educational and cultural level. After World War II, the influence of Soviet experiences and practical activities can be felt in the field of adult education in all the countries, and these experiences are sometimes directly transmitted into the other countries without readjustments. Under the influence of these experiences, new forms of adult education were formed in most of these countries (for example, cultural centers and societies for propagating scientific knowledge). In most of these countries, the state took over responsibility for adult education, and this led to the centralization of the system and the strengthening of the role of the state in this field of education.

In many of these countries, the philosophy of lifelong education is accepted and adult education is regarded as the most important part of it. The 1960s marked a series of reforms of education as a whole, in accordance with the conception of lifelong education. Through these reforms adult education became a part of the unified system of education. On the basis of these reforms, educational legislation that sanctioned such trends of development was enacted. The conception of lifelong education was developed in theory, especially in Poland and Yugoslavia.

Similarities among the systems of adult education in these countries are apparent in the functional linking and interaction of educational and cultural institutions, the school and postschool path to education, education that leads to the acquiring of officially recognized degrees, and those forms of cultural-educational activities that mark a person's way of life. This linking is particularly noticeable in Hungary, Rumania, and Czechoslovakia, where special attention is paid to the participation of all citizens in hobby and cultural activities.

In all these countries the need for linking labor and education is emphasized, which has special significance from the standpoint of adult education. The economy and social services as a whole (factories, businesses and industries, and institutions) have become an important factor in adult education. A whole microsystem of adult education is constituted within the economy, directed not only at training working people for functions of labor but also for managing labor and enriching one's inner life. This kind of situation greatly contributes to the democratization of education as a whole.

During the last twenty years in most of these countries, empiricism has been dominating the field of adult education. Attempts have been made to put adult education on a scientific basis and to determine by scientific methods its specific aspects, to find the most efficacious methods of education, to establish scientifically an organization of cultural and educational institutions, and to base the creative practical activities in this field on theory. In most of these countries, the universities have started playing an important role in research on the problems of adult education. This can be said particularly of Poland, the GDR, Hungary, Czechoslovakia, and Yugoslavia.

Research has produced a body of knowledge that has enabled the intensification of professional training of adult educators at universities and other institutions of higher learning. In most of these countries, the conception of the need for training personnel for cultural-educational work with adults has prevailed. In most the adult educators are trained at universities where this is the major subject or is offered at the level of postgraduate studies. Naturally, the approaches and solutions are not uniform, but there is a noticeable general tendency toward professionalization of adult education in all these countries.

To note the similarities in the systems of adult education in

European socialist countries is not to deny the differences among them. These differences derive from the socioeconomic and political position of each country, from their historical development, and from their level of economic and cultural achievements. The differences derive from the strategy and characteristic ways of development of socialist societies, which have a direct effect on the system of adult education. In most of these countries, the conception of centralist planning is dominant and there is an increased role of the state in the field of adult education. In Yugoslavia a socialist self-managing society is being developed, and therefore the role of the state in the field of adult education is decreasing. Such a policy increases the role of organized labor in education, bringing decision making in adult education closer to those who need it most. This distribution of responsibility has a direct influence on the program orientation of adult education.

The historical development of each country I have discussed has had an effect on the structure of the system of adult education, and therefore in some countries we come across certain institutions that do not exist in other countries. This gives the system of adult education its unique aspects in the organizational and program sense in each country.

Differences in the systems of adult education also derive from the differences in the theoretical conceptions and scientific attitudes to the founding of adult education. There are two dominant standpoints: one by which the theoretical framework of adult education is found in pedagogy or its branch, adult pedagogy (Czechoslovakia, the GDR, the Soviet Union, and Rumania) and the other by which the theoretical framework of adult education is found in andragogy (Hungary, Poland, and Yugoslavia) as a relatively independent science that includes a whole system of andragogic disciplines. The second standpoint also supports the thesis that there is a general science dealing with education (Poland and Yugoslavia) or anthropogogy (Hungary), which is divided into pedagogy and andragogy. Theoretical discussions that may eventually result in establishing greater similarities of concepts have been led on these various concepts existing in certain countries (Czechoslovakia, Hungary, and Yugoslavia).

The differences in theoretical conceptions bring about differences in training personnel for work in the field of adult education. These differences are reflected in the levels and approaches to training cadres: major studies (Czechoslovakia, Hungary, the GDR, Poland, and Yugoslavia), postgraduate studies (USSR), or just shorter courses and seminars (Albania). The differences are also reflected in the division in the training of personnel for the field of culture and the field of education, as is the case in the Soviet Union.

The differences do not represent anything negative in the development of the system of adult education; on the contrary they give the system of each country specific characteristics and special qualities. In each country universal values that contribute to the world treasury of theoretical thought on adult education are crystallized. This means the systems of adult education in European socialist countries should be regarded as a unity with differences and not as a uniformity and that from these differences come new possibilities for the development of the theory and practice of adult education.

Chapter Four

Professionalization in Adult Education in the Federal Republic of Germany and the German Democratic Republic

Joachim H. Knoll

Before comparing the Federal Republic of Germany (FRG) and the German Democratic Republic (GDR), I must point out an anomaly. This chapter study is comparing not an aspect between two nations but an aspect between two parts of the same nation. It is a nation, moreover, that has had an anomalous history. Although the origins of the development of Germany as a peculiar culture are as old as those of England, France, and Spain, Germany was not unified until 1871. Its subsequent rapid industrialization and the expansionist and imperialist policies of its emperor resulted in World War I, which left the German people exhausted and defeated.

Whatever chances Germany, reconstituted under the Weimar Republic, had to become a nation that was democratic domestically and cooperative internationally were dashed by the worldwide economic depression that began in 1929. Social tensions reached such a point that President Paul von Hindenburg could form a parliamentary government only by accepting the support of the National Socialist party. Hindenburg made Adolph Hitler chancellor in January 1933. Within three months the Reichstag gave Hitler dictatorial powers. Less than seven years later Hitler's policies had resulted in World War II.

After the war the boundaries of a completely defeated Germany and the lines dividing it into two parts (East and West Germany and East and West Berlin) were drawn by the occupying Allied powers. The conflict between the Soviet Union on the one hand and the United States, Great Britain, and France on the other hand had begun even before Germany's unconditional surrender in May 1945, and Germany was the main arena of this conflict. Since 1949, Germany has been divided into two states, the FRG and the GDR, with the precise status of West Berlin unclear but intimately tied to West Germany.

In May 1949, the people of West Germany adopted a constitution similar in structure to that of the old Weimar Republic except that the states (*Länder*) have much more power and the federal republic much less. The FRG, with its own armed forces, is a member of the North Atlantic Treaty Organization (NATO). The FRG became a full member of the United Nations in 1973. With the help of the United States and by joining the European Common Market, West Germany has become one of the leading industrial powers of the world.

In May 1949, the people of East Germany adopted a constitution, superseded by one adopted in 1968, similar in structure to that of the USSR, with highly centralized powers and highly collectivized economic and social life. The GDR, with its own military forces, although Soviet forces are still stationed there, is a charter member of the Warsaw Treaty Organization and a member also of the Council for Mutual Economic Assistance. The GDR became a full member of the United Nations in 1973.

In recent years the GDR and the FRG have established relations that encourage mutual trade and facilitate movements of visitors between the two parts and zones. However, the division is more than a political demarcation and an ideological difference. It is physically marked by a 4.8-kilometer cleared, policed zone and the formidable Berlin Wall. Although the peoples of both parts of Germany have accommodated to the situation imposed by external powers, they do not regard the division as natural or permanent.

These remarks are intended to remind the reader that beneath the differences or similarities in one aspect of adult education that can be discerned, strong, deep binding forces are at work that must be seen in the perspectives of hundreds of years, not just of recent decades.

Having sketched the historical background, I shall now provide a general characterization of adult education, the professionalization of adult education, and the comparative study of adult education in the two parts of Germany; describe the present situation of reform tendencies in the FRG and the GDR; discuss the professionalization of adult education and its substantiation in the FRG and the GDR; and draw a few conclusions.

General Characterization

The term *adult education* is generally applied in German usage to two fields: practical adult education, which in the FRG is pluralistically constituted (folk high schools, church, trade union, and party political institutions), and to the academic discipline whose object of research is adult education. In the interest of a precise definition of the scientific pursuit of adult education, the terms *adult pedagogy* (*Erwachsenenpädagogik*) (used mainly in the GDR and other socialist countries and less in the FRG), and *andragology* or *andragogical science* (used in the Netherlands, Yugoslavia, and less in the GDR and FRG) or *science of adult education* are adopted. The term *university adult education* characterizes those activities that in English-speaking countries are referred to as *uni-*

versity extension and *extramural activities*, that is to say, programs
of various forms in which the university presents itself to the public
and whereby scientific disciplines make manifest their social relevance or societal serviceability.

This chapter deals with a single aspect of this topic. I selected the problem of professionalization because it is carried out
by the universities and teachers' colleges. Accordingly, I do not
discuss activities related to in-service education. The system of
adult education in the FRG is pluralistically organized; churches,
labor unions, and political parties are managing their own agencies
for adults. Due to this structure there is a widespread in-service
training, which is the responsibility of the agencies and not necessarily linked up with the universities. To give an example, the
German Folk High Schools Association has developed its own
courses for those aiming at a position at a folk high school. In this
course the practical methods and measures required to fulfill a job
in a folk high school are taught. In speaking of professionalization,
I do not include the training of civil servants for jobs in adult
education. Persons seeking administrative jobs within, for instance,
evening institutes are educated either within the local community
administration or in addition at special schools (administration
schools, *Verwaltingsschule*) and are not specifically prepared for the
administrative duties in adult education. But this does not exclude
the professional adult educators who are introduced into the field
of administration. Program planning, curricula design, counseling,
and training the part-timers are under the direction of those who
have been professionally prepared to be adult educators. These
remarks are especially directed to readers who are not acquainted
with the German systems of adult education.

This chapter complements and is complemented by parts of
several others in this book—Chapters Three, Five, Six, and Ten.

Adult Pedagogy as a Discipline. The science of adult education,
or adult pedagogy, did not establish itself in the FRG and the GDR
as an independent subdiscipline of educational science until after
World War II. Up until this time scientific issues of adult education
were pursued within the framework of general education (today,
educational science). This applied in particular to the period of the
Weimar Republic (1919–1933), during which adult education first

began to be regarded more intensively and consciously as a legitimate field of educational research. As early as the nineteenth century one can cite lectures, seminars, and publications in the university sphere devoted to the themes of popular education (*Volksbildung*), national education (*Nationalerziehung*), and the popularization of science. Historians of nineteenth-century education have begun to take an increasing interest in this aspect (Dräger, 1975).

Two basic assertions are generally accepted today: first, that the scientific pursuit of adult education presupposes an educational context, that is, adult pedagogy constitutes an autonomous subdiscipline of pedagogy or educational science. Second, recognition is also claimed—particularly by those authors whose interpretation of adult education is primarily societally oriented—for the pertinence of adult education not only to educational but also to social science (Axmacher, 1974; Feidel-Mertz, 1975; Mader, 1976). Without prejudice to such an undoubtedly justifiable differentiation, adult pedagogy presents itself institutionally as a subdiscipline of educational science, and as such it enters into the increasingly particularized domain of educational science, whose various branches include general educational science, history of education, comparative study of education, vocational and economic education, social education, recreational education, remedial education, school education (again subdivided into its various forms), and adult education. There is also consensus that adult pedagogy has entered, or should enter, into a process of development represented in the programmatic formula "From Pedagogy to Educational Science," which advocates a reorientation of the objects and corresponding procedures of educational research, that is, the transition from interpretative hermeneutic procedures to primarily empirical methods. This new directional impetus has not, however, come to imply a complete disengagement from the nineteenth-century foundations of educational theory but rather aims at broadening the scope of its fields of inquiry and research activities (Brezinka, 1972).

Generally speaking—and this applies to the FRG, the GDR, and other German-speaking systems, such as those of Austria and Switzerland—adult pedagogy is regarded as a subdiscipline of a freshly surveyed educational science and as such is expected to employ the standard procedures of its fellow subdisciplines.

It thus seemed appropriate to orient the comparative study of adult education toward the already established procedures and groundwork of comparative education. In the FRG, and one may say in the GDR as well, the opinion prevails that the issues, procedures, and repertoire of methods of comparative education may also be applied to the comparative study of adult education. An exception may be the use of microanalytical procedures, which are perhaps better suited for comparisons of structures and educational content of school types. On the occasion of the Third Quinquennial Conference of the International Congress of University Adult Education in Accra in 1976, Titmus postulated that various problems dependent on economic, systemic, and societal conditions are determining factors of the content of adult education and that even if basic conditions are relatively similar, curricular precepts cannot be as stringently constituted as in the school system (Titmus, 1976a). To give a concrete example, analyses of mathematics courses such as those studies carried out under the International Project for the Evaluation of Educational Attainment (Schultze, 1970) cannot be applied to adult education, as in this field such heteronomically determined educational objectives are not ostensibly stipulated—even if these objectives are de facto similar. The often-expressed reservations against Bereday's macroanalytical global approach in application to comparative education should not interpose in the comparative study of adult education (Bereday, 1967).

Methodology. Leaving aside for the moment qualifications of this nature, one might say the comparative study of adult education could model its research methodology after the current stage of development of comparative educational science. It would not be necessary for comparative adult education research to repeat the history of comparative education research, whose stages have been systematically described by Answiler (1971) as the following: first, the subjective-impressionistic phase—with, for instance, reports of educational journeys; then the objective-descriptive phase—the period of monographic studies in foreign education that may be termed classical; and, third, the analytical-expressive phase.

Comparative education may have analyzed its methodological profile, but studies along the lines of this profile are in fact still relatively sparse. Surveying the situation in West Germany, we find the majority of studies are intersystem descriptions or comparisons, in particular, comparisons between the FRG and the educational systems of the Eastern European countries. Dissertations in the GDR are with few exceptions limited to intrasystem comparison. The study of comparative adult education has followed the initiative of adopting the range of methods and issues of comparative education and complementing them with perspectives intrinsic to adult pedagogy. This was also a basic premise of the Nordborg conference of 1972, a meeting initiated by the International Congress of University Adult Education (ICUAE), UNESCO, and the Danish Ministry of Education, at which there was not only discussion on methodological questions but also the first appearance of completed research projects (Syracuse University, 1972). The ICUAE World Conference in Accra in 1976 established this as a point of reference in the topic "Widening Access to University Adult Education" (Knoll, 1973).

As to the scientific penchants of adult pedagogy in the FRG, there are only a few university chairs or research institutes that concern themselves with international aspects of adult education. Broadly speaking, adult pedagogy in West Germany, after a phase of having had educational policy as a prompter to decision making (in development of educational leave, professionalization, and curricular systematization), has swum with the current of a widespread tendency in higher education policy and courted prowess in the field of theory, barring the way to an international, more pragmatically interpretable study of adult education. The hypothesis is occasionally put forth that, contrary to the thinking of the 1920s, the international aspect has diminished in importance and now only the practitioner of adult education participates in international discussion (Knoll, 1976).

Currently, research and teaching of adult pedagogy, insofar as they pertain to international perspectives, are still dependent upon English-language publications, which claim to exemplify not only methods but also possible procedures in the comparative study of adult education (Bennett and others, 1975). In the relevant foreign publications the approach and techniques of comparative education are adopted; in the FRG such publications—monographic treatises as well as articles in periodicals—are still primarily part of the objective-descriptive phase of foreign studies in adult education (Knoll, 1976). This does not, of course, represent a qualitative judgment but merely a qualifying statement with reference to methods. These methodological demarcations, which imply the step from juxtaposition to comparison has not been taken, are also to be found in the studies of the GDR. Here examples may be cited from the publication *Vergleichende Pädagogik* (*Comparative Pedagogy*).

Present Status of Reform Tendencies

Even a primarily structural comparison of the adult education systems of the GDR and the FRG must take into account the manifold differences in economic and geographical factors. The statistical yearbooks of both states show the following vital statistics: population of the FRG, 61.45 million, area, 248,576 square kilometers; population of the GDR, 16.89 million, area, 108,178 square kilometers. One must then also point to the differences in economic and political commitment. The FRG is a member of NATO, the European community, and other international and supranational, Western-orientated bodies. The GDR belongs to the Warsaw Pact countries and to the socialist economic community, Council for Mutual Economic Assistance. Both states have prominent places in the aforementioned supranational organizations on account of their high degree of industrialization and a high export rate in proportion to the size of their economy.

Of greater consequence are the ideological contrasts against the background and on the basis of which the education systems of both countries have developed. Apart from these differences, reforms in the field of adult education have not by any means been synchronized. While the GDR with its Law on the Uniform Socialist System of Education of February 25, 1965, reached, so to speak, the end of a phase in educational reform, the FRG was only just embarking on the "realistic turning point" reform in its system of adult education (Knoll and others, 1967).

Significant milestones on the path to a reform of adult education in the FRG—from 1970 onwards termed *further education,* this in itself denoting a new concept—are the following documents, which are only a small sampling from a wide range: On the Situation and Function of German Adult Education, Report of the German Education Committee; Structural Plan of the Education Commission of the German Education Council, 1970; Comprehensive Plan for Education of the Federal and State Commission for Educational Planning, 1973; and First Further Education Act of the State of North Rhine-Westphalia (Gernert, 1975).

In addition to these documents, I must mention the manifestos of 1963, 1966 and 1968 of the German Folk High School Association (*Standort- und Selbstverständniserklärungen des Deutschen Volkshochschulverbandes*); the proposals of the 1960s on educational policy made by the adult educationists Picht, Schulenberg, and Knoll; the Social-Liberal Coalition's Education Report and Government Declaration (*Bildungsbericht und Regierungserklärung der sozial-liberalen Regierungskoalition*) of 1969–1970; and the preliminaries to the adult education acts of the federal states that have appeared in the interim either as bills or as ratified acts, beginning with that of North Rhine-Westphalia (for example, Bavaria 1974, Bremen 1974, Hesse 1974, Lower Saxony 1970, and Saarland 1970). The acts of 1970 reflect a traditional understanding of adult education, not having been in a position to presage the developments that led to the widely accepted concept of further education.

Professionalization and its Substantiation

What holds true in the comparison between West German and East German adult education also applies to the process of professionalization: The GDR, having gotten off to an earlier start, has taken the lead. In the GDR it was recognized relatively early that a rationalized system of adult education with a stringently constituted curriculum requires adult educators with the necessary academic qualifications who are well versed in applying these to the practice of adult pedagogy. Thus training and refresher or in-service training programs for full-time adult educators were developed at an early stage, these being still today quantitatively and qualitatively superior to those available in the FRG (Siebert,

1970b). Moreover, educational policy in the GDR has not fallen prey to the supposition that adult education must present itself as being completely divergent in content and method from school education. On the contrary, the simple reasoning has prevailed that the methodology and didactics of adult teaching must in the first instance relate to school teaching, the specific features characteristic of adult learning, then, of course, being taken into consideration. In the FRG the conjecture was long entertained that youth education and adult education were in principle things apart and that consequently didactics and methods for adult education must be developed separately.

Both systems have recognized that the profession of the adult educator requires specific training on an academic level. Assuming the activities and function of the adult educator can be divided into subject expertise on the one hand and competence in educational management on the other (educational and career advisory responsibilities and curriculum planning), professionalization in the GDR puts more emphasis on the former function and in the FRG on the latter.

Pursuing the significance of the issue of professionalization in the thinking of our times, it would appear at first that this particular question is of no consequence. It emerged from my search of dictionaries, in particular of educational ones, that professionalization was not to be found as a problem complex in its own right. In short, educational encyclopedias in the FRG and the GDR do not as a rule carry an entry entitled "Professionalization." In such works the contemporary position of discussion on professionalization is at any rate not recorded. From my own personal engagement in scientific policy making, a comparison with journalistic science seems appropriate, as in this discipline too the malignant question of what its academics can actually do in practice hangs in the air. Journalistic science has been involved in social scientifically based discussion about professionalization to a greater extent than has educational science (Kepplinger and Vohl, 1976). Here it is mainly the wide range of English-language material on professionalization that is utilized, including earlier works (Vollmer and Mills, 1966). An intensive search of recent encyclopedic works reveals just one newly published West German lexicon with an entry "Professionalization of Educational Occupations" (Wehler, 1973). However, nowadays if one reads in new works under the heading of "Adult Education," one usually finds mention of the problem of professionalization (Starke, 1970).

Meaning. In such contexts German usage makes a distinction in nature and content between professionalization (*Professionalisierung*) and occupationalization (*Verberuflichung*). Occupationalization characterizes the tendency toward conversion of part-time or secondary occupational activities to full-time employment. Among other definitions of professionalization is Mader's (1976, p. 127): "Professionalization means a process of specific qualification for a function in adult education. The premise must be made that those employed in adult education have indeed specific qualifications in their own particular teaching subjects, but that these qualifications are of unspecific relevance to the teaching, planning, and consultative function of adult education. It is therefore the task of professionalization on the one hand to orientate these unspecifically acquired qualifications toward the specific conditions of adult education, and on the other hand to make the sphere of further education itself, of which the employees have a pragmatically acquired working knowledge, the subject matter of their training and continuing education." This definition presupposes that the subject expertise required for teaching must first be acquired—for example, by means of an academic study course—and that this expertise should then be functionalized for the specific requirements of adult teaching by means of a supplementary or complementary course.

There are postulators and models of an integrated first degree for training adult educational personnel, with parallel practical courses to compensate for the deficit in applied knowledge. Both training models exist in the GDR: first, an academically conceived secondary training course subsequent to an academic primary course—in combined use of correspondence and direct study —and, second, adult pedagogy as a first degree course. In the FRG —insofar as degree courses in educational science specializing in adult education are at all available—the training of adult educators is effected through first degree courses. Apart from these the sponsors and institutions of adult education offer as an additional qualification for adult educators a short-term study course. The idea of an additional degree or diploma in adult education (*Zusatzstudium*) has recently been favored in the literature on this topic. If one wanted to bring about the combination advocated by Mader, to orient the study of the individual subject toward the requirements of adult teaching, it would be a logical consequence to complement the relevant branches of science with a didactic structure specially geared to the characteristics and needs of adult education. A degree course in physics would thus be coupled with the study of the didactics of physics in application to adult learning. The GDR has gone some way in this direction with the establishment of faculties or departments of subject didactics for the essential subjects taught to adults. At present the FRG is still only fragmentarily aiming at this transportation of pure subject expertise into expertise in teaching the subject to adults (Schultze, 1970).

Entrance Requirements. Literature on professionalization and the reality of practice in the FRG and the GDR presupposes an academic course of study is a *sine qua non* for a post in adult education (further education and adult qualification) (Schulenberg and others, 1972). Exceptions to this rule are activities that demand practical or artistic skills.

There are no stringent stipulations as regards entrance requirements for prospective adult educators in the FRG. From a legal point of view, a post in adult education is not necessarily dependent on examinations or certificates. If, however, one traces the course of recommendations, reports, and legal provision on adult education, a tendency toward professionalization and occupationalization can be clearly discerned over the past twenty years. But these testimonies are as a rule couched in terms that cannot be interpreted as an unequivocal vote for any one particular form of training. The German Education Committee (*Deutscher Ausschusz für das Erziehungs-und Bildungswesen*), an independent panel of experts, declared in 1960: "The training of full-time folk high school teachers . . . must, in collaboration with the universities, be so governed that the quality and freedom of their work be secured" ("Zur Situation . . . , 1966, p. 921). The German Education Council (*Deutscher Bildungsrat*) the board of experts succeeding the German Education Committee, also expounds in its structural plan (*Strukturplan*) (*Deutscher Bildungsrat* . . . , 1970, p. 212) on the "qualification of teaching staff" and bemoans among other things the fact that educational policy and reform are confronted with the difficulty that the available statistics and analytical studies on further education are not sufficiently informative and that reliable data on further education staff do not exist. The work of the German Education Council formed the basis for the Federal and State Commission for Educational Planning (*Bund-Länder-Kommission für Bildungsplanung*), a body that, as a result of modifications to articles 91a and b of the Federal German Constitution, set limitations on the educational and cultural autonomy of the West German states in favor of cooperation between the federation and its component states. The *Bildungsgesamtplan* of the Federal and State Commission for Educational Planning is more explicit on admission requirements for adult educators, but here it should be mentioned that the second recommendation of the Conference of Ministers for Culture and Education (*Kultusministerkonferenz*) published in 1971 had already proposed modalities of training for adult education personnel. The federal and state commission, which in fact also advocates supplementary qualification for part-time adult educators (*Bund Länder Kommission* . . . , 1973, pp. 64–66), quite frequently refers in its recommendations on qualifications for full-time teachers to a "supplementary course of study in educational science specializing in adult education."

Legislation on further education in West Germany also makes no precise definition of forms of training and entry qualifications beyond the established principle of a first degree (Gernert, 1975). Even though the GDR's system of adult qualification—and with it professionalization—may be regarded as having been more or less consolidated since the act of 1965, there are still some measures outstanding as far as regulation of the details of professionalization is concerned. While provision has been made for the training and in-service further education of full-time personnel in first degree and supplementary study courses, it has only been since 1965 that improving the competence of part-time adult education staff has become a subject of interest and target of action. Thus in 1971, a compilation of the issues of adult pedagogy and psychology appeared, a practical handbook specially geared toward the needs of part-time staff (*Beiträge zur Erwachsenenquali-fizierung* . . . , 1971). Then again in a parliamentary statement of 1970, the People's Chamber (*Volkskammer*) of the GDR, referring to adult education generally, decreed in a clause on the aspect of professionalization: "The principals of working collectives (*Arbeitskollektive*) must be qualified for the management of the training and further education of the workers" ("Decree of the People's Chamber . . . ," 1970). As the GDR has a uniform and centrally controlled system of education, its legal directives are to a great extent rigidly compounded. Among the laws, resolutions, and decrees of the People's Chamber, the Council of State (*Staatsrat*), and the Council of Ministers (*Ministerrat*) pertaining to adult qualification in the widest sense, are the following directives: Principal Responsibilities of Clubs and Cultural Establishments in the Five-Year Plan (D 111/6), Further Education for Teachers (J/1/27), Further Education Courses for Teaching Staff of Out-of-School Establishments (J/1/28), Employment of Staff at Institutions of Vocational Education (K/11/8), Programs for Further Education (J/1/48), and Statutes of Employment for Teaching Staff in Popular Education (K/111a/4).

Thus, while in the GDR professionalization and its related modalities of training are for the most part legally provided for, in the case of the FRG one can only describe professionalization as being at an early stage of development, albeit with a plurality of training courses of widely diversified content. In the foreground of discussion on qualifications for admission to a teaching post in adult education are the "Conceptual Directives for the Diploma Examination in Educational Science," which also provides for specialization in adult education ("Declaration of the Conference of Ministers . . . ," 1969). On the basis of these parameters, diploma courses specializing in adult education have since appeared at teacher training colleges (*Pädagogische Hochschulen*) and universities. These may be classed as first degree training courses for further education personnel. Regulations governing supplementary courses, however, do not as yet exist. In fact only after the *Rahmenordnung* ("Conceptual Directives") was introduced did questions began to be raised on training situation, requirements, and professional role and identity. The *Rahmenordnung* had omitted any precise job definition or the necessary activity profiles. Conceptual directives and a study course had been developed without sufficient reconnaissance work on job description and professional opportunities (Weiss, 1975). In pursuance of questions of this nature, discussion on the basic issues of professionalization has also become more intensive in West Germany. Summings up of the status quo and of opportunities for development are being carefully scrutinized (Vath, 1975).

Definition. On the basis of an analysis of the relevant Anglo-American literature, Vath (1975, pp. 19–20) names the following characteristics as determinative of professions and thus, broadly speaking, of professionalization: "integration of practitioners of the profession into an organized body; observation of an ethical professional code; application of specialist expertise based on theoretical knowledge; training of a specialized nature; acquisition of a degree or diploma as a prerequisite for entry into the profession; and esprit de corps as a basic professional principle."

The *Rahmenordnung* for the diploma in educational science specializing in adult education has by no means been adopted by all West German universities. For example, at the University of the Ruhr in Bochum, adult education may be studied only for M.A. and Ph.D. degrees or for the state examinations for entry into the teaching profession at secondary level, that is, for teachers at establishments of general secondary education (*Realschule, Gymnasium*) or vocational education (*Berufsbildende Schulen*). It was argued at this university that these examinations, which usually require two or three individual main subjects, equip their graduates with a wider scope of professional serviceability. But both universities of the federal armed forces (*Hochschulen der Bundeswehr*), at Hamburg and Munich, have introduced diploma courses in educational science specializing in adult education, albeit with the so-called "compulsory optional subject" carrying such weight that the candidate is assured of the opportunity to acquire sufficient expertise in a teaching subject (Knoll and Siebert, 1968). In the debate on professionalization, references to foreign models are comparatively rare, both in the FRG and in the GDR (Knoll, 1974).

The fact has by no means been dismissed in the FRG that the diploma in educational science specializing in adult education poses manifold problems and that it shows promise of being advantageous but at the same time encounters difficulties in practice. The sheer extent of discussion in the press following the introduction of the diploma course was of itself impressive (Burmeister and others, 1976; G. Buttler, 1975; G. Buttler, 1976; Buttler and Buttler, 1974; Buttler and others, 1974; Buttler and others, 1975; I. Buttler, 1976; Kemner and Kurze, 1979; Kuhlenkamp, 1976; *Materialien zur Studien* . . . , 1975; Schweiz, 1975; Siebert, 1974, 1975).

In both the FRG and the GDR, activity profiles—and study content—are being broadened to embrace not only the more traditional fields of competence of further education (vocational, political, and general) but also the international dimension. Thus the German Folk High School Association has established a section for adult education in developing countries to coordinate and document the manifold activities of adult educational practice in the Third World. Similar external activities can be perceived in the GDR (Fischer, 1975).

Increasing Support. Adult education (further education, adult qualification) enjoys a high degree of prestige in FRG and GDR educational policy. Expenditure on adult education is classed in both systems as an economic investment. The rates of increase in this context are either subdivided into the separate sectors or documented as overall figures. Inter Nationes, for example, an information agency associated with the FRG Foreign Office, writes, "In 1976 the governments of the eleven states of the Federal Republic of Germany allocated 1.8 billion DM for expenditure on art, culture, and adult education, that is to say, 80 million more than in 1975; 322 million DM were allocated for adult education and public libraries" (*Bildung und Wissenschaft*, April 1977, p. 64). The GDR also evidences considerable augmentations (Lenzko, 1975).

The *Bildungsgesamtplan* of the Federal and State Commission for Educational Planning (1973) made the following prognostications with regard to future developments: "Graduation of costs in further education: 1970—179 million DM; 1975—362 million DM; 1980—553 million DM; 1985—709 million DM."

The member states of the FRG, insofar as they have passed legislation on adult and further education, have committed themselves to such an extent that these forecasts will very likely be exceeded.

An important impediment to making comparisons between the GDR and the FRG is the fact that even institutions bearing the same title are endowed with different responsibilities. For example, the folk high school of the GDR is primarily responsible for courses leading to school-leaving qualifications, that is, for granting subsequent to school leaving the graduation certificates of the ten-grade polytechnical high school (*Polytechnische Oberschule*) and the twelve-grade extended high school (*Erweiterte Oberschule*). Enrollment figures in this particular field will decrease in direct proportion to the degree of correction to this requirement for compensatory forms of education. An ideal comparison between the folk high schools of the FRG and the GDR is thus rendered impossible on account of their different responsibilities and functions.

Conclusion

In this chapter I have compared adult education in the FRG and the GDR. Others have done this, too (Niehuls, 1973; Siebert, 1970a). Such attempts must use as their principal point of comparison a structural analysis of institutions, participants, educational content, and communication forms. This procedure has meanwhile been criticized by GDR educationists, who, on the publication of our survey of the system of adult education in the GDR (Knoll and Siebert, 1968), declared the system of adult education could only be interpreted in the light of the educational goal—the socialist personality—as described in the preamble to the GDR act of 1965. Thus they claimed the system of adult education could not be adequately appraised from a structural analysis.

However, I hypothesize that there are convergent phenomena of structure and content inherent in the composition and objective requirements of highly industrialized nations. In this case one must make allowances for the fact that educational objectives beyond the demands of performance and efficiency are relegated to a position of lesser importance. There are only limited possibilities of comparison between, as it were, a monolithically constituted system that presents itself as a scientifically substantiable integral whole (GDR) and a system whose very constitution is pluralistically rooted and whose educational objectives are manifold (FRG). On the basis of this hypothesis, tendencies toward reform bearing a high degree of similarity, immanent in or transcending the systems, can be summarized as follows:

transition from "subjective education needs" to "objective educational needs"
increasing stringency in curricular precepts
systematization of educational subject matter
vocational orientation of adult education
more intensive standardization and coordination in adult education institutions
establishment of adult education as a sphere in its own right within the state education system
adult education as a public responsibility and as the obligation of state and communal bodies
application of the psychology of learning to the practice of adult education (unit system principle, integration of vocational, general, and political education)
introduction of a certificate and qualification system
increasing professionalization

These elements of reform have already been implemented or at least adumbrated, and traits in the FRG and the GDR in these spheres bear a resemblance to each other. The process of reform in the GDR was brought to an interim standstill by the act of 1965, after which subsequent legislation has merely been of a particularizing nature. In the FRG these elements of reform in adult education did not govern educational policy until after 1970, when corresponding demands began to be made on the educational political scene. A start on the relevant legislation was made at the end of 1974.

If, on the basis of the forgoing analysis, one were to include other German-speaking countries such as Switzerland or Austria (Kemner and Kurze, 1979), one could justify the hypothesis that highly industrialized countries have similar structural modalities of professionalization. Austria and Switzerland too are in a process of evolution from having been principally agrarian nations to becoming systems in whose economy industrialization plays an increasingly important role. The development of adult and further education runs in synchronization with this process. In the face of such economic changes, the debate on professionalization becomes more intensive. Both countries are closely following the path of West German discussion on professionalization, without, of course, adopting training modalities as practiced in the FRG. It is to be expected that characteristic national forms will develop in these countries.

This chapter may have shown that ideological preoccupations in highly industrialized countries are often sacrificed to practical necessities. It may also have demonstrated a structural convergence between the GDR and the FRG, which are both experiencing the strength of world economic forces and in which the demands of their respective competitive situations triumph over their *Weltanschauung*.

Chapter Five

Adult Education Organizations in a Comparative Context

E. M. Hutchinson

In this chapter I consider adult education organizations at national (or national-divisional), regional, and international levels both as an essay in comparative study and as an indication of the contribution these bodies can or could make to the continuance and extension of such study.

At the international and regional levels the organizations in question are, first, those established to stimulate and support the provision of learning opportunities for adults in more than one country and, second, bodies concerned with particular sectors of society in various countries. Such organizations may provide training facilities for functionaries and teachers by way of conferences and seminars, but in general they do not give services to the public at large. Examples of the first group are the Interna-

109

tional Council for Adult Education, the African Adult Education Association, the European Bureau of Adult Education, and the Asian-South Pacific Bureau of Adult Education. Examples in the second category of organizations are the International Congress of University Adult Education, the International Institute for Adult Literacy Methods, the European Center for Leisure and Education, the International Federation of Workers' Educational Associations, and the International Cooperative Alliance.

These and similar bodies have been created largely by individuals and independent voluntary effort—the International Institute for Adult Literacy Methods was an exception. But they are increasingly likely to be in contact with and to receive and reciprocate practical help from some intergovernmental bodies, notably UNESCO, the International Bureau of Education (IBE), or the International Labor Organization (ILO). At the regional level there are also such UNESCO-instituted bodies as the Regional Center for Functional Literacy in Rural Areas for the Arab States and the corresponding body in Latin America.

Categorization is more complex at the national level. For the purpose of this chapter, national organizations are deemed to be those that promote and stimulate adult education by more than the direct and immediate provision of learning opportunities for groups and individuals. (The term is used loosely to include also those that serve only a part of a nation, such as in England and Wales as distinct from the U.K., English-speaking Canada, and Tasmania but that serve not only their areas but a national function as well.) They are the principal bodies the International Council for Adult Education had in mind in organizing the first Conference of National Organizations for Cooperation in Adult Education at Wansfell Adult College, England, in 1974. The report of that conference (*National Organization for Cooperation* . . . , 1975), although relatively cursory, is one of the few sources of general information and assessment of the significance of such organizations, as will be apparent from the use I shall make of it. The Adult Education Division of UNESCO is currently trying to improve the flow of information and to produce international directories, but at this time the only region for which a reasonably clear picture is available is that served by the European Bureau of Adult Education. A third and much improved edition of its *Directory of Adult Education Organizations in Europe* was published in 1978.

National Organizations

"The initial hypothesis," states the report of the Wansfell conference,

> was that some national mechanisms or some combination of means are required in every region and country:
> * to foster recognition and attention for the special needs and services of adult education
> * to help link up adult education within the entire educational system and learning community—adult education seen within the perspective of lifelong learning
> * to persuade governments, intergovernmental agencies and non-governmental organizations to provide more adequate resources
> * to help establish and maintain high standards of performance
> * to develop improved means of communication and to encourage training and research
> * to found adult education as a response to the needs of the nation and the human family (*National Organizations for Cooperation* . . . , 1975, p. 3).

The report also quotes from the conclusions of the international symposium on *Functional Literacy in the Context of Adult Education* held in Germany in 1973:

> * in view of the need for permanent provision for adult education, governments should take a long-term view and establish the necessary institutions and structures
> * coordination should not seek to impose uniformity; rather it should aim at linking educational activities with the solutions of the problems of the nation and the individual
> * such coordination may be achieved through national boards and councils and appropriate committees at various levels. Institutes of adult education and adult education associations also have a vital role (*National Organizations for Cooperation* . . . , 1975, p. 4).

The functions that must be performed by any organization that aspires to fulfill the role envisaged in these generalizations will necessarily include some or all of the following:

- maintaining a documentation center and library
- taking responsibility for the issue of recurrent and occasional publications
- organizing regular meetings between representatives of public and private organizations that give direct service to the public at large
- arranging congresses, conferences, seminars, and other group meetings accessible to substantial numbers of functionaries, teachers, and other people employed professionally or voluntarily in giving such service
- initiating and/or undertaking enquiries at various levels of detail to a point that may justify the use of the term "research"
- fostering and in some circumstances undertaking the training of practitioners of adult education at various levels
- serving as a point of first reference for people, whether from home or overseas, seeking information about national or local aspects of adult education provision
- serving as a center of advocacy and appraisal in relation to the policies of central and local government (*National Organizations for Cooperation* . . . , 1975, pp. 67).

These functions cannot be performed at any level of seriousness without an adequate base and the employment of a cadre of appropriately qualified staff. If these criteria are rigorously applied, the number of such organizations is not as yet very large.

Types of National Organizations

The Wansfell Report exhibits a certain confusion in distinguishing between the organization of provision for adult education and organizations specifically established for the performance of functions related to it. This is not surprising since this confusion represents the actual situation in the field. In response to inquiries, a large number of countries will claim that adult education is organized through the national ministry responsible for all forms of education and that, at the same time, the ministry provides the documentation, information, and representational functions characteristic of a national organization defined as such. If there exists within the ministry a section specifically concerned with adult education, there may be substance in the claim. All too often there is not, but the protocol of intergovernmental organizations, of which UNESCO is the outstanding example in this field, is such that it is scarcely possible to say so. It would be invidious here even to identify them except by negation since sources of positive information are imperfect and the margin of possible error is large.

At the other extreme are those organizations actually titled National (or State or Provincial) Associations, Councils, Institutes of or for Adult Education, with formal constitutions and status and defined ranges of activities operating independently of government departments and claiming independence, even if, as is commonly the case, they accept financial support from public funds for both the maintenance of the organization itself and for the performance of special services of inquiry, research, or experiment. Their number, as we shall see, is quite small, and they are largely concentrated in northwestern Europe and North America, with a few in India and Australasia responsive (for historical reasons) to British example and influence. Even so, they are far from uniform in structure and pattern of relationships, with public and independent bodies directly providing educational services for adults. It is noticeable that they seem to be most effective in countries that are relatively small geographically, for example, England and Wales, the Netherlands, and Switzerland, which are also countries with long traditions of representative democracy and a multiplicity of independent associations for community purposes. In the Scandinavian countries, which certainly share those characteristics, the long-standing autonomy of influential popular or people's movements for adult education—Folk High Schools, Study Circle Associations, and People's Universities—has tended toward an unwillingness to delegate any substantial functions to formal national organizations of the kind under discussion, although they exist at least in name in Denmark, Finland, Norway, and Sweden. With the exception of Finland, these are countries of exceptional ethnic, religious, linguistic, and cultural homogeneity, and it might be argued that shared attitudes and established and effective government support for adult education reduce the need for agencies to focus on the claims of the providing bodies.

It seems clear, however, that it may be equally if not more difficult to create a central body of common acceptance in countries with strongly marked internal divisions of political structure or religious affiliation. No such body exists in either the Federal Republic of Germany (FRG) or Austria, although in both countries there are very large, effective, and publicly recognized agencies of adult education. In both these countries the largest autonomous, nonconfessional, but publicly recognized and aided adult education organizations at local levels, the *Volkshochschulen*, have federated at provincial and thereafter at federal levels to form powerful national associations—the *Deutscher Volkshochschul-Verband* and the *Verband der Osterreichischer Volkshochschulen*, respectively. Externally, they are often regarded as comprehensive national organizations, and they do in fact perform many of the functions appropriate to such bodies, but they exist in parallel to confessional bodies, particularly those connected with the Roman Catholic church, that have very large bodies of adherents and maintain strong national organizations.

Under the FRG constitution, power to legislate on education is given to the *Länder* (provincial) governments, and several of them in recent years have passed new acts concerning the promotion of continuing education. One such is the Act in Land Baden-Wurttemberg of December 1975 (*Adult Education Legislation . . .* , 1976, pp. 111–117), which provides among other things for the establishment of a Land Board of Continuing Education to include representatives of a wide variety of providing agencies. Similar developments in other *Länder* may well create a situation in which a representative federal body would become necessary. In his comparative study of professionalization of adult education in the FRG and the German Democratic Republic (GDR), Knoll in Chapter Four gives some significant examples of voluntary associative activities in the FRG.

In Switzerland and the Netherlands, where religious and provincial divisions are equally marked, there are alternative and overriding historical pressures contributing to national unity, and in both countries central organizations for adult education have been established with representational support from strongly entrenched sectional providing bodies.

The general character of adult education organizations can be reasonably inferred from the historical, political, and economic configurations of different countries. Where adult education emerged as a popular force associated with political and social reform in a unitary state, there is a greater likelihood that in its later development those responsible for its promotion will see advantage in creating a strong national focus even though they may have reservations about the extent of power that should be delegated to it or the terms on which it should seek or receive governmental interest and support.

The position is very different in emergent ex-colonial states, where adult education is likely to be encouraged and developed on any scale only if it appears to those in power that it will contribute directly to preconceived political and economic aims. If there is a central agency, it is most likely to be a national board or council constituted and in essence controlled by the central government. There are good examples in British ex-colonial territories such as Kenya, Tanzania, Singapore, and Malaysia.

Neither would one expect to find a voluntarily created body in Russia or the countries closely associated with it (which Savićević treats in Chapter Three). One will, however, certainly find some approved center, such as the Higher Institute for Research in the General Education of Adults in Leningrad or the Department of Adult Education of the faculty of philosophy of the Charles University in Prague, as well as sections or departments of appropriate government departments.

The three English-speaking continental countries—Australia, Canada, and the United States—present formidable problems of analysis and understanding to the outside observer. All of them are federal countries in which education as a public responsibility is a function of the separate states or provinces. This has not prevented the establishment of independent organizations claiming to serve as national focuses for the promotion and servicing of adult education. The position is complicated, however, by ethnic considerations in Canada, so there exist both a Canadian Association for Adult Education and L'Institut Canadien d'Éducation des Adultes, and by the varying attitudes in state or provincial areas. Thus in three Australian states there are statutorily established boards or councils of adult education, only one of which has shown much disposition, through its responsible officers, to support the independent Australian Association of Adult Education. In the

United States large injections of foundation support did not enable
the first national association, the American Association of Adult
Education, founded in 1926, to become sufficiently firmly based to
withstand wartime dislocation. New efforts, again supported by
foundation money after 1950, came up against the reluctance
of the established representative bodies of university extension
services and administrators of public school adult education to risk
being overshadowed by a powerful national organization. In more
recent years the Adult Education Association of the U.S.A. has, for
purposes of cooperation, become one of the eighteen members of
the Coalition of Adult Education Organizations.

Organizational Patterns. The character of a national organization depends on the general pattern of adult education provision in
a particular country. Historically, their establishment was associated in the first place with claims for the importance of independently provided adult education, universities being conceived,
after the British pattern, as "independent." People with this orientation created the British Institute of Adult Education in 1921, and
their example was influential in the setting-up of the first American
association in 1926, the Canadian association in 1935, and the
Indian association in 1939. These early associations consisted of
individuals, and it was only through the affiliations of such individuals with public or private agencies that the national associations
had contact with them. In Britain the shift from an individual to an
explicitly agency-supported national association came with much
difficulty soon after the Second World War, and the experience of
the body then constituted, which quickly became the present
National Institute of Adult Education (England and Wales), was
regarded in the subsequent constitution of a similar agency in
Scotland (1950), and of national agencies in Australia (1960), the
Netherlands (1966), and Ireland (1969). The problem of finding
an appropriate basis for the formation of fully effective national
organizations has not, in my opinion, been solved in Canada or the
U.S.A. Elsewhere the trend in recent years has been toward the
creation of such bodies by government decision and action or the
conversion of formerly independent organizations into public
ones. Paralleling this trend has been the increase in legislation
governing adult education, which Titmus and Pardoen document

in Chapter Six. Table 1 gives some idea of where and when various types of national organization have been established in the past half century.

Table 1. Decades of Founding

Pre-1940	1941–1950	1951–1960	1961–1970	1971–
Canada[a]	Austria[c]	Australia[a]	Brazil[c]	Botswana[d]
England[a]	France[c]	Costa Rica[b]	Iran[b]	Ghana[a]
India[a]	Germany[c]	Guyana[a]	Ireland[a]	Norway[b]
New Zealand[e]	Tasmania[b]	Israel[a]	Kenya[b]	Belgium[b]
USA[a]	Scotland[a]	Singapore[e]	Netherlands[a]	Baden W.[b]
	Thailand[b]	Switzerland[a]	Nigeria[b]	
			Sweden[a]	
			Tanzania[d]	
			Zambia[e]	
			Yugoslavia[a]	

[a] Independent
[b] Governmental
[c] Claiming to act as
[d] University
[e] Independent superseded or supplemented by governmental

Although incomplete, this summary establishes the accelerating growth in the number of countries having national or national-divisional organizations of some kind or at least making public claims to having them, and the growth, particularly since the 1960s, in the number established by government action or decision. Of the eleven bodies recorded as in existence in 1950, only two were primarily governmental. By the mid 1970s, thirteen of thirty-two were in that category. This development was probably stimulated at least in part by the experience and recommendations of the second UNESCO-sponsored international conference on adult education in Montreal in 1960. The need for national organizations to promote cooperation, nationally and internationally, and to serve as communication channels and information agencies was then recognized and recorded, and it was emphasized again in the recommendations of the Tokyo conference twelve years later. Recommendation 30 (*Final Report* . . . , 1972) on that occasion invites member states (among others) to "establish research and documentation centers dealing with adult education with a view to facilitating international research and the diffusion of professional information; and encourage the creation of associations of adult education in order to enable their members to keep themselves well informed through systematic programs, seminars, and specialized libraries."

Examples. It may be useful to see if these broadly stated tasks are reflected in the claimed character and purposes of some of the organizations of nations or divisions of nations already mentioned. The Canadian Association for Adult Education, for example, in its annual report for 1974–1975, presents a summary of its objectives as:

> to represent the interest of adult learning in Canada and in the world community;
>
> to facilitate communication and interaction among practitioners and adult learners between the various provinces and regions of Canada;
>
> to offer critical examination and evaluation of the effectiveness of existing programs of adult education and citizen participation in Canada;
>
> to encourage those interested in adult learning to speak and act together in pressing matters of joint concern;
>
> to identify priorities among the unmet needs of adults in Canada for continuing education opportunities;
>
> and to encourage established institutions to adapt programs and priorities in response to new needs.

The National Institute of Adult Education (England and Wales) defines itself as "an advisory and consultative body reflecting nationally the interests of organizations, institutions, and individuals in the provision of adult education." In fulfillment of this principal objective, it claims the functions of promoting understanding with a view to cooperation between the associated bodies by convening conferences and meetings, encouraging experiments and initiating inquiries, maintaining a library, publishing and distributing journals and other printed materials, providing meeting places, and developing cooperative relations with people and organizations in other countries and internationally. Although the institute has a substantial record of action under all these heads and has a large measure of acceptance by its constituent bodies both public and private, steps were taken in 1977 to implement a recommendation from a national committee of inquiry that had reported five years earlier that a government-initiated national advisory council should be established in parallel. It is now operative as the Advisory Council for Adult and Continuing Education. This is in keeping with the trend mentioned earlier and with, for example, the provision made in the Norwegian Adult Education Act, 1976 (*Adult Education Legislation* . . . , 1976, pp. 87–92) for the establishment of a Council for Adult Education as an advisory body for the Department of Education.

The Swiss Federation for the Education of Adults operates in a country containing twenty-six cantons, each of which is largely independent so far as concerns the provision of education. To secure any kind of common front among the large number of independent bodies, confessional and lay, that promote adult education, of which thirty-two are members of the federation, is a task of great delicacy. The federation is described as having no party-political or confessional attachments and as existing to

> promote the interests and sustain the efforts of its member organizations;
>
> extend and adapt the educational system so that each individual can pursue education throughout life (according to a system of *education permanente*);
>
> make available to the public and to the authorities specialized information relating to all matters, general and specific, concerning the education of adults;
>
> and keep all who collaborate in the education of adults in touch with new developments at home and abroad, by the provision of such training courses as will enable them to perform their tasks more effectively.

The Netherlands Center for Adult Education describes itself briefly as a center for cooperation and study in the field of adult education offering advice and promoting coordination of activities in research, training, documentation, and publications.

The difference in tone among these statements, with their emphasis on promotion of cooperation between independent providing bodies and advice and service to people working with them, and the equivalent statements of some of the governmental bodies is notable. Thus the duty of the Kenya Board of Adult Education is to advise the minister and coordinate activities in the field of adult education. According to its twenty-fifth anniversary brochure, the Adult Education Board of Tasmania was created in 1948 to

> advise the minister on matters of general policy with respect to adult education;
>
> investigate and report upon any matters . . . that may be submitted to the board by the minister;
>
> plan and supervise the administration and development of adult education in this state and to assist other bodies actually engaged in adult education . . . ; and
>
> take such steps and make such recommendations to the minister, as the board may think necessary or desirable, for the purpose of coordinating the activities of bodies engaged in adult education.

In both Kenya and Tasmania leadership is assumed to be vested in central government, and what is sought is coordination by the exercise of authority rather than cooperation to be achieved through persuasion and stimulus. Nevertheless one doubts whether, in practice, the distinction is as sharp as the formulas would suggest. Experience teaches that the character and attitudes of the individuals who serve as principals, secretaries, or directors may be more important than formal terms of reference.

In Zambia the board, established in 1973, is designated "advisory," but it has the task of "coordinating" field activities. In this it has the support of the preexisting, voluntarily created Adult Education Association of Zambia. In addition it is empowered to undertake research and to serve as a clearinghouse for information and as a link with agencies outside the country. It can also issue publications.

How do these examples of similarity and difference, culled mainly from geographically smaller areas, relate to the position in the U.S.A.? In a summary prepared for the Wansfell meeting, the

Adult Education Association of the U.S.A. was described as having been established in 1951 by the American Association of Adult Education and the Department of Adult Education of the National Education Association. Its aims and objectives are "to be a national organization dedicated to development of unity of purpose in the adult education movement; production of available knowledge about adult education; continuous effort to alert the nation's key leaders and general public to the need for continuing education; the establishment of a home base for those who make adult education their work."

Essentially the association, like its predecessor body, is a forum for activists who see their roles as adult educators transcending their specific employments in universities, independent organizations, or the public schools system. As such they are a minority, the greater part of their colleagues finding such mutual support as they wish in the narrower focus of, say, the National Association of Public Continuing and Adult Education or the National University Continuing Education Association. The linking of these organizations themselves, which would parallel the structural character of most of the European national associations, is a task that has been assumed since 1964 by the Coalition of Adult Education Organizations, the Adult Education Association being itself a constituent member of the coalition. Clearly, there are geographical, historical, and constitutional factors involved that really do not have any parallel elsewhere.

Functions. Underlying all differences of structure, purposes common to practically all national organizations are those of collecting and disseminating information—the maintenance of libraries and documentation centers and the publication of regular and occasional publications. At least fourteen of the organizations are listed as national key centers of documentation concerning adult education in the *Directory of Documentation and Information Services in Adult Education* UNESCO published in 1977. Three centers of outstanding excellence are those maintained by the Swiss Federation, the Netherlands Center, and the New Zealand Council. The National Institute in England is now in the process of developing its large library resources, which have hitherto been underutilized for lack of adequate finance.

National organizations are not, however, the only documentation centers. A considerable number of universities, through their extension or adult education departments, have large collections, and documentation centers are inevitably maintained by federal or state departments of education and are frequently recorded as having special sections devoted to adult education as a whole or to special aspects of it. Examples are the Educational Resources Information Clearinghouse and the New York State Clearinghouse of Resources for Educators of Adults at Syracuse University.

It is in the dissemination, rather than in the storage, of information that national organizations have roles of outstanding importance. In most countries there are plenty of journals concerned with education generally, but the space given in them to adult education, however that term is interpreted, is usually minimal. Wherever adult education is substantially developed through independent associations or institutions, there is likely to be a proliferation of news sheets and sometimes more substantial publications addressed to participants or adherents of the promoting movements, and these can be valuable sources for the understanding of adult education in an unfamiliar environment. But the journals that take it as their task to provide a continuing commentary, review, and record of theory and practice in the special field of the education of adults are produced overwhelmingly by national organizations or their regional or international counterparts. Journals incorporating "adult education" in their titles have been published by national organizations in the U.S.A. and U.K. for half a century. The Journal of the Indian Association has reached its fortieth anniversary. The *Deutscher Volkshochschulverband* publishes not only *Volkshochschul im Westen* but also a trilingual (English, French, and Spanish) half yearly journal for adult education in Africa, Asia, and Latin America under the title of *Adult Education and Development. Éducation Permanente*, the quarterly journal of the Swiss Federation for Adult Education, now in its thirteenth year, is produced with parallel texts in German and French. The more substantial national organizations are able to produce regular publications aimed at different readerships: *Adult Education* and *Lifelong Learning: The Adult Years* (formerly *Adult*

Leadership in the U.S.A.) or *Adult Education, Teaching Adults,* and *Studies in Adult Education* in Britain. Other valuable recurrent publications, unlikely to be available without the sponsorship of permanent organizations, are directories, yearbooks, and bibliographies, which may be historically interesting but are quickly misleading if not regularly revised and kept up to date. This is to say nothing of the output of reports and memoranda arising from research and inquiries conducted or supported by the organizations themselves or by their constituent members.

Another mode of communication and stimulus to cooperation is the holding of conferences, particularly at the national level. Such events are easy to satirize, but one need only have been a guest at such an encounter in one of the great continental areas, for example, Australia, the U.S.A., or Canada, or in ex-colonial African countries, to know how heartening they are to many of the participants who by the very nature of their local engagements often work with very little day-to-day mutual contact and support.

Nor is the value of effective national organizations confined to the services they render to the immediate national communities. Assistance is commonly given to other nationals in the organization of study tours, help with research projects, and facilitating personal contacts and access to libraries and documentation centers. This extension on a personal basis paves the way for formal links with regional and international organizations, which, on the evidence to date, are unlikely to achieve very much unless they are firmly related to sympathetic and effective national organizations.

International, Regional, and World Associations of Adult Education

It is certainly not widely known to the present generation of adult educators that a World Association of Adult Education existed from 1919 until 1947, although it was effectively silenced by the war of 1939–1945. Initiated by Albert Mansbridge, the founder of the British Workers' Educational Association, it attracted interest and support in at least North America, northwestern Europe, Czechoslovakia, and India. By "support" I mean that certain individuals, having more or less close associations with operative organizations, took part in its activities and secured financial support for it from charitable foundations, particularly in the United States. The evidence of its activities rested largely on its publication of quarterly bulletins, still a valuable historical quarry, although there was a short-lived quarterly publication of a more substantial and scholarly kind. Admirable people were associated with this enterprise, but since its overall tone was very much *de haut en bas*, it was always suspect in circles specially devoted to workers' education. The progenitor of the British National Institute of Adult Education was envisioned by its creators as the British element of the world association, and the first association in the U.S.A. had links with the world association from its inception. It is a normal commentary on human frailties that the secretary-directors of the British and U.S.A. national bodies preferred to organize their personal contacts directly, rather than through the machinery ostensibly created to help them.

The world association was able to finance a number of traveling scholarships, and useful reports were produced by their holders. Its biggest single achievement was the mounting of a world conference in Cambridge, England, in 1932. Not until the Tokyo conference of 1972 was there an adult education assembly with participants drawn from so wide a variety of countries. A large volume of contributed papers was issued, and an equally voluminous report was issued subsequently.

UNESCO Conferences. But "the winds blew and they were scattered." Working with the barest minimum of secretarial service, the world association disintegrated under the impact of war. When UNESCO convened the first postwar conference of adult education at Elsinore in 1949, only one person referred to the former existence of the world association.

Although delegates from the U.S.A. to the Elsinore UNESCO conference sought to promote the establishment of a continuing international organization, the overwhelming consensus was in favor of looking to UNESCO itself to fulfill the role. That view still commanded majority support at the second UNESCO conference in Montreal in 1960, although by then most of those concerned were a good deal less starry-eyed about the potentialities of UNESCO for adequate and effective service. But whatever their hesitations, they could not at that time see any serious alternative. As already noted, however, the need for appropriate *national* organizations was endorsed. By then also the European Bureau of Adult Education had begun to show that useful work could be done across national borders at a level less ambitious than that of the whole world. Although the initiatives in setting up the latter were personal and independent, the activists, aware of past experience, were insistent that the bureau could become firmly based only if it engaged the interest and support of the operating agencies and the established correlative machinery (so far as it existed) in different countries. It has now persisted for twenty-five years with a slow and steady expansion of its range of publications, studies in increasing depth, and promotion of personal contacts by the organizing and promoting of conferences and seminars, by the maintaining of regular meetings of its steering committee, and by biennial assemblies.

That this has been possible has been largely due to dedicated service by G. H. L. Schouten, its honorary secretary, and the financial support his reputation has made it possible to secure from the Dutch Ministry of Culture. But in Holland and the U.K. in particular, links with national organizations of adult education have enabled the bureau to forge connections with a very wide range of the national operative agencies, which in turn has made it possible to look to them for direct financial support and the use of their influence in seeking financial and other support from governmental and private agencies. This pattern of organic growth, a putting down of deep roots into the subsoil of the working agencies of adult education in different countries, is indispensable to the development of the reciprocal relations that both justify and give value to the creation of such regional organizations.

No one who has firsthand experience will underestimate the difficulties of developing such reciprocal relations, and Europe is obviously not the most difficult area in which to work. Writing of developments in the decade after the Montreal UNESCO conference of 1960, I noted in 1970 in reference to the formation of the African Adult Education Association, "the difficulties of sustaining a firm and continuing relationship between the thinly scattered forces of adult education are at least as formidable as they are in

Asia and Oceania. Problems of intercommunication in Europe or North America become insignificant when set against the African situation with its fantastic varieties of ethnic and linguistic groups—within which mediation almost inevitably takes place through the imported languages of the too recent colonial past" (Hutchinson, 1970, p. 52).

International Council of Adult Education

Against this background one has to consider the foundation in 1973 of the International Council of Adult Education and to estimate its possible future value. The first phase of its existence repeats the pattern noted earlier in relation to many national organizations, the European bureau, and the prewar world association, in that its establishment was made possible only by the skillful and sustained advocacy of a small number of people masterminded by J. R. Kidd of Canada. Operating first from the Canadian Association of Adult Education and later from the Ontario Institute for the Study of Education and building on his chairmanship of the Montreal UNESCO conference and subsequent UNESCO contacts, by the later 1960s, Kidd had a unique personal knowledge of structures and personalities in adult education in many countries. The creation of a multilanguage journal, *Convergence*, under his editorship was a valuable precursor to the discussions of a wider circle, made possible by the attendance of leading figures from many national organizations at the UNESCO conference in Tokyo in 1972.

Although there were sufficient affirmative voices to provide a starting point for a formal organization, there was a very large measure of scepticism and outright hostility. Writing as editor in *Convergence* in 1973, I commented, "We face a difficulty that those with the most relevant experience of attempting to improve cross-national communication in limited areas may be most skeptical about attempts to do the same thing on a world scale. They know too well the realities of the difficulties and they will be hesitant if they feel they are being asked to contribute time and energy to large but vague objectives" (Hutchinson, 1973, p. 2). This was, I think, a fair estimate of the attitudes of many of my colleagues in the European Bureau of Adult Education, and they were certainly not unique. A more serious difficulty, however, since such hesitations are amenable to persuasion by performance, was the sheer absence of regional organizations in most parts of the world and even of national correlating bodies of any substance in the great majority of countries. Moreover, countries with single-party governments who commonly treat intergovernmental organizations, UNESCO in particular, as bases for political and ideological struggle are unlikely to engage themselves seriously in building up a system of free exchange of knowledge and of people as its carriers.

This means that for a very considerable period, whatever may be the formal constitution, the International Council of Adult Education will rest on the commitment and efforts of individuals and on what they can bring with them by way of support from the operative agencies with which they are associated. It is unlikely they will be able to bring much money, which means the council will have an inadequate, overworked, and underremunerated central secretariat, unless the lack of financial support from associated bodies can be made good by contributions from charitable foundations or intergovernmental agencies. Substantial funds have been received from the W. K. Kellogg Foundation and the Canadian International Development Association. Such contributions are not likely to be available in perpetuity, but they have in fact been the indispensable source of initial support. Committed associates have been able to raise funds or provide logistical support for enterprises administered jointly by them and the council. On this basis the *Deutscher Volkshochschul-Verband* has facilitated meetings of the council's governing body; the National Institute of Adult Education in England has provided a base for the conference of national organizations for cooperation in adult education convened by the council in 1974; and many agencies were persuaded to commit themselves to aiding the international conference mounted in Tanzania in 1976. In trying, as it is now doing, to strengthen regional linkages in major areas of the world, the council is consciously contributing to its own survival and development.

My five years experience on the council indicate that many initial hesitations have been overcome. What I said ten years after the Montreal conference about failure to live up to the terms of the "declaration" then published seems applicable to this stage of the development of the international council. "There is no point in being unduly depressed by such facts. Those of us who choose to work in the margins of contemporary history may be forgiven if, at times, we clothe our sense of urgency in rhetorical terms . . . we shall be culpable only if we mistake the words for the facts and withdraw in disillusion from the slow persistent effort to bring the two into closer alignment, much of which must still be done in our immediate national situations."

Many people recoil from a large concern with "organization." They associate it with "bureaucracy," used as a perjorative term and a dehumanized concern for means without regard to ends or the imposition of individually unsought ends by illegitimate means. It is idle to deny such dangers exist and are too commonly demonstrable, but they frequently arise from a failure of those who rightly criticize to engage themselves effectively in freely sought cooperation. The rising tide of concern worldwide for "life-associated" rather than "school-completed" education makes it imperative that those who believe there are scope and need for nongovernmental as well as governmental action in later learning and recurrent education and who believe the two are mutually supportive shall combine their forces and assert their combination in formal but flexible ways. That, as I understand it, is the primary intent of the International Council for Adult Education, seeking not to supplant but to support and cooperate with other specialist bodies such as the International Congress of University Adult Education or the International Federation of Workers' Educational Associations on the one hand and UNESCO, the ILO, or the IBE on the other.

Conclusion

From this survey of national and international associations of adult education, I conclude that the best of good intentions and the most selfless of voluntary service will not, by themselves, suffice to support such bodies. To have a continuing and developing existence, they must be formally institutionalized and firmly linked to the institutionalized framework of adult education as it actually exists in the several countries.

Chapter Six

The Function of Adult Education Legislation

Colin J. Titmus
Alan R. Pardoen

This chapter focuses on legislation (including state decrees or orders that, although not called laws, have the force of law) that in whole or in part, explicitly or implicitly, by initial design or subsequent application promotes or regulates the education of adults. We are concerned here mostly with western nations.

After dealing with definition, we discuss influences in laws governing adult education, trends in these laws, and these influences and trends in the laws concerning adult education of England and Wales, France, and Norway. Then we draw some conclusions concerning the comparative examination of laws concerning adult education.

Definition

We have adopted the *Exeter Papers* definition of adult education: "Adult Education is a process whereby persons who no longer

attend school on a regular and full-time basis (unless full-time programs are especially designed for adults) undertake sequential and
organized activities with the conscious intention of bringing about
changes in information, knowledge, understanding or skills,
appreciation and attitudes; or for the purpose of identifying
and solving personal or community problems" (Liveright and
Haygood, 1968, p. 8).

We have not restricted the concept of adult, as the *Exeter
Papers* do, to persons over twenty-one years of age because that
does not conform to contemporary international practice in adult
education, and the restriction is found little, if at all, in legislation.
We have been impelled to broaden the definition by the lack of
uniformity in the use of the terms *adult* and *adult education* not only
internationally but within countries and by the variety of legal and
administrative tradition and practice that, with other factors, some
of general force, some specific to individual states, have created a
great diversity of legal measures applicable to adult education.

In the United Kingdom adult education has traditionally
meant nonvocational, noncredit courses. Although the expression
is now given wider meanings, it is also frequently used in the old
sense. France has never developed a concept of adult education as
a distinctive sector of education, and the phrase has not achieved
general usage. Neither of these states has passed adult education
legislation framed in those conceptual and linguistic terms.
Reference to a recent report of the European Bureau of Adult
Education indicates that comparatively few states have (European
Bureau of Adult Education, 1974).

Some nations, including the United Kingdom and France,
have described the education to be provided not in terms of the
public for which it is intended but in terms of its relation to initial
education. Thus the United Kingdom and in recent years some
provinces of the Federal German Republic (FRG) speak of *further
education*, while France prefers *continued education*. Where legislation applies to a limited kind of education, one finds terms indica-
tive of the purpose of the provision—*industrial training* (United
Kingdom), *vocational education* (Austria, France, and FRG), *social
advancement* (France and Belgium). The people for whom it is intended are named in terms of function—workers, employees, per-

sonnel, not adults. Where provisions of a law extend beyond the field of adult education, for example, by applying also to preadults or by covering activities outside its scope, other terms such as *leisure-time education* (Denmark) or *the promotion of culture* (Solothurn Canton, Switzerland) may be employed.

Influences in Adult Education Laws

Laws governing adult education in a country are influenced and their course determined by many factors, among them whether the country is governed by a common law code or a civil law code, the nature and terms of its fundamental constitution, whether it is a unitary or a federal system, and the degree to which its powers are centralized. Moreover, the recent growth in laws governing adult education must be examined to discern its causes and the purposes and effect of such legislation.

Common Law versus Civil Law Codes. Most countries of the Western world tend to base their legal systems on some variation of common law (case law) or civil law (code law). The English system, upon which that of the United States of America is founded, is the classic example of the first. Common law is a product of continuous process over centuries, during which time it was never under attack and always founded in local and national custom; a country depends on the decisions rendered by judges in precedent cases to interpret the laws. The administration of the law has tended to be decentralized, through a hierarchy of national, regional, and local courts, in which judicial arbitrariness was held in check by a jury and by the process whereby lower court decisions may be appealed to higher legal authority.

In the Middle Ages most of mainland Europe, lacking a tradition of strong central authority to give legitimacy to the law, looked to Roman law for its basis. Roman law provided a set of principles not derived from native custom but from a code that had ensured uniformity of law and its administration throughout the diversity of the Roman Empire. Napoleon, confronted by a need to build a new legal system in France after the chaos of the French Revolution and to impose uniformity upon the disparate parts of his own empire, caused to be drawn up a written code of legal principles rooted in the Roman tradition. In theory all laws necessary are to be found within the covers of the Napoleonic code. All decisions are made not according to precedents laid down by previous cases but according to what the code says. Legal systems based on such a written code are to be found in France and Belgium. They are characterized by precision, strictness, rigidity, and centralization of legal interpretation and administration.

It is to be expected that differences of legal systems will show themselves in adult education legislation, and so they do. It does not seem, however, that one can make significant generalizations about the form and scope of laws relating to the education of adults according to whether the legal system is a code or a common law one. Too many other variables come into play.

Nature of the Constitution. One variable is the nature of the state's constitution. Is it written or unwritten? The United Kingdom is a common law country whose constitution has evolved in an unwritten form in a process similar to that of the legal system. France is a code law state with a written constitution. The United States has a legal system based on the common law but has a written constitution also. A constitution of the common law kind tends to be more flexible and evolutionary than one of the code law kind, whose content and limits are set by the words used. Interpretation may change, as the decisions of the United States Supreme Court show, but within more formal limits than those imposed by an unwritten constitution, which is based on precedent not of judicial decisions but of constitutional practice.

A constitution, by specifying the rights and duties of citizens and those, both legislative and executive, of government, may have a restrictive effect on legislation by limiting the field of government action to only those rights and duties. Some years ago the right of the state of Illinois (U.S.A.) to fund adult education was challenged on the grounds that such an action infringed the state constitution. The form and content of legislation may be affected in other ways. The current French constitution, approved by referendum in 1958, stipulates that some classes of law, including educational ones, shall state the fundamental principles of legislation, while decrees and orders, issued by the responsible minister without reference to parliament, shall prescribe the details of a law's application (Pickles, 1962). To some degree French adult education legislation reflects this approach. In particular the 1971 Law on Vocational Education within the Framework of Permanent Education has spawned a multiplicity of applicatory texts.

Unitary versus Federal States. The nature and number of laws in a state are further influenced by whether it is a unitary or a federal one. In a unitary state, lawmaking is vested in the central government, although it may, at its discretion, devolve some minor powers to make bylaws upon regional or local authorities. Denmark, Sweden, Norway, and Holland are unitary states. In a federation the constitution makes a more even distribution of legislative functions between the federal government and the governments of the states or provinces that compose the federation. Education is usually a responsibility of the provincial governments, not of the federal government. In the FRG and Switzerland, for example, general adult education is the subject of laws passed by member provinces.

There are some exceptions to this division of powers between federal and state governments. The federal government of the Union of Soviet Socialist Republics and of other Communist federal states, such as Yugoslavia, control all educational policy through legislation, leaving member republics to legislate for its implementation. In most federations, whether Communist or not, vocational education, to be discussed, tends to be subject to federal law. The Austrian federal law of March 21, 1973, on the promotion of adult education and public libraries from federal funds, resembles part B of Public Law 94-182, October 12, 1976 (Mondale Act), of the United States Congress in that the federal government enters the field of adult education to supplement the resources available from state and private initiative without infringing on states' legislative rights.

The practice of Communist countries conforms to their general principle that federal or central government shall exercise close control over the development of all areas of national life. But non-Communist countries also are concerned with vocational education. The Austrian and United States laws may be seen both as forming part of a general trend toward greater participation by central government in the determination of national social and

economic policy and as recognizing the importance of adult education as an instrument of that policy.

Degrees of Centralized Power. The nature of laws is influenced
by the degree to which national or provincial administration is
centralized. Legislation in a centralized state concentrates powers
of decision making in the hands of government, even in matters of
merely regional or local significance. A detailed and rigid structure
of administration for the exercise of these powers can be and often
is written into laws or statutory orders. The more decentralized a
state is, the more the responsibility for administrative and even
policy decisions is devolved upon provincial and local authorities.
Legislation reflects this, tending to lay down procedures in general
and flexible terms. Centralization in administration goes with code
law systems, as in France and Belgium. Common law countries,
such as the United States and the United Kingdom, devolve more
authority upon provincial, county, or municipal authorities. Adult
education laws are influenced by the pattern of the country but
more by a general trend toward decentralization because of factors
specific to adult education, which we shall discuss later.

Trends in Adult Education Laws

The influences discussed can be seen operating in recent
general changes in laws concerning adult education.

Recent Growth. Of the sixty-five laws, statutory orders, and
decrees listed in *Adult Education Legislation in Ten European Countries*
(1976) and its supplement, all of which were enactments still wholly
or partially in force when the study was conducted, only four are
dated before 1950 (two each from Switzerland and the United
Kingdom), more than three quarters have come into force since
1965, and almost two thirds belong to the years from 1970. From
this one may deduce that states are finding it increasingly necessary
to legislate in the field of adult education—for the first time or to
replace older laws and regulations with ones more suitable for
contemporary conditions. In passing the lifelong learning provisions of Public Law 94-182, the U.S. Congress was therefore joining an international trend. This surge in lawmaking has provided
a body of material for study that was lacking until the last two

decades, since many, perhaps most, of the measures to be found in the European bureau list had no predecessors. There was either no legislation treating adult education or else none fulfilling the function of these modern measures. Related to the recent growth in legislation, one should note, as Hutchinson does in Chapter Five, that most of the national or divisional associations of adult education have been formed since 1951.

As one attempts to understand the recent growth in legislation, two general questions spring to mind. Why legislate for adult education? Why this spate of laws and orders now?

The first question may seem either too naive or else to be plumbing depths of philosophy and political science out of place in this chapter. (After all, why legislate for anything?) But it is neither. Adult education did not wait for legal regulation in order to begin. In Great Britain, mechanics' institutes had been in existence for thirty years and the adult Sunday school movement for a much longer time when the government's Science and Art Department issued the first regulations on adult education. These measures offered financial assistance from state funds to science courses because it was believed necessary to encourage the training of more highly skilled craftsmen in order to meet foreign industrial competition.

State as Provider or Facilitator. The British experience and the laws of other countries give an answer to the first question: Legislation is introduced into adult education when the state enters the field as either a provider or a facilitator. This comment introduces the second question: Why have there been so many laws and orders concerning adult education in recent years? The answer is that governments have perceived the need to bring about certain changes through involving themselves in adult education. This involvement is a recognition of the importance of adult education or of some sector of it. In practice the condition of the state's commitment, at least in the Western world, is finance. The state considers adult education important enough to warrant spending money on it and regulates adult education through the control of expenditure.

But if adult education existed without state monies, what purpose is state intervention supposed to serve? It is clearly always to introduce a new element into the situation. The state legislates to achieve change, generally of an expansionist kind. The state may add to what is already there or create opportunities for learning of new kinds. For example, the Swedish Order Concerning Municipal Adult Education (1968) lays upon municipalities the duty to offer to adults the possibility of pursuing their secondary studies up to the level that has been open to children since the extension of the period of compulsory schooling, in 1962, from seven to nine years.

Purposes. Legislation may promote the growth of existing activities by making arrangements for distribution of subsidy to organizations—as the Belgian (Flanders) Royal Decree of March 24, 1967, on Subvention of Activities of National and Regional Organizations on Behalf of Adult Education in the Dutch Language does—or by making mandatory what was previously optional, as England's education act of 1945 did for local authority provision. Or legislation may make it easier for individuals to participate in adult education, as is done by Belgian, FRG, and Swedish laws on paid educational leave.

Adult education law also regulates the new programs and functions it sets out to create. It may, however, be seen primarily as a change agent rather than a regulatory one. Regulation is needed because of innovation. The perception of need for change has provoked the rush of lawmaking in the last two decades. The factors that have led to the evolution of the principle of lifelong education have pushed states to legislate for the growth of adult education. One cannot generalize and say these factors are always the cause of the legislation, although chronologically it would seem possible. Some laws can indeed be seen as conscious steps toward the achievement of a national system of lifelong education—the stated aim of all French educational laws and orders for a decade. The legislation in other countries shows little sign of having been conceived on such a comprehensive theoretical base. For example, the Industrial Training Act, 1964, and the Employment and Training Act, 1973, both United Kingdom measures, do not seem to have a theoretical basis.

But if a causal relationship between the concept of lifelong education and the quantity of adult education legislation cannot be generally established, that both have been the product of the same pressures is more certain. The idea behind the pressure can be stated in two principles: Education should offer to all individuals equal opportunities of achieving the highest and widest degree of self-development of which they are capable, and education should meet the needs, both social and economic, of society seen as a collective unit. It has become increasingly clear that a formal system of schooling that ends with high school and higher education that ends in adolescence or the early twenties are unable to meet the requirements. Efforts to achieve equality of educational opportunity, notably through the introduction of secondary education for all, have not succeeded. The increase in the growth rate of knowledge, particularly insofar as it has led to a very rapid social and economic change, has meant that much of what is learned in initial education becomes obsolete, what needs to be learned had not been discovered when one was at school, and new problems and opportunities that cannot be foreseen and prepared for in childhood or adolescence arise in later life.

Economic Growth as a Goal. The implication is that for an amelioration of the situation, one should look to postinitial education, hence the concept of lifelong education and the increase in legislation for the education of adults. A few examples will show adult education laws influenced by the principles previously cited and responding to the needs of social and economic change. The Norwegian Adult Education Act, 1976, says in its first paragraph, "This act shall contribute to providing adult persons with equal opportunities to acquire knowledge, understanding, and skill, which will improve the individual's sense of value and personal development and strengthen the basis for independent achievement and cooperation with others in working and social life."

The Austrian Federal Law on the Encouragement of Adult Education and Public Libraries out of Federal Funds, 1973, puts at the head of its catalogue of activities that may be promoted under its provisions political, social, and economic education and continuing vocational education—in other words, fields of study of value to society, not merely to the individual. Provision designed to respond to conditions created by economic change is to be found in most vocational training laws, as in the Union of Soviet Socialist Republics Model Order for the Education and Further Qualification of

Workers Directly Engaged in Production, 1968. It lays down that workers put out of work by, among other things, mechanization and automation of production, shall be retrained for new jobs.

Specific Objectives. If the purposes of adult education can be stated in broad terms as change and regulation for growth, there appear to be a number of more limited goals to be attained as steps to the wider end. No single law or order sets out to achieve them all, and none of the goals is unique to one country, but taken together they offer a picture of the range of immediate objectives at which adult education legislation aims.

A law may seek to establish the purposes of adult education (Lifelong Learning Act, U.S.A., 1976, and Adult Education Act, Norway, 1976); it will seek to ensure they are achieved. It may situate adult education in educational policy as a whole (Education Act, England and Wales, 1944, and Basic Principles of Legislation on the Education of the People, USSR, 1973).

Adult education law can prescribe which department of the government's executive branch shall be responsible for adult education—not necessarily the Department of Education. In Holland there is currently uncertainty whether adult education should be added to the regular education system, coming under the Ministry of Education and Science, or remain with the Ministry of Culture, Recreation, and Social Welfare. The fact that responsibility for adult provision may be divided among a number of departments—in France among Youth and Sports, Education, Universities, Labor, Vocational Training, Agriculture, Health, and Defense, to name but a few—is both a reflection of ad hoc historical development and of the breadth of the field. Ministries have established themselves in various areas of adult education as they have had to meet certain needs within their purview. Legislation has confirmed them in their role and sought to provide the means for resolving conflicts of interest between them.

Division of powers is also laid down between central government departments and provincial and local authorities. The Adult Education Act (Norway, 1976) and the Act Concerning Leisure-Time Education (Denmark, 1968) are two of a number of laws that set out areas of national, regional, and municipal responsibility.

Where functions are prescribed and relationships between institutions are determined, appropriate administrative forms and structures are created or defined. In 1974, the FRG provinces of Bavaria, Breman, Hesse, and North-Rhine Westphalia all passed laws in which considerable attention is devoted to forms and structures.

Legislation does not ordinarily forbid provision of learning opportunities or prohibit organizations from providing. Its thrust is toward encouraging or ordering activities for adults to be offered. Where it obliges, the obligation is laid upon public bodies (Act Concerning Municipal Adult Education, Sweden, 1968). In cases where the participation of adults is desired but they are to be left some freedom as to the extent and nature of their action, measures are laid down to encourage them to do so.

Laws and Voluntary Organizations. Private organizations are not obliged to offer adult courses, but they are frequently encouraged and assisted to do so. In most countries adult education was initiated by voluntary bodies, which achieved a high level of development before government or local authority entered the field. Growth of the amount intended by government could be achieved only by the injection of public resources, but for reasons of political principle, expediency, and efficiency, it has been considered important to maintain the presence of private enterprise, at least in Western countries. The law helps to do this, as in the case where folk high schools are given a privileged position in some FRG provinces. The Danish Leisure-Time Education Act both ensures that instruction is offered to adults and protects the interests of voluntary organizations by specifying they shall provide it. If they do not do so, then and only then municipal authorities must take over the responsibility. The prevailing trend in the allocation of responsibility and power is toward decentralization, both vertical (from central to provincial and local government), and horizontal (from public to private bodies). One would expect this in countries like the United States and the United Kingdom, but it can also be seen in centralizing states. Comparison with school legislation will make the point. There is uniformity in school provision and organization, and private schools play little part in countries such as Denmark, Belgium, or France. In contrast there is a clear attempt in adult education law to devolve authority and responsibility into local and private hands.

This may be explained in part by historical accident: Law has continued and confirmed a situation already existing when it was passed, since it made sense to build on what was there rather than to pull down and rebuild from scratch. But it conforms to the realities of adult education in other ways. Since participation is voluntary, it is a buyer's market. It is a must, to attract learners, to offer what they want. Adult needs are diverse and vary with local circumstances. Placing responsibility for programs at the local level and sharing it between public and private bodies is expected to ensure a more sensitive response to public demand.

Laws Setting Priorities. Although all adult education may be a good thing, legislation suggests governments consider some learning activities to be of more value than others. One cannot be dogmatic about this. If law prescribes or encourages growth in one sector while ignoring another, it may be that the one is considered to be neglected while the other is flourishing without government intervention. There are three sectors that, above all others, appear to receive specific attention in laws and orders: instruction in the formal school and higher education curriculum, as either a compensatory or complementary measure; cultural activities, often of an all-age nature; and vocational education.

For example, Danish, Norwegian, and Swedish laws already mentioned emphasize the provision of secondary education for adults. Measures like the Royal Order Establishing Conditions of Recognition and Grant to House Culture and Cultural Centers, 1970, which applied to French-speaking parts of Belgium (a similar order applied to the Dutch-speaking districts), and laws for the promotion of cultural life, passed by several cantonal governments in Switzerland, provide for the second sector.

The third sector, vocational education, is the one almost universally considered the most important. Special taxes on employers finance it in both the Industrial Training Act, 1964 (United Kingdom), and the Law on Vocational Education within the Framework of Lifelong Education, 1971 (France). These and measures introduced by other states make it the most favored financially. Where, as in the Norwegian Adult Education Act, 1976, and some FRG provincial legislation, some vocational training is excluded from the provision made, this is done because other laws deal with it generously. General practice takes much training for work out of the educational ministry and puts it under the labor or unemployment ministry. It is, indeed, an instrument of economic planning, designed to achieve jobs for those being trained and to supply adequate skilled labor where it is required in the economy. This is why, although the general trend is toward decentralization of decision making and provision, organization of vocational legislation is controlled at the national level. In federal states much of the law covering it is federal, as in the Federal German Promotion of Work Act, 1969, and the Swiss Law on Vocational Education, 1963.

Training Adult Educators and Union Leaders. There are two other sectors that receive special attention in law: the training of adult educators and labor union training. Before the recent spate of adult education legislation, few countries paid much attention to the first field. Hardly any practitioners had been specifically educated for their adult educational function, although many had been trained as schoolteachers. The United States was ahead of the rest of the Western world in the training of adult educators. The growth of adult education, which legislation was intended to stimulate, called for a much greater number of organizers and educators. It was estimated in France that the implementation of the agreement between unions and employers that was the basis of the 1971 vocational education law would require four thousand full-time and forty thousand part-time educators within three years. If the expenditure on adult education were to be fully effective, they would have to be trained. Legislation has therefore been passed to create the means, previously nonexistent in most cases, for the training to be done. The Lifelong Learning Act (Sec. 133) authorizes the assistant secretary of the United States Department of Health, Education and Welfare "to assess, evaluate the need for, demonstrate, and develop alternative methods to improve training and retraining people to become educators of adults." The Austrian Federal Law on the Promotion of Adult Education, 1973, allows the federal government to found institutions for the training of adult educators. These two examples indicate a tendency for central government to enter directly into this kind of work, as into other vocational education.

Labor education differs appreciably from other forms of adult education. In the first place it is one of the longest established forms of adult education. Second, it is undertaken by the unions or by other organizations on their behalf and under their supervision. The intrusion of the state into the direct organization and provision of courses would be unacceptable to them. But since unions play a crucial role in economic and social life, government has an interest in the training of union members and particularly officers. Its concern finds expression in law through measures to subsidize the union's training activities or to make it possible for union members to participate in them through financial assistance and other help, such as educational leave (Employment Protection Act, United Kingdom, 1975, and Law Granting Unpaid Leave to Workers with a View to Encouraging Workers' Education, France, 1957).

Motivating Adults to Learn. Whatever arrangements legislation may lay down to ensure that courses are available for adults, they serve no purpose unless people attend them. Whether they are intended to promote individual or collective good, it is individuals who must be given the means and the will to participate. For adult education is often stated in law as a right of every person, often a need, but it is never laid down that adults are legally compelled to undertake learning activities. In the sense that to undergo training or further training is a condition of the exercise of certain professions, or social roles, an element of coercion may exist, but it is not to be found in law. The state desires adults to continue learning; it is both contrary to principle and, in Western countries, politically impracticable to resort to compulsion. In legislation, therefore, the individual is encouraged and enabled to study.

When laws decree courses be offered, give help to build adult education centers, and support the training of educators, they fulfill an enabling role. But they go further. They help to make provision known by authorizing expenditure on publicity (Adult Education Law, 1974, Hesse, FRG); they offer some courses free (Order Concerning Municipal Adult Education, Sweden, 1968); and they authorize the offer of positive incentives to study in the form of certificates or diplomas for the successful completion of courses (Law for the Regulation and Promotion of Further Education, North Rhine-Westphalia, FRG, 1974). To meet the argument that adults cannot be expected to combine sustained study with a full-time job, more and more states are introducing legislation that establishes each worker's right to paid leave from work in order to study. Among them are Sweden, Belgium, Italy, France, and some provinces of the FRG. In doing this they are implementing an International Labor Organization resolution.

Paid educational leave now appears to have high priority in adult education legislation. Laws that establish employees' right to paid educational leave, compelling employers to release them so they can participate, are a recent development. Normally, adult education law places only public, not private, organizations under compulsion. The other notable exception to the norm is the imposition on employers of taxes to pay for vocational training.

State Money as Control. With limited exercise of obligation on organizations and on potential students, government exercises influence on adult education mainly by the way it spends money. The financial clauses of laws and orders demonstrate this principle. They encourage provision and participation by decreeing or authorizing expenditure. By channeling central government grants through provincial or local authorities and allowing these authorities discretion in their allocation, the laws decentralize power (Rate Support Grants Regulations, United Kingdom). By ordering local authorities to meet a fixed share of the cost of adult education (Adult Education Act, Norway, 1976), the laws lay responsibility upon them.

It is mainly by decreeing for what money shall be available and on what conditions that legislation fulfills its important functions of regulation and establishing priorities. The Norwegian Adult Education Act authorizes special subsidies to programs for handicapped persons, persons with a particularly weak fundamental education, or persons with particularly heavy family obligations; to some labor union courses; and to other designated programs. By the conditions under which payments in lieu of earnings are made to workers taking educational leave, the French Law on Vocational Education, 1971, ensures leave will be taken almost exclusively for vocational training. By singling out for review "the organization and design of funding for pre- and postretirement training and education for the elderly," the Mondale Act, United States, 1976, also establishes a priority.

Laws in England and Wales

From the point of view of education, the United Kingdom does not form a single legislative unit. Scotland and Northern Ireland have their own laws, which show significant if not fundamental differences from those that relate to education in England and Wales. We consider only the laws and regulations that apply to England and Wales.

There are four basic measures currently in force: the Education Act (England and Wales), 1944; the Industrial Training Act, 1964; the Employment and Training Act, 1973; and Further Education Grant Regulations, 1975.

The 1944 act was intended to bring about an overall reorganization of the national education system, for the first time under a minister of education. In so doing, the act prescribed important measures for the education of adults. The minister would oversee national policy, but under his control and direction local education authorities (counties and some large municipalities) would have the duty to secure the statutory provision of public education organized in three stages, primary, secondary, and further, to meet the needs of the population of their area.

Each authority (Section 41) was obliged to secure for persons over compulsory school age adequate provision of full- and part-time education and of "leisure-time occupation, in such organized cultural training and recreative activities as are suited to their requirements." In drawing up the scheme of further education provision that was to be submitted to the minister, each was to consult with universities and nonstatutory bodies that provided further education in its area and should consider the expediency of cooperating with voluntary associations.

Primary, secondary, and further education, like other local authority services, were to be financed by local taxation (called "rates"), supplemented by a general subvention from the state.

Under further education (grant) regulations (which have been periodically amended) issued by the minister of education, universities and national associations may receive direct subsidy from the state toward the cost of providing tuition in courses of "liberal adult education." The minister may also make grants to voluntary organizations.

Role of Local Government. These measures are principally the product of over a century of adult education development and of an even longer administrative tradition. By laying responsibility for provision upon local authorities and by the terms in which the law was phrased, which left it to be decided locally what form the "adequate" opportunities for postschool leisure-time occupation should take, the 1944 act continued previous educational legislation and British practice in the administration of public services.

Suspicious of concentrating power in the hands of central government, the British have made it a matter of principle to establish strong local government with considerable independence of action. Indeed, the 1870 Education Act, which made primary schooling compulsory in England and Wales, was opposed on the grounds that it would be an unacceptable infringement of local power of decision.

Nevertheless, central government has a long history of intervention in adult education, but until the 1944 act, its actions were permissive, not mandatory, and confined to areas where local initiative was inadequate and needed help. From the nineteenth century, economic pressure in the form of foreign industrial competition stimulated the government to support technical and manual education, at first by grants and then by legislation that permitted county and borough councils to devote local taxation to it.

It was not until the beginning of the twentieth century that the government, conscious that working-class adults needed general education above primary level, passed legislation to allow local councils to offer general as well as technical education for adults and made direct grants to universities for extension work and to the Workers' Educational Association (WEA). By this time adult vocational instruction had over fifty years become absorbed in the national provision of technical education. The term *adult education* was limited to nonvocational studies of a liberal nature, and only university and WEA classes of this nature, deemed necessary for individual self-fulfillment and for the exercise of the duties of citizenship, qualified for government grant. By differential financing the government had helped to create this separation of the vocational from the nonvocational.

The 1944 Education Act and further education grant regulations up to the present day have perpetuated the separation of terms. The unrestricted range of postschool instruction, which local authorities were to provide, was called *further education;* the expression *adult education* was used only for those liberal studies universities and the WEA were to be encouraged to continue providing, subsidized as before by the central government. It should be noted here that legislation has not been monopolistic in intent. Local authorities were to "secure provision" of further education, not necessarily to provide it themselves. They were indeed encouraged to find a place in their schemes for voluntary bodies, which had been major providers for over a century.

Steps Toward the Welfare State. It may appear from the forgoing that the 1944 act and the further education regulations merely regulated existing practices whose origins lay in the nineteenth century and earlier. The law made, however, two important innovations: Further education was to form, with primary and secondary, an integral part of the statutory education system; and local authorities were not permitted, they were compelled, to make provision for it. The second was a logical consequence of the first, and both may be seen as a normal development of educational history. That they came when they did, though, may be attributed to the Depression years of the thirties and to the Second World War, which engendered an idealistic determination that the social injustices of those years should not be repeated. The education act was the first of the series of laws that from 1944 to 1946 built a British "welfare state." Its purpose was to create equal educational opportunities for all. A government report after the First World War (Ministry of Reconstruction, 1919) had already seen universal and lifelong adult education as a national necessity, but its recommendations had been only partially implemented. In the social climate of 1944, it was possible to override local resistance in the name of national need.

England and Wales established further education as an integral part of their formal education system before most other countries—perhaps because organized education for adults there began early—largely to meet the requirements of the Industrial Revolution. It had a comparatively uninterrupted development, evolving steadily toward the idea of equal opportunities without the violent class conflicts many other countries experienced. The legislative framework laid down in 1944 has continued to appear adequate, except in one area, that of adult vocational training.

Vocational Training. Under the pressure of technological and economic change, the United Kingdom, like other countries, has conformed to a common pattern, already noted, by using vocational training as an instrument of manpower policy, by passing specific laws to regulate it, by taking it out of the field of education and placing it under the Ministry of Employment, and by imposing a degree of centralization not found in other laws regulating education (in the sense that the laws apply to Scotland and Northern Ireland as well as to England and Wales). These laws do, however, show national as well as international characteristics.

The United Kingdom needed national machinery to promote adult vocational training. Government intervention was required, since commerce and industry had not created such machinery for themselves. Nevertheless, enough of a free enterprise philosophy was retained for it to be widely felt that vocational training was the business of business, not of government. There was also a continuing commitment to the devolution of power rather than to its concentration in ministerial hands. The result of these influences is to be seen in the compromise of the Industrial Training Act, 1964, which set up an industrial board for each major sector of economic activity. Each board was composed of representatives of employers and trade unions in equal numbers and of some civil servants. It was left to each board to draw up a training policy for its sector and to see that the required facilities existed and did its best to expand appropriate training. A board had no power to compel employers to train. It did have the power to impose a levy on employers to finance training. Each board was free to fix the rate of levy, and employers could deduct from their taxes the amount they spent on training.

In effect the law was only mildly coercive, since employers were free to decide whether to train or not and, through their representatives, had a say in the wielding of the stick of levy and the carrot of levy relief. Also, authority was to be devolved. The minister could in practice exercise little supervision over the boards, which operated quasi-independently, so there was no over-all policy. Moreover, even with nearly thirty boards, some sectors of the economy and many individuals were not affected by the provisions of the act.

To make a more effective instrument of labor market policy, Parliament passed the Employment and Training Act, 1973. Under its terms a Manpower Services Commission (MSC) was created, with two executive arms, the Employment Services (ES) and the Training Services Agencies (TSA) to coordinate employment and training. The Industrial Training Boards were retained, but they were subject to closer supervision by the MSC. The latter could, moreover, make such provision of training for employment, through TSA, as it deemed necessary, even in fields served by a board. In the name of efficiency, the law increased centralization of authority and government intervention in training. But it still avoided placing the exercise of authority directly under the minister. Ultimately, it lay with him, but effectively decisions in policy and execution were to be made by the MSC, a ten-man body composed of representatives of employers, unions, local authorities, other educational organizations, and a chairman appointed by the minister.

Adult education legislation in the United Kingdom reflects the slow evolution of a stable society without extreme social conflict, whose tradition has been to keep authority with local rather than central government. Nevertheless, the central government has reluctantly intervened increasingly in adult education as it has become more important to national life.

Laws in France

In France legislation had a very different beginning. Since 1789, French history has been characterized by revolution, near revolution, foreign invasion, extreme conservatism, radicalism, and class divisions within a continuing tradition of strong centralized government and weak local authority. The dominant and mainly conservative bourgeoisie has feared the working class for its revolutionary record and has tended to resist attempts to increase its power (in contrast to Great Britain, where the predominant policy has been to educate the workers to exercise their power within the existing social and political system). Therefore adult education, until recently intended mainly in both countries for the working class, has met fairly general approval in Britain but has been a matter of political controversy in France and only half-heartedly promoted (although the first law on the subject dates from 1836). Legislation of 1884 empowered public primary schools to offer evening classes for adolescents and adults. However, having flourished until 1914, after the First World War these classes died of the neglect from which all primary education suffered. At the turn of the century, a short-lived attempt to establish people's universities on the model of British university extensions foundered on the rocks of class enmity and unsuitable methods.

Out of these experiences grew the myth that workers would not attend formal courses. Although it would not be true to say there was no education of adults, by the beginning of the Second World War, provision was sparse, unregulated by legislation. The term *adult education* and the concept of it as a distinctive sector of education were not even in common currency. Instead there had developed the notion of *popular education*, which denoted all organized social, recreational, and intellectual activities outside the realm of home, school, or work for people of all ages from the cradle to the grave. Emphasis in popular education was placed on youth, and the only educational opportunities for most adults, particularly of the working class, were to be found in the voluntary associations.

The call for social justice, stimulated in France as in Britain by the Second World War, engendered a move for greater educational opportunities for working people, but such opportunities were not to be achieved through establishing formal adult classes, of which there had been no tradition, but by the development of informal popular education. There was, however, no legislation to promote this type of activity. None of the short-lived French governments up to 1958 was strong enough to pass major laws on education; and education remained controversial in a still-divided country. More important, perhaps, was the attitude of the proponents of popular education to central government in general and the public education system in particular.

After the wartime Vichy regime's takeover of popular education for political indoctrination, the proponents of popular education blamed the public school system for the working class educational disadvantagement. It was rigidly and bureaucratically directed from Paris, inflexible in organization, formal in method, and ill suited in content to working-class needs. Popular education therefore would be quite otherwise: locally and democratically based, flexible, informal, and run by volunteers. Legislation in the French tradition would centralize, formalize, and limit freedom. The promoters of popular education required of government only that it provide financial support without strings—for which there already existed machinery in a law that had been enacted with no thought of application to education.

The Law on the Contract of Association, 1901, had laid down that two or more persons could form a nonprofit association for any legal purpose without prior authorization. They acquired corporate legal status, however, only by registering the organization at the nearest prefecture (local office of central government). Among the benefits the association might receive from this action are subsidies from central or local government. Popular education associations, all voluntary, therefore needed no other laws.

The government has acquiesced in the role assigned to it. It has been able, by the giving or withholding of grants, to influence provision and, in order to obtain action that it desired, to combine with private bodies to form new associations under the 1901 law. A number of regulations has been issued, but the only legislation on popular education affecting the education of adults has been a law (1961) giving the right to leave from employment to persons wishing to undergo popular education.

A similar law had been enacted in 1957 to encourage trade union training, but as in other countries such activity was treated as a special case. Otherwise organized courses of study for adults were not considered important enough during the Fourth Republic to need legislation, even if a government had been able to enact it.

Laws of the Fifth Republic. Only since Charles de Gaulle brought in the Fifth Republic in 1958 have governments had the conviction and strength to legislate for adult education. Under the same pressures and for the same purposes as in the United Kingdom and in nations of the industrialized world, a series of laws on adult vocational education was passed—of which the culmination and summation was the Law Organizing Continuing Vocational Education within the Framework of Lifelong Education, 1971.

Common pressures tend to produce similar responses. Like the law in the United Kingdom, the French law took vocational education out of the Ministry of Education's hands, appointed a committee to decide national policy, and involved employers and trade unions. It did not oblige employers to train, but it encouraged them through a training tax that was to operate in a fashion similar to the one in Britain.

But within broad resemblances marked differences existed. The French law emphasized the individual's rights and needs, his access to higher levels of culture as well as his continuing need for occupational competence throughout life, and it encouraged every kind of organization, public and private, to see that adequate provision was made. The British acts of 1964 and 1973, concentrating on the economy and immediate work skills, made no mention of lifelong education; but the United Kingdom had already made provision for the individual and general education and had a national lifelong organization through further education laws. France had no such measures and was trying, belatedly, while concentrating on vocational training, to create machinery for general adult education as well.

In accordance with the historical differences in administrative practice, French law centralized power in government hands more than the British did. Policy was to come from Paris, decided by ministers and civil servants. Employers and the unions were to be represented on committees that advised on policy; they were not to make it. The rate of training tax was fixed by government. There was another difference between French and British legislation. Whereas the latter placed responsibility with one ministry, the former laid it with a committee of ministers directly under the prime minister. This reflected a wider view in France of the scope of adult training, a higher estimate of its status, and perhaps a recognition of interministerial rivalry.

Paradoxically, French training was to combine traditional direction by centralized government with the operation of an open market in provision. It was to be the subject of freely negotiated contracts between suppliers and consumers, mainly government and employers. Competition was to be encouraged. The combination conformed with the philosophy that was credited with France's economic success of the 1960s. In comparison also, in accord with a national tendency, British training has devolved but has been operated as a public service.

Right to Paid Educational Leave. The most distinctive feature of the 1971 French law was the establishment of the right, albeit subsequently limited by decrees and orders, of each employee to paid educational leave from work. What distinguished this measure from other countries' legislation of the same kind was its scope, potentially if not actually unlimited, and its timing, since it predated other Western European laws. It sprang from a collective agreement won from the national employers' federation by the unions after the social unrest of 1968 and was made law by a government anxious to promote participation in adult education, which was new to the thinking of most Frenchmen. Most countries were moving toward paid educational leave, as has already been mentioned. That it came as soon as it did in France was not unconnected with a tradition of imposing social change by legislation, the zeal of a government newly converted to adult education, and the readiness of government and employers to make concessions to workers after the shock of recent near revolution. Conversely, the fact that the United Kingdom has not yet established paid educational leave as a general right may be because government has still preferred persuasion to compulsion; has been under no pressure from the unions, which have had other priorities; and has experienced the complacency of a long-standing national provision of adult education. Moreover, France, unprecedently prosperous in 1971, could afford such a course; Britain, beset by deep-rooted economic problems, thought it could not.

Laws in Norway

Developments around the world indicate a lack of uniformity among nations regarding how adult education is defined and what activities are to be included. There has been a movement in recent times away from providing the traditional, fragmented program of adult education opportunities and toward supporting the notion of lifelong learning so well expressed in *Learning to Be* (Faure, 1972). Continuous education in Scandinavia has historically been a way of life (Gage, 1975). Consequently, it seems logical to look to this part of the world for a likely subject to review. Norway, out of concern for increased equality and democratization among its people, made a legislative leap into the realm of lifelong learning in the 1970s.

The historical evolution of adult education legislation in Norway can be linked quite closely to the general growth of democracy and agrarian reform that began in the nineteenth century. There were many reasons that prompted the development of these events at this particular time. Many of the central practices of feudalism had been on the decline for some time. The French Revolution had a profound effect on the newly constituted government, which had separated from Denmark. The abolishment of land-based servitude made it possible for peasants to move freely from one district to another. The tenant farmers became free landholders, and many moved their dwelling place away from the confines of the villages to be closer to their fields. Consequently, the typical Norwegian landscape, with its scattered farms and small landholdings, began to evolve together with a populist belief in education. This historical background laid the basis for legislative mandates in Norway.

The pattern of modern day adult education legislation in Norway seems to fall into three distinct time intervals: 1935–1963, 1964–1975, and 1976 to the present. A brief survey of legislation in Norway follows in an attempt to trace the evolution of legal responsibility away from localized adult education activities toward a comprehensive act oriented toward lifelong learning.

First Period. The first period encompassed the following pieces of legislation: Norwegian Library Act of 1935, Norwegian Football Pools Act of 1946, Norwegian Library Act of 1947, Correspondence Schools Act of 1948, Folk High School Act of 1949, and University Act of 1956.

Perhaps one of the most unusual pieces of legislation passed in Norway during this time concerns the financing of adult education facilities. The Norwegian Football Pools Act of 1946 set up a publicly owned company, Norsk Tipping A/S, which has a monopoly over the revenue derived from these activities. Its board and managing director are nominated by the king, and the Ministry of Church and Education supervises its operation. By law its operating surplus is distributed for the use of building community centers and recreational areas. Organizations across Norway have found financial support from these funds to be indispensable in their work with adults (Lyche, 1964).

The first Norwegian library act was based upon the premise of a matching grant system from the central government and the local authority concerned. This system led to rather difficult conditions due to the unequal distribution of resources among the localities involved and precipitated the passage of the Library Act of 1947. (Affecting cultural and adult education work, this legislation is considered by many to be the most important law passed up to that time.) The act stipulates there shall be a public library in every municipality and every school shall possess a school library (Lyche, 1964).

In 1948, the Norwegian Parliament passed the Correspondence School Act, which requires the subject matter and educational content of all correspondence courses be approved by the Ministry of Church and Education. This act created a Council on Adult Education to advise the Ministry of Church and Education on recognition of courses and the supervision of correspondence schools. Teaching by correspondence in Norway plays a very important role in adult education, both in voluntary educational organizations and for personal enhancement in the army and merchant navy (Lyche, 1964).

As early as 1934, the Norwegian Farmers' Association (*Norges Bondelag*) had pushed for a separate law relating to folk high schools. The Norwegian folk high schools were heavily influenced by the Danish philosopher and educator, Nicholas Severin Frederik Grundtvig (1789–1872). The development of democracy in both Denmark and Norway is deeply indebted to Grundtvig. He advocated the theoretical position of "free popular education," believing democracy could survive only if the masses were educated. Mass education was to be voluntary, based upon a broad cultural foundation. This conceptual framework is similar to later movements that developed in the United Kingdom and the United States under the nomenclature of liberal adult education. The parliament passed the Folk High School Act in 1949. The term *folk high school* signifies all county schools, folk high schools, and private youth schools that have as their purpose the provision of further education in general subjects; thus it excludes schools that provide technical training or prepare their students for examination certificates. According to this law both the buildings and the curriculum of a school must be approved by the Ministry of Church and Education if it is to receive a state subsidy; the students must be at least seventeen years of age; and the principal and the teachers must have been trained at a training college, university, or other specialized school. The law further requires the state to provide five sixths and the county one sixth of the money needed for the expenses of these schools (Lyche, 1964, p. 19).

One other Norwegian act deserves mention because of its impact on extension education in institutions of higher education. The University Act (1956), relating to the University of Oslo, was amended to recognize university responsibility in the field of adult education. Perhaps the most important result of the amendment was the establishment of the University Office for Extension Activities at the University of Oslo. This office acts as a contact center for all institutions and organizations needing help and advice in finding lecturers, teachers, or any sort of information that might assist them in their adult education work (Lyche, 1964).

Second Period. The second legislative period was marked by the approval of the Norwegian Parliament of the *Stortingsproplsisjon* No. 92 (1964–1965) *Om voKsenopplaering* (Storting Proposition No.

92 [1964–1965] on Adult Education) on April 9, 1965. Through its policy statements on key educational issues, this document bridges the gap between prior legislation on adult education and the embodiment of an early lifelong learning proposal. The Storting Proposition No. 92 declares that general educational and vocational education are equal: "The adult training is aimed at giving each individual the best opportunity during his adult life to satisfy his desire for knowledge and to qualify him for his vocation and community life in general. Adult training must be placed on an equal footing with other forms of education. For the purpose of this report, adult training means all education that is not part of initial education. According to this definition, the concept of adult training comprises all general education and specialized and vocational training that adults seek to obtain after having gone to work for some time. General education and specialized training should be placed on an equal footing as regards leave of absence and economic support. So far as possible, existing educational institutes should be utilized for adult training too (*Storting Proposition . . .* , 1964–1965, p. 3).

Since 1965, state grants have been provided annually to the field of adult education under a separate chapter (Number 295) in the state budget. Appropriations covered state support for teachers' salaries, study materials, and administrative services, as well as courses for adults in municipal and county educational institutions. The state provided 65 percent of the total expenditures; the remainder was covered partly by grants from municipalities and counties, partly by the educational institutions, and partly by the fees paid by participants.

In 1966, a separate department for adult education was established within the Norwegian Ministry of Church and Education. The Department for Adult Education is responsible for the administration of the fields of adult education to which state support is granted under chapter 295 of the state budget. The Council for Adult Education was also nominated in 1966 as an advisory body to the Ministry of Church and Education. The council consists of representatives of the Joint Committee for Study Work, the Norwegian Employers' Confederation, the Norwegian Federation of Trade Unions, the manpower authorities, the public school system, the vocational schools, the university and colleges, and the mass media (Ministry of Church and Education, 1972, p. 7).

The Storting Proposition No. 92 also strongly emphasized the role of libraries and mass media in adult education. This framework provided the necessary legislative background for the Library Act of 1972, which increased allocations from the state, counties, and municipalities to library services. Public libraries are now considered not only loan centers for books but also "mediatheques" and centers of study for adult education activities (Ministry of Church and Education, 1972, p. 7).

The Storting Proposition No. 92 can be summarized by listing some of the main principles advocated for the development of adult education—lifelong learning in Norway:

1. Adult training should be equated with other types of education. It should therefore be developed with a view to providing facilities for adults to obtain advanced education, general as well as vocational. General education and vocational training of adults should be interrelated and equalized.
2. Persons should have an opportunity to document their knowledge and skills, regardless of how they were obtained.
3. The educational facilities and equipment of the various schools must be employed in adult training as far as they are compatible.
4. The problems of pedagogy and method entailed by the training of adults must be made the subject of scientific study. Personnel attached to adult training facilities must have pedagogical education suitable to their functions in this field.
5. The school system will have the responsibility of training adults who aim at passing complete examinations. Preparations for partial examinations from vocational or specialized schools and preparations for partial examinations and study work in general should be handled as much as possible by the adult education organizations.

Third Period. The third and most recent legislation interval was marked by the passage of the Norwegian Adult Education Act of 1976, Norway's first comprehensive piece of legislation on adult education and lifelong learning. Its strength lies in a clarification of the roles and responsibilities associated with adult education—lifelong learning among governmental agencies (state, county, and municipal), governing bodies (state, council, and educational), and industrial organizations. The approach of the legislation is to reorganize the distribution of adult education activities under the centralized conceptual framework of lifelong learning spanning all levels—primary fundamental education, regular fundamental education, vocational training, and postwork education.

The major purpose of this act is to develop a higher degree of equality and democratization within the population as a whole. It was felt that educational policy had to be adjusted to suit the increased demand for information and knowledge outside the traditional educational delivery system. One central goal of the legislation is to stimulate informal learning on the part of the population at large so as to provide possibilities for both personal and career development for all Norwegians. "The purpose of adult education is to help the individual to attain a more satisfying life. This act shall contribute to providing adult persons with equal opportunities to acquire knowledge, understanding, and skill, which will improve the individual's sense of value and personal development and strengthen the basis for independent achievement and cooperation with others in working and social life" ("The Norwegian Adult Education Act," 1977, p. 2).

The comprehensive nature of this legislation with respect to lifelong learning can be evidenced by the broad range of activities it will regulate. The law on adult education will coordinate the following activities:

voluntary studies in organizations and institutions that are eligible for subsidies;

fundamental education at the primary and secondary levels that is especially organized for adults;

alternative types of fundamental education for adults at all levels;

postwork education and short courses, not forming part of the fundamental education, in secondary schools and at institutions for higher education;

short-term courses for adults at folk high schools, vocational training for adults as part of the labor market policy; and

training given in connection with a company, and other education offered for adults based on a special evaluation ["The Norwegian Adult Education Àct," 1977, p. 6].

A few key aspects of this legislation have already been highlighted in an effort to depict the transformation of the lifelong learning influence over the traditional fragmented barriers to program development (age, physical condition, occupation, educational background, and leisure time) in adult education. Fundamental education, either complete or partial training at primary, secondary, or at higher levels, should give the core ingredient for further self-managed learning throughout the rest of life. By placing fundamental education at a higher priority than other types of adult education, it was felt the work toward lifelong learning would be stimulated. Practical experience in Norway has shown that people receiving a good fundamental education are more motivated for further education and seek jobs that stimulate their interest for continued learning ("The Norwegian Adult Education Act," 1977, p. 2).

Similarly, postwork education is used within the context of recurrent education methodology where adjustment, renewal, and increased fundamental education is closely associated with the practical experience of adults. This proposed framework satisfies the need for alternating among education, work, and other activities (Eide, 1973).

While the relationship between general education and vocational education seems to be stressed, it should be emphasized that lifelong learning in all sectors of society is covered by this act, as evidenced by the section of the law dealing with handicapped persons. Paragraph 24 of the act indicates that matters relating to handicapped persons should be given special priority. Educational institutions and organizations involved with study circles are encouraged to develop relevant courses in accordance with this act. For adults living in institutions for the handicapped, special arrangements can be made for the institutions to receive subsidies and organize the training ("The Norwegian Adult Education Act," 1977).

The general priorities of the Norwegian law imply that many of the activities that previously have been independent and conducted separately will now be coordinated. This means all types of fundamental education for adults at different levels will now be financed almost entirely by the central government, regardless of who organizes it. The subsidization of study work in companies and the National Association of Industries will be totally covered by the state. For all other types of adult education, a public subsidy will be granted at the rate of 80 percent of the total cost prescribed. The participants' fees will therefore be a regular contribution. Eighty-percent subsidies will be granted to the following types of adult education: postwork education at secondary schools and at higher education institutions, voluntary study circles in organizations, courses for adults in folk high schools, and courses arranged by industry and by the National Association of Industries.

The Norwegian Adult Education Act of 1976 makes its contribution to lifelong learning by clarifying the duties and responsibilities of governmental, educational, and industrial agencies; by developing educational offerings relevant to adults with practical backgrounds in work and community life; and by introducing financial arrangements intended to stimulate people in the direction of lifelong learning. The financial basis of this legislation is directed toward an overall development of lifelong learning without any special emphasis being placed on an educational philosophy or segment of society. Thus this legislation becomes an instrument toward increased equality between general education and vocational education, between the young and the elderly, between men and women, and in the distribution of resources.

The full impact of the May 18, 1976, legislation on adult education has not yet been felt in Norway. To be sure, many problems regarding long-term developments associated with lifelong learning are not answered. A better coordination of the legal system as it applies to education in society seems necessary. The area of educational leave needs additional clarification (Edding, 1973). However, this state of affairs does not in any way negate the true meaning of this landmark piece of legislation. Its main contribution has been to integrate lifelong learning into the total educational and governmental system of Norway.

Conclusion

We have demonstrated the value to comparative studies of an examination of the legislation relating to adult education. It is a rich field for cross-national studies. The conscious and deliberate involvement of government in the field, the rapid and significant increase of this involvement in the last two decades, the forms it takes, and the purposes it is intended to serve reveal the growing interest and involvement of the government. There are advantages and dangers in society's recognition of the value of adult education the spate of modern legislation reflects. Adult educators cannot do without, in fact have long sought, government involvement in adult education, but it brings risks, notably to the freedom of action of the educator and to the range of effective choice of the individual learner, which may be sacrificed or at least restricted in the name of social policy, of which adult education may be perceived as an effective instrument. Perhaps the most interesting feature of the laws examined is the concern displayed by the legislative branch of a number of Western European governments to maximize the support that the executive branch may bring, while clearly setting limits to its functions, whether at the central or local level, in order to protect the freedom of the individual and of voluntary associations and to minimize the danger of abuse of public authority.

However, one final word of warning may not be out of place. Laws prescribe what may or shall be done; they are evidence of intention, not proof of realization. The student of comparative adult education who takes the word for the deed may be sorely led astray. Between the enactment and implementation may be a broad gap, which is an important subject for comparative studies.

Chapter Seven

Educational Technology in Comparative Adult Education

Donald P. Ely

This chapter describes the role of educational technology in the design of instructional programs for adults in three settings. The context for the comparative analysis of this role is focused on three adult education programs—in prerevolutionary Iran, the United Kingdom, and the United States. The specific aspect of each program studied is the design and delivery of courses in formal and nonformal settings. General principles for development of adult education courses in these settings are derived from the case studies.

Before turning to the case studies, I define educational technology, indicate its use in formal and nonformal education, sketch its emergence as a part of total instructional design, outline the educational technology approach, indicate the kinds of problems it can solve, and specify the elements common to open learning.

What Is Educational Technology?

Definition. When the term *educational technology* is used, the primary meaning for most people refers to the "things" or products of our technological society—the "hardware" and "software," the machines and media, and the equipment and materials. That interpretation is indeed so widespread that the Presidential Commission on Instructional Technology in the United States offered it as a commonly held definition: "the media born of the communications revolution that can be used for instructional purposes alongside the teacher, textbook, and blackboard . . . television, films, overhead projectors, computers, and the other items of 'hardware' and 'software' " (Tickton, 1970, p. 7).

While that definition bears some semblance to actuality, the second definition, much less known and accepted, offered by the same commission expresses my emphasis: "[Educational technology] is a systematic way of designing, carrying out, and evaluating the total process of learning and teaching in terms of specific objectives, based on research in human learning and communication, and employing a combination of human and nonhuman resources to bring about more effective instruction" (Tickton, 1970, p. 7).

The second definition emphasizes process rather than products. Audiovisual media are included in a subset of the larger process definition. The movement toward emphasizing process is the first and probably the most important trend in the use of media for instruction. It provides a *context* in which the media play an integral role rather than setting the media aside as separate entities. In the process definition the media become part of a systematic design to deliver information to users. Mere delivery of information, in whatever format, is insufficient; effective delivery must deliberately embody both the user's purposes and his analysis of the audience who will be receiving the information. This concept of total instructional design is expressed also by Ryan in Chapter Nine, where he expounds the elements of program design and program development. The process definition undergirds all I have written throughout this chapter. To consider media *qua* media is to look at solutions in search of problems.

One can easily become caught up in the glamor of the media

without realizing they exist as a means of communication. Some media-oriented people tend to analyze such new devices as videodiscs, cable television, satellite transmission, and minicomputers in terms of possible applications rather than to consider the communication problems that need to be solved. Their logic carried to the extreme creates delivery systems in search of users and content to communicate.

Formal and Nonformal Education. The use of educational technology as means in a process has been evident in educational programs, both formal and informal, in many parts of the world. Formal education refers to "the hierarchically structured, chronologically graded 'educational system,' running from primary school through the university and including, in addition to general academic studies, a variety of specialized programs and institutions for full-time technical and professional training" (Coombs, Prosser, and Ahmed, 1973, p. 11).

Bowers (1972), Grandstaff (1973), Schramm (1973), and others define nonformal education as any organized activity outside the established framework of the formal school and university system that aims to communicate specific ideas, knowledge, skills, and attitudes in response to a predetermined need.

As increasing numbers of adult students sought advanced education opportunities through formal education channels, it became increasingly apparent that these institutions could no longer accommodate the demands upon them. Therefore nonformal education approaches have been considered and adopted in some countries to meet the demands for further education. In these cases formal education is being delivered through nonformal means. The distinctions between formal education and nonformal education begin to blur at this point.

Educational Technology. Heretofore, formal and nonformal education had looked to audiovisual media to deliver instruction to audiences in remote locations and at unconventional times, for example, through broadcast television (Schramm, 1973) and audiocassettes (Colle, n.d.). In these cases the concern was for mechanisms for delivering information that would overcome barriers of time, space, and location. The emphasis was still on the media as media. The distributive property of media (Edling and Paulson,

1972) permitted transport of an event through space and offered a simultaneous and identical experience to thousands or even millions of potential learners. However, the quality of the experience and its relationship to other events and materials were not always considered. For example, there might be a television broadcast of a lecture with little attempt to take advantage of the medium through appropriate visual embellishment. Another program might present information without regard to specific actions to be taken by the learner at the conclusion of the hour. It became increasingly apparent that the medium was merely distributing messages from a source with little regard for audience needs and without providing a context for the program.

As the limitations of media were realized, there were educational problems of greater magnitude emerging that brought about a reassessment of media's role in adult education. New pressures for providing educational opportunities, particularly to those capable of benefiting from higher education, limited faculty resources, and lack of facilities resulted in the development of new ways to provide alternative educational services. At the same time adults not concerned with higher education were seeking opportunities to requalify themselves for employment as their skills became obsolescent or as the need for new training arose. Some were seeking to remedy the deficiencies of their basic education (MacKenzie, Postgate, and Scupham, 1975).

It was clear that the simple use of media to distribute information was insufficient to meet the educational challenges for adults, yet it was evident also that media had to play some role in the overall design of instruction. In the early 1960s, educators and educational technologists introduced programmed instruction into the field. During that period the field of educational technology emerged with an emphasis on the definition of behavioral objectives for instruction and the use of a wide range of media in both stimulus and stimulus-response modes. Educational technology had moved from the position of a solution in search of problems to a problem-oriented field that could offer a series of alternative solutions.

Approach of Educational Technology. Stamas (1973) has developed a number of "models" that illustrate how technology approaches problems. These models take into account most of the variables inherent in the processes of teaching and learning. The educator (1) specifies content and objectives in relationship; (2) assesses the entering behaviors of the learners; (3) designs a learning experience by decisions concerning strategy, the organization of groups, the allocation of time, the selection of space, and the selection of resources; (4) conducts the learning experience with the learners; (5) evaluates the performance in terms of the students' subsequent behaviors; and, completing the cycle, (6) feeds back the results of the evaluation into plans for the future. The point is that the media are only one of the resources to be selected. However, the potentialities and limitations of the specific media and the way they are related to each other and to other elements require great precision in all the steps of the system.

The systematic approach to instructional design provides educational technology users with a context they had not previously considered. In turn, the varieties, capacities, and range of the instructional media have made them one of the most important elements going into the total process of developing institutional designs.

The "selection of media" element in the model infers that a full range of media be considered and that those media that will contribute to the implementation of the objectives should be selected. Beyond selection is the actual designation of the way the media are integrated into the fabric: as basic sources of content, as enrichment, or as facilitators of the learning process when used for pacing or sequencing instructional events.

The use of educational technology as a part of total instructional design has enabled educators to offer courses to adults who have not previously been able to attend courses in formal settings.

Problems. Most adult learners are already occupied in full-time jobs. Many need to upgrade or update their skills to maintain their current positions, to change careers, or to advance in their professions. The day-to-day demands do not often permit further study. Also some have courses available in their area but not offered at convenient times. Even if opportunities are available at the right time, the costs of further education may be prohibitive.

The overcoming of these and other limitations has brought about a number of educational opportunities for adults that permit an individual to pursue a course of study without going to an educational institution on a regular basis. These courses operate on an independent basis whereby individuals select their own time and place and proceed at their own pace. Each of these programs uses the educational technology approach with media as an integral element of the course design. Such programs are referred to as *open learning*. The rationale for open learning programs and examples of programs in thirteen countries are described in MacKenzie, Postgate, and Scupham (1975).

Common Elements in Open Learning Programs. Almost every open learning program has six characteristics:

Multichannel sources are used for presentation of a common core of experiences. The medium may be broadcast television or videotape, radio or audiocassettes, films, books, or combinations of several media.

A *referrable document*, such as a workbook or text designed for the course, is used in conjunction with the common experience as a guide for the learner.

Student response that requires overt participation in the learning experience is built in. Workbooks or programmed instruction sequences require written responses; group discussions or group projects are often organized to ensure responses; individual experiments are sometimes part of the design; and systematic tests and other evaluations of progress are given.

A *tutor* or counselor is available for consultation or assistance. This person-to-person liaison may be available at a specified location or by telephone. Itinerant tutors sometimes move about a designated area and are available on certain days.

A *final examination* is required to demonstrate competence.

A *reward* or recognition of successful completion is given to the successful learner. This may be course "credit" or a certificate of completion.

Case Studies

Chicago, U.S.A. The city of Chicago was faced with burgeoning enrollments in its postsecondary institutions in the mid 1950s. Chicago's TV College, established in 1956, is believed to be the oldest remote-study program using educational technology as the basis for its course delivery system.

TV College may be the most successful television-based adult education program of all times. More than two hundred thousand students have taken courses; over a hundred thousand have received college credit; more than five hundred degrees have been awarded; and over twenty-five hundred students have received two-year Associate of Arts (A.A.) degrees with one semester or more being completed through TV College. In addition to the students who enroll for credit, an average of ten thousand "casual" viewers watch each program (Zigerell and Chausow, 1974).

The study guide for each course is closely tied to the television program. Television is the primary source of the course content, although most courses have required textbooks and mail-in assignments. Programmed instruction is also used in some courses.

In the preparation of each TV College course, the instructor has much more autonomy and responsibility than his counterpart in the British Open University or the former Free University of Iran. Television instructors prepare the study guides and work with TV College producers in the preparation of each program. There is no course team, as was the case in the United Kingdom or Iran, but the producers have developed some of the competencies of instructional developers, and the assistance of the TV College central staff in matters pertaining to course design is available.

Televised courses are not appropriate for all students in all situations. Even where they are appropriate they must be revised from time to time to accommodate changes in the content, changes in the society, and changes in the student body. Zigerell and Chausow (1974, p. 33) point out, "TV College Staff has long known that instruction aimed at the unconventional learners must be systematized and made up of varying and complementary components. The future of TV College lies in becoming part of a larger whole—or instructional technology system—which will supply systematic, innovative instruction for all kinds of learners, on and off campus."

United Kingdom. After four years of intensive planning and development, the Open University began its course offerings in 1971. As of 1976, more than five thousand persons have been graduated. The Open University began as a postsecondary program for adults over the age of twenty-one and has retained that age as the lower limit for entrance. It aimed to reach individuals in the country who were intellectually able to do university-level work and who had been denied the opportunity because of the need to enter the work force after secondary school or because of limited space in universities. In 1976, over one third of the fifty-five thousand registered Open University students were housewives and technical and clerical personnel.

The Open University is probably the best example of educational technology on a national scale in practice. The heart of the operation is the course team, which, according to the report of the Planning Committee, is to set in motion "teaching operations drawing on different media but using a systems approach with the learner as the key figure" (Scupham, 1975, p. 339). An Institute of Educational Technology (IET) was established for this special function to provide specialized personnel who are involved in course design, construction, and evaluation. The academic staff is primarily concerned with course content. "The staff of the IET is concerned with the formulation of objectives, with performance tests, with the developmental testing of course material through its use with sample groups, with assessment and examination, with the conceptual difficulty, grading and continuity of courses, with student feedback, and with the necessary modification of courses" (Scupham, 1975, p. 332).

The combination of the IET, subject matter specialists, and the BBC producers has yielded unique and highly effective courses using a full spectrum of instructional media. The primary carrier of information is print—in the form of textbooks, readers, and workbooks. Television and radio broadcasts are used extensively as secondary sources of information and as pacing devices. Some recordings are used for courses in music, poetry, drama, and foreign languages. Science courses often provide laboratory kits. There are over two hundred computer terminals located in study centers for student use. Face-to-face meetings occur during the summer for many courses (about seven days) and through tutors and counselors in study centers. Self-help groups are also organized. Correspondence is used to assess performance.

An extensive research program considers the marketing of the Open University, the status of students, the relevance of various types of media to instruction, and the effectiveness of teaching methods (Bates and Moss, 1975).

Whenever programs for adult learners, using the principles of total instructional design and integrated use of educational technology, are considered, the Open University should serve as the touchstone.

Prerevolutionary Iran. In 1971, the Ministry of Science and Higher Education in Iran realized enrollment in institutions of higher education had increased fourfold since 1963 and the demand was steadily increasing. Higher percentages of students from urban areas were enrolling than from rural areas. Educational opportunity at the postsecondary level was being denied to many young people. The need for trained manpower was increasing at the same time.

After a period of extensive study, the Ministry of Science and Higher Education decided to establish the Free University of Iran, based largely upon the design of the British Open University (Beardsley, 1975). The first students were enrolled in 1977.

Like the British Open University, the principal medium of instruction during the initial years was to be the correspondence text, supported, amplified, and supplemented by television, radio, broadcast notes, textbooks, home experiment kits, tutors, audiocassettes and videocassettes, summer schools, and a computing service. The courses were to be designed by teams of subject matter specialists, educational technologists, radio and television producers, writers, and evaluators.

Special emphasis was placed on local and regional centers where learners would obtain assistance in self-directed study and receive stimulation for continued study. The relatively remote locations of learners might have led to isolation and depersonalization, which is common to most learning-at-a-distance systems. Broadcast resources were to be made available in local and regional centers since many homes do not have radio or television receivers. "It is believed that much of the success of the university will depend upon the extent to which three basic needs of the students are met: (a) the need to learn how to study effectively and efficiently on

one's own; (b) the need for general advice, help, and encouragement; (c) the need for assistance to set up and run self-help
groups" (Beardsley, 1975, p. 198).

Although there are no data regarding the outcomes of the
Free University's program (and, of course, its future is clouded by
the revolution in Iran), it was planned and has taken into account
some of the unique cultural and geographical characteristics of
Iran. It used the concept of total instructional design and the integrated procedures of educational technology to carry out its plan.
The strong influence of the British Open University makes it
a likely candidate for comparative studies when a degree of
normalcy returns to Iranian educational institutions.

Comparative Aspects of Educational Technology

From the case studies described it can be seen that the common elements mentioned previously run through each program.
Further exploration of other similar adult education programs reflects most of the same features. Other programs include external
degrees in Australian universities, the extramural studies program
of Memorial University in St. Johns, Newfoundland, Canada; the
Centres de Téléenseignement Universitaire in France; Everyman's
University in Israel; correspondence education augmented by
broadcasting through the Japanese Broadcasting Corporation
(NHK) and the Ministry of Education in Japan; the Correspondence Course Unit in the Institute of Adult Studies at University
College in Nairobi, Kenya; the Television Agricultural High School
in Poland; correspondence education in the Soviet Union; and the
University of Mid-America in Lincoln, Nebraska, U.S.A.

Each of these programs was established to provide educational opportunities to adults who are unable to attend courses in
formal institutional settings. The programs permit individuals to
work on their own, at their own pace, and at a place of their own
choosing. They assume some degree of motivation on the part of
the learners and give only minor assistance in helping individuals
to use self-study procedures.

All programs use a variety of instructional media, emphasizing printed materials and strong support from broadcast television

or radio. Supplementary printed materials and recorded materials are often available. The cost per student is somewhat less than with students studying in conventional institutional settings.

Almost all the programs have engaged in careful design of the courses and procedures to be followed by the learners. This systematic design has taken into account most of the variables that affect learners who are studying at a distance. The principles of total instructional design with the integrated use of educational technology have been used in course development.

Total educational design should be based upon solid research, and the results of an educational experience should be followed by careful evaluation. Such evaluation is not possible unless the factors that evaluation depends upon have been included early in the design (Gerlach and Ely, 1971).

Research and Evaluation

Research is "careful, critical, disciplined inquiry, varying in technique and method according to the nature and conditions of the problem identified, directed toward the clarification or resolution (or both) of a problem." *Evaluation* is "a judgment of merit, sometimes based solely on measurements, such as those provided by test scores, but more frequently involving the synthesis of various measurements, critical incidents, subjective impressions, and other kinds of evidence weighed in the process of carefully appraising the effects of an educational experience" (Good, 1973, pp. 494, 220).

By these definitions most of the studies involving the use of educational technology in adult education have been in the area of evaluation. In a review of research on audiovisual media to teach adults, Campeau (1971, pp. 100–101) established the following set of seven major criteria to select studies for her review: comparative effectiveness studies, utilization studies, basic studies, production studies, military research, attitudinal and motivational research, and media-preference research. After identifying over twelve hundred research references, she found two hundred worthy of further study. Of these only about a dozen studies were found to meet the criteria, and most of these dealt with programmed instruction.

Armsey and Dahl (1973, p. 17) also point to "the lack of conclusive research" in educational technology.

No evaluation had been made of the Free University of Iran before the revolution. The Open University has conducted extensive evaluations of its program (Bates and Gallagher, 1975). Many of them have been published in professional journals (Hawkridge and Coryer, 1975). TV College conducted comprehensive evaluations during its first four years of operation and occasional studies after that time (Zigerell and Chausow, 1971).

The evaluations that have been conducted by the programs listed here vary in purpose, style, and format. It is difficult to draw conclusions from such a collection of studies. However, the authors of *Open Learning* indicate there are four types of evaluation research that are generally carried out: (1) background research, which is concerned with the information needed to establish the case for the program; (2) formative research, which is conducted to determine the extent to which a product "works"; (3) summative research, which is concerned with final results; and (4) policy research, which determines the extent to which the program is meeting its original goals and to recommend adjustments for future overall operations (MacKenzie, Postgate, and Scupham, 1975, pp. 47–50).

It is really too early to make recommendations based on "hard" research, but certain generalizations of a heuristic nature have been made. The authors of *Open Learning* give some guidelines:

> The system must guide a student by eliciting, interpreting, and analyzing goals at the beginning point and throughout the student's contact with the program of instruction.

> The system must formulate learning objectives in such a way that they serve as the basis for making decisions in instructional design, including evaluation, and in such a way that they will be fully known to, accepted by, or capable of modification by students.

> The system must facilitate the participation of learners without imposing traditional academic entry requirements, without the pursuit of an academic degree or other certification as the exclusive reward.

To provide the flexibility required to satisfy a variety of individual needs, the system should make it operationally possible to employ sound, television, film, and print as options for mediating learning experiences. The system should use testing and evaluation principally to diagnose and analyze the extent to which specified learning objectives have been accomplished. In other words, the system should be competence-based.

The system must be able to accommodate distance between the instructional staff resources and the learner, employing the distance as a positive element in the development of independence in learning [MacKenzie, Postgate, and Scupham, 1975, pp. 16–17].

For the most effective teaching and learning, the uses of media were never sufficient unto themselves. This is true of the older media (which are so familiar they often are not regarded as media), such as the lecture, the book, and the blackboard. It is true of the newer media, such as films, radio, and television, which at first educators tended to use by themselves as though there were some special magic in them. Experiences during the fifties and sixties led to three related discoveries. One was that to be effective, all media, old and new, have to be used within the total concept of instructional design, with a precise knowledge of how the strengths of each medium, alone or together, can be combined. The second discovery was that an understanding of the appropriate use of the various media make total instructional design more precise and flexible. The third discovery was that total instructional design appropriately using the several media, including the new ones, vastly increases the number of persons who can be provided with opportunities to learn that fit their circumstances.

Chapter Eight

Reaching Unreached Adults

Kwasi Ampene

The important role adult education has played, and is still playing, in the development process of many countries has been too well documented in the history of the movement to need recounting. Being a citizen of a Third World country and an educator, I am fascinated by what has been achieved in some countries and the possibilities that exist for transforming some aspects of life in the less-developed countries through adult education. For instance, the achievements of Bishop Nicholas Grundtvig and the influence the folk high school system has had on Denmark and other countries should be an inspiration and a guide to some developing countries, particularly in Africa, that are grappling with problems of national unity. Similarly, the Mechanics Institute of Great Britain and the American cooperative extension movement played significant roles

175

in the development of the economies of these countries. In Eastern Europe the tremendous strides that have been achieved in the economic, cultural, and social fields have been due in no small way to the emphasis placed on adult education, as Saviĉević documents in Chapter Three. And in Africa a notable leader, Mwalimu Nyerere of Tanzania, is acting on the conviction that purposeful progress can be achieved only through the use of adult education.

It is this a priori case for adult education as a necessary tool for economic, political, and social development that makes it imperative to survey the extent of the world's population still to be reached with purposeful programs of adult education. Therefore my objectives in this chapter include identifying groups of persons still outside the pale of functional adult learning opportunities, examining efforts to reach the unreached adults through literacy programs and postliteracy programs, examining efforts to provide a favorable literacy environment and suitable functional reading materials in vocationally oriented programs and programs offering opportunities for recurrent education, suggesting strategies for reaching more of the unreached adults, and drawing conclusions.

Unreached Groups

Adults who are still to be reached by adult education and to whom opportunities to learn functional skills must be extended can be grouped under five headings: the illiterate, the functionally illiterate, the literate without functional skills, the well educated who lack motivation and opportunities for recurrent education, and women.

Illiterate. A broad survey of adult educational opportunities in the world shows that the majority of adults who have not yet been reached with any programs of modern adult education are in the Third World countries. This is not to say that in these countries there were not (and still are not) traditional arrangements through which the people were socialized according to traditional requirements. However, these arrangements of socialization, which were sufficient for life in simple circumstances, are no longer adequate for raising the quality of living in modern terms.

There are many channels of communication for bringing

educational programs to individuals or groups. And in view of the enormity of the task of reaching as many adults as possible, the written word is yet to be employed in reaching all the millions who need relevant education to improve their quality of living. Indeed, as the majority of the people in Asia, Africa, and Latin America are illiterate, such educational programs as reach them are either by word of mouth or through the radio. However, the radio, as an extension of the oral method, has its shortcomings, and its effectiveness in bringing about change in behavior depends on such opportunities for reinforcement as discussion groups, simulation, and, most important of all, the written word.

While no one would claim literacy per se can bring about progress, illiteracy has a high association, almost a unit correlation, with the basic blights that adult education attempts to eradicate: poverty, hunger, ignorance, diseases, and overpopulation. It is therefore tempting for many planners trying to reach the unreached to assume the preferred medium is the written word, notwithstanding the fact that more people join the ranks of the illiterates than are made literate every year. Stressing literacy in development programs implies sympathy with all who have faith in education as a powerful tool for social change. In Chapter Five Hutchinson's documentation of the growth of national or divisional associations of adult education since 1960, in Chapter Six Titmus and Pardoen's observation that legislation concerning adult education has burgeoned since 1950, and in Chapter Three Saviĉević's accounts of the provisions made for adult education by the socialist countries of Eastern Europe all attest to the strength of the faith in education as a tool for change. In the less-developed parts of the world, there is a feverish activity to step up the campaign against illiteracy because, although the proportion of literates is increasing, the absolute number of illiterates is expected to rise. UNESCO figures show that about 800 million people, as of 1977, were illiterate and that in 1980, the number of illiterate adults would exceed 820 million, although the world's illiteracy rate might have dropped to 29 percent (UNESCO, 1977, p. 2).

Thus the first category of unreached adults, numbering over 820 million and representing about one fifth of the world's population, is to be found mostly in Africa, Asia, and Latin

America. Although one does not rule out the possibility that some of the world's 800 million illiterates are reached through other channels, such as television, radio, loudspeakers, drama, and simulation games, the concern being expressed is that until persons are able to explore the options open to them by knowing where to go for help, by being able to find out some things for themselves, and by reading the relevant literature, they are not equipped to be self-reliant in the lifelong process of learning. As Ryan says in Chapter Nine, literacy is now conceived not as an end in itself but as a means to other ends.

Functional Illiterates. It is common to think illiteracy is a problem only in the less-developed countries, but recently there have been some alarming discoveries in the industrial countries, too. In the U.S.A., for instance, the problem of illiteracy has been identified among poor blacks, Puerto Ricans, isolated poor whites, such as those living in the Appalachian Mountains, and migrant Mexican workers. In addition to illiterates, a large number of Americans, estimated at about twenty-five million, have not sufficient literacy and numeracy skills to function adequately in their industrialized environment, hence the federally funded adult basic education program, which aims to raise the educational level of such persons to high school educational attainment in certain key subjects.

Similarly, Bullock (1975, par. 2.4, p. 12) has revealed there are about two million functionally illiterate people in the United Kingdom. These are persons who after leaving school at fourteen have not been reached or have not taken advantage of opportunities for continuing education; as a consequence their skills have declined.

The existence of such a large number of people who are no longer able to read and write adequately in what could be considered a highly literate environment underscores a problem in efforts to eradicate illiteracy, namely, that if new literates are not stimulated by their environment to use their skills to read readily available materials, such as a community or new readers' newspapers, or to fill out government forms, they will soon lapse into illiteracy (UNESCO, 1977, p. 4). This happens in about a decade with respect to persons who have had some education in an industrial society. In the less-developed countries, with minimal literacy environment, especially in the rural areas, one assumes it is a common fate for persons with only a little education—such as youngsters who terminate their education after three to six years of schooling—to lapse into illiteracy.

Therefore the second group of unreached adults found in both the industrial and less-developed countries is semiliterate or functionally illiterate persons who have lost literacy and numeracy skills acquired at school or elsewhere either through disuse or through lack of maintenance, such as the reading of interesting material and the lack of stimulating literacy environment. To this group may be added the increasing number of "early school leavers" in some developing countries, usually youngsters with no more than three to six years of formal school who "drop out," due to lack of opportunities to continue, into an illiterate environment and lapse into illiteracy.

Literates Without Relevant Skills. A third group of unreached adults, found mostly in the developing countries, consists of young adults aged sixteen and above who have been educated largely with an academically oriented curriculum that misfits them for their environment. Such persons, usually educated for ten to fifteen years in a colonial pattern of education that paid little or no heed to the challenges of the environment, may be able to read and do simple calculation fairly efficiently. But they are poorly equipped for making a living in a rural and nonindustrial environment. Indeed, it is no exaggeration to say they have been educated "out of" instead of "for" their environment, hence their exodus from the rural to urban areas in the hope of finding white-collar jobs for which they have the basic skills of reading, writing, and numeracy.

This group is of great concern to almost all governments in black Africa. The following declaration illustrates the extent of the concern and suggests a remedy for the situation, namely, orienting the curriculum toward work. Delegates declared that the major task of education was "to educate the young while at the same time awakening in them a critical awareness of the status of their peoples and developing in each individual the values of work, progress, and the cultural values of their civilization; . . . to provide a new form of education so as to give school close ties with work; such an education, based on work and with work in mind, should break down the barriers of prejudices that exist between manual and intellectual work, between theory and practice, and between town and countryside" (UNESCO, 1976, p. 30).

While awaiting the outcome of the innovations suggested in the African ministers' declaration, many African countries appear to have lost control over the situation of school leavers; Ghana's education service admits that about 120,000 youngsters aged fourteen and above join the labor market, willy-nilly, every year with unemployment running at 13 percent (Ghana Government, 1977, p. 3). The reputation of black Africa for having the fastest growing urban population in the world is partly due to the fact that the school leavers, usually on the encouragement of their parents, leave for the cities in search of employment.

The desire to migrate to the urban areas is further aggravated by the fact that the "good things of life," such as clean water, electricity, good housing, and entertainment places, are largely concentrated in the urban areas. This is the result of the development pattern followed by the colonial administrations, which, naturally, aimed at providing these amenities in areas where their administrative officials lived. Wages for colonial administrative officers and other employees were higher than what the peasant in the rural area could make from farming or fishing, thus the higher premium put on formal education that was (and still is) in many developing countries the only channel to do a "European" job with high wages and the relatively comfortable life in the cities. As if to make matters worse, almost all countries in Africa after achieving independence rushed into giving more of the colonial type of education to their people, with the result that they now have large populations of fairly well educated young adults who cannot find white-collar jobs and are unwilling to take to farming or other manual and productive occupations.

The declaration of the African Ministers of Education, quoted earlier, shows beyond doubt that governments in Africa are aware of the problem and some efforts are already being made to arrest unemployment and migration of the youth by reforming the curriculum and structure of educational systems to be based on work with work in mind. For instance, in Ghana's efforts to reform her educational system, the government declares the following to be among the objectives of the new structure and content of education for preuniversity courses:

> the development of practical activities and the acquisition of manual skills;
> the development of the qualities of leadership, self-reliance, and creativity through the promotion of physical education, sports and games, cultural and youth programs;
> the study of indigenous languages, science, and mathematics [Ghana Ministry of Education, 1974, p. 1].

Similarly, at the Seventh Commonwealth Conference held in Accra, Ghana, in 1977, many "country" papers of participating commonwealth nations showed the same concern for getting their educational systems to respond to the challenges that face their countries.

The following excerpts illustrate this point:

Uganda: Since the majority of children who enter primary schools do not continue to secondary, there is increasing emphasis being placed on integrating practical skills in areas of agriculture, crafts, home economics in the academic program.

Nigeria: Among the objectives of universal primary education are developing in the child the ability to adapt to his changing environment; giving the child opportunities for developing manipulative skills that will enable him to function effectively in the society within the limits of his capacity; providing basic tools for further educational advancement, including preparation for trades and crafts in the locality.

India: Some strategies to be adopted to reform the education will be . . . a thrust through nonformal and school education for achieving universal primary education, attack on adult illiteracy, and a qualitative change in approach to education, that is, development of programs of less formal and bookish curricula, problem and function-oriented learning, cultivation of wider social, cultural, and personal awareness, a stress on work experience and vocationalization of higher secondary education. The link between education and life, needs and aspirations of the people is to be reinforced with students, teachers, and schools participating in productive and developmental activities in surrounding areas.

From the forgoing quotations it is clear that some serious thinking is going on about adapting the content and structure of education borrowed from European sources to local needs and particular circumstances of each country. However, it has already been pointed out, at least in the case of Ghana, that thousands of reasonably well educated young adults join the labor market each year with no particular skills to sell. The question that may be asked is, what is being done in these countries where there is an acute problem of unemployable but educated young adults to make such persons employable through programs of adult education and training?

Well Educateds Lacking Motivation and Opportunities for Recurrent Education. There is some argument about which is the most desirable term for describing the necessary continuous learning a well-educated person has to do in order to adapt fittingly to changing circumstances. I have adopted *recurrent education* because of the interpretation Houghton and Richardson (1974, p. x) give to it, namely, "Recurrent education . . . must not rely on preconceived programs of study that, as far as the process of living is concerned, have little obvious relevance but whose major function is the elevation of some individuals over others. Recurrent education must be learner-centered in every sense of the term and the role of the teacher changes from that of purveyor to that of facilitator."

The process of learning emphasized by Houghton and Richardson, which is lifelong and oriented toward the solution of problems, should be most actively encouraged among the leaders in every society. However, given the circumstances of the less-developed countries, where the responsibility for innovative leadership is great and rests with the educated minority of the population, whose education has been in the tradition of a foreign educational system, the need for recurrent education, or even re-tooling of some educated persons to make their leadership effective, hardly needs any emphasis.

The need to encourage educated persons in the developing countries in particular to be constantly on the alert to seize every opportunity for recurrent education should be given priority consideration by governments and international agencies concerned with development. I am not suggesting some persons in this group are not already involved in recurrent education of various types, such as participation in conferences of professional bodies. I am concerned there be a well-organized and comprehensive program that will serve as many persons as possible on a continuing basis.

Women. Although all of the groups previously mentioned are made up of both men and women, all too often when they are considered simultaneously too little attention is given to important differences between their needs. I emphasize that women need special attention because, owing to various practices and prejudices, they have not received equal consideration with men in the provision of educational opportunities. In almost every country where illiteracy is a serious problem, there are more women than men illiterates. There are also fewer women than men enrolled in all cycles of education in the less-developed countries. Now that educational opportunities are becoming increasingly available, housekeeping chores prevent women in the developing countries from participating as actively as men in literacy and other educational programs. Sometimes when determined mothers take their nursing babies to literacy classes, they have to leave because the babies cry. Thus, while traditional arrangements or religious regulations might have prevented women in the past from having modern education, today the lack of such things as day nurseries, baby-sitters, efficient transportation, and some labor-saving devices in the home frustrate women in their efforts to participate in adult educational programs.

Despite the various obstacles that make it difficult to reach women with adult education programs, their role in the economies of some developing countries is marvelous. In Africa, for instance, women do as much work on the farms as men, and in some cases, as in Ghana, there are more women farmers than men. In West Africa the "market women," as they are called, control a vital section of the distributive trade—taking merchandise to the rural folks and bringing foodstuffs from the rural areas to the urban dwellers. In addition they perform their traditional role as mothers and homemakers. It is this vital role they play in society that led Emma Kwegir Aggrey, the pioneer Ghanaian educationist, to counsel his countrymen in the late twenties to take the education of women seriously because, he said, if you educate a man you educate one person, while if you educate a woman you educate a whole nation. It is the multiplier effect of the education of women that makes it regrettable, particularly in the developing countries, that in all categories of persons still to be reached with adult education programs, women are in the majority.

Efforts to Reach Unreached Adults

There is hardly any member government of the United Nations Organization that does not appreciate the importance of investing in the education and training of its people as part of its development process. Even in countries where the tradition of adult education has long been established, reviews of existing systems are being carried out and new strategies devised to reach more people with adult education programs. For instance in the United Kingdom, a comprehensive review carried out by a committee under the chairmanship of Lionel Russell recommended the doubling of the budget for adult education to reach at least two million more people (Russell, 1974, p. 15).

As far as the developing countries are concerned, the following statement by the president of the World Bank, Robert McNamara, is typical of policies being pursued by agencies such as UNESCO, the International Labor Organization, and the Food and Agriculture Organization, which work in close collaboration with these countries:

> In the five-year period 1974–1978, the World Bank and its affiliate, the International Development Association, intend to increase their support for education development. They will do so in the conviction:
>
> that every individual should receive a basic minimum education as soon as financial resources and the priorities of development permit;
>
> that skills should be developed selectively in response to specific and urgent needs, by training the right people, both urban and rural, for the right jobs—both in the modern and traditional sectors;
>
> that educational policies should be formulated to respond flexibly to the need to develop educational systems (nonformal, informal,

and formal), so that the specific requirements of each society might be met; and

that opportunities should be extended throughout an educational system for those underprivileged groups who have been thwarted in their desire to enter the mainstream of the country's economic and social life. This must include most equitable access to education for the poor, the ill-fed, women, and rural dwellers and must provide, as well, a better chance to advance from the classroom to the place of work [World Bank, 1974, p. ii].

Some governments in the developing countries, encouraged by international agencies, are making efforts to reach the unreached adults in their countries with education supported by action in the fields of agriculture, nutrition, population planning, and health.

Literacy Programs. Projections regarding the progress of literacy programs in the face of increasing world population in South America, Asia, and Africa are not encouraging, despite the efforts being made to provide educational opportunities for both the young and the old. For instance, as earlier alluded to, as the population increased to 4,500 million in 1980, the world's illiterate population also increased from 800 million in 1977 to 820 million in 1980. This seems like a losing battle because population growth in the countries having high illiteracy levels is faster than the rate at which people become educated through both the formal and nonformal systems. For instance in Africa, where population growth is about 3 percent per annum, the adult illiteracy rate will be down from the 74 percent to 67 percent by 1980, but the actual number of illiterates will apparently have increased by millions (International Institute for Adult Literacy Methods, 1975, p. 2).

It was this trend of more and more people joining the illiterate group each year because of population growth that led to the launching of the Experimental World Literacy Program (EWLP) in eleven countries (seven in Africa, three in Asia, and one in South America) from 1965 to 1975 (The UNESCO Press UNDP, 1976). The purpose of the program, supported jointly by UNESCO and the United Nations Development Program, was to evolve an effective approach toward overcoming the problem of illiteracy. In an honest and critical appraisal of the results of the experiment, the experts reached a number of conclusions that should help improve the organization of literacy projects as well as the learning aspects and thereby reduce costs per learner.

Three of the conclusions are of particular interest in view of some of the problems I have already raised. First, with regard to functionality of the curriculum, it was found that the nearer the content of the learning task was to the actual life problems of the learner, the higher his motivation and rate of learning. Second, 75 percent of the learners were between fifteen and thirty-four years old, and vocationally oriented programs, generally in agriculture, were organized for 91 percent of the one million learners who were reached in the EWLP. This finding is encouraging in that the learner perceives literacy to be of immediate use and accepts the possibility of literacy helping to increase his or her economic productivity. The profile of the "successful" participant described in the EWLP report seemed to be to one who could "actively seek information likely to help solve mainly personal problems, generally posed in vocational terms; prefer such activity to participation in formal community organizations; take full advantage of his new literacy and numeracy skills to maintain personal bank and savings accounts; and aspire to reduce the size of his or her family in exchange for the prospect of a higher material living standard" (The UNESCO Press UNDP, 1976, p. 178).

The third finding that gives hope for a group already indentified as needing to be reached in a substantial way is the fact that women accounted for about 55 percent of all EWLP enrollment. As they were equally involved in the vocationally oriented programs, it shows that with adequate motivation and support from the male population and governments, women, who form almost half of the population in many Third World countries, can contribute effectively to national development.

There are indications, therefore, that in almost all countries in Asia, Africa, and Latin America where there is massive illiteracy, some effort is being made by governmental as well as voluntary agencies, both national and international, to reduce the illiteracy level. Certainly, the awareness that illiteracy is a drag on national progress exists. But an observation in the EWLP report—namely, the lack of commitment on the part of governments to allocate resources or display sufficient determination to reduce illiteracy—makes one wonder whether the absolute numbers of illiterate persons will fall, given the present rate of education and population growth. And given the constraints of resources and the high drop-out rate as observed during EWLP, it seems illiterates shall be with us for a long time to come. However, the determination of countries such as Tanzania and prerevolutionary Iran to reduce the illiteracy level provides some hope and inspiration for other countries that may have the willpower to make the effort.

Postliteracy Programs. The most regrettable aspect of contemporary education, especially in the developing countries, is the large number of people, both youngsters and adults, who relapse into illiteracy or become functionally illiterate because of lack of further educational opportunities to consolidate their literacy skills and apply them to the ordinary business of living. The high drop-out rate in literacy programs has already been identified in the EWLP. In Ghana, for instance, about half the number of children who enroll in schools have not completed more than six years of schooling. As their mastery over skills at that stage is minimal and they drop out into an illiterate rural environment, their chances of remaining literate after a few years are very slim.

I therefore use the term *postliteracy* to cover all programs that attempt to consolidate literacy skills acquired either in adult literacy classes or in primary schools with a view to increasing the level of education and making it functional.

An aspect crucial to the maintenance of literacy skills is the extent to which the environment encourages the neo-literate to use his literacy skills and the extent to which appropriate reading materials are made available to help exercise and maintain his functional literacy.

Literacy Environment and Functional Reading Materials

It may be assumed an industrial environment is stimulating for neo-literates, but a closer look at the situation reveals this is only superficially true. Apart from street signs and billboards carrying persuasive messages to consume this or that commodity, the industrial environment makes very little provision for the neo-

literate whose ability for comprehension is rather low and therefore needs to be fed gradually with simple words and sentences.
What is even more important is the opportunity for neo-literates to
practice their skills by reading simple materials that affect them
directly. But regrettably, such matters as insurance and sales
agreements are framed in such legal language that neo-literates are
all too grateful to the sales agent who only requests them to "sign
here." The telephone, which may be a blessing in many ways, does
not encourage neo-literates in the industrial environment to try
their skill at writing because within seconds they can be in touch
with someone a thousand kilometers away more intimately than if
they had written. Libraries and museums, which adult educators
look upon as stimulators and resources for independent learning,
usually stock materials suitable for children and very literate
adults; hence the neo-literate rarely visits these places. In short the
industrial environment today does very little to promote continuing literacy on an informal basis for the neo-literate.

The literacy environment in many developing countries,
especially in rural areas, has not yet reached the level I have
described as unsatisfactory in the industrial countries. The situation is further complicated by the language of literacy, which may
be a local language, not being the same as the official language,
which may be a European language—acquired during the colonial
era. Thus neo-literates hardly get the opportunity to use their
language of literacy in any official way such as completing forms at
government offices and banks. Furthermore, street signs and other
public notices, when available, are usually in the official language,
which neo-literates can neither read nor write. Newspapers and
magazines, which are well known as media for informal or inci-
dental learning, are usually available only in the official language,
and it requires considerable educational background to comprehend the content of such resources.

However, notable efforts are being made in some developing countries to provide suitable materials in the form of functional
readers—for example, the reading materials for the neo-literate in
the functional literacy project of Tanzania. (Some rural newspapers in local languages have also appeared or reappeared in such
countries as Mali, Kenya, Ghana, and Togo to provide interesting

and current information for neo-literates.) A few governments have also adopted a national language that is the language of literacy as well as the official language. The efforts of Tanzania and Kenya in legislating for Kiswahili as the national and official language of their countries are commendable. It should be pointed out, however, that the multiplicity of languages in many African countries and the political upheaval that may result from an attempt to elevate one of the local languages as the national and official language have not encouraged governments facing the language problem to attempt to resolve it. Also, the access such languages as English and French provide to international communication has been considered too great an advantage to be sacrificed in the development of indigenous languages, although this need not necessarily be the case.

Vocationally Oriented Programs. Persons already identified as needing programs of training that will equip them with skills needed in actual life are school leavers who have acquired basic academic education at the elementary school level or beyond. As such persons are usually well provided for in the industrial countries, in this section I emphasize issues involved in training opportunities for industry and agriculture in the nonindustrial countries.

Since the most important sector in the economics of the nonindustrial countries is agriculture and related cottage or small-scale agro-based industries, one would expect the emphasis in training would be to attract school leavers into agriculture. In the past, although there was the realization that agriculture was important, the attractions of the urban areas were so great and the white-collar opportunities there for the few educated persons so extensive that training for agriculture did not receive the emphasis it needed. In some areas of Africa where the white man had decided to settle permanently, such as Kenya and Zimbabwe, the question of training Africans to be modern farmers did not arise because it was not envisaged the African would become an independent, prosperous modern farmer: He was to provide cheap and unskilled labor on European-owned farms. Now, of course, the position has changed in some of these countries (Kenya, Tanzania, Uganda), but the system of ownership in some of the countries has tended to favor the rich African instead of making it possible for young school leavers to work on the land as modern farmers. In Tanzania, where socialism has been the basis for social reconstruction since that country gained independence, opportunities are offered for school leavers to engage in scientific agriculture in cooperatives at Ujamaa settlements (communes). Tanzania has also embarked on the provision of folk high schools of the Scandinavian type in all administrative districts of the country. This is a promising development that will provide training facilities and equip young persons with skills needed in the immediate environment.

The government is the main agency for providing opportunities for training and further education in the less-developed countries. There are, however, many voluntary organizations, for example, church organizations and proprietary agencies. But the efforts of these voluntary organizations are very much limited by their resources, so governments in most developing countries may be considered the most important brokers.

Some governments are very progressive in matters of adult education and training; others conceive of education only in formal academic terms, with the result that even technical education has tended to emphasize undergraduate courses in subjects such as engineering and architecture. As the graduates from such academically oriented courses are paid a lot more in wages and salaries than middle-level technicians, many developing countries are short of skilled masons, mechanics, plumbers, and other artisans who are often more useful than, for example, a university trained engineer.

Opportunities for Recurrent Education. In English-speaking countries in Africa, which were former colonies of the United Kingdom, the advent of higher education after the Second World War brought with it extramural departments attached to the university colleges that were established (Nigeria, Ghana, Sierra Leone, Uganda, and Kenya). The objective for establishing the extramural departments was to provide opportunities of recurrent education for the educated sections of the general public who could follow a lecture and participate in subsequent discussion in the English language. Persons attracted to these lectures were therefore the educated minority, although of varying educational background. The success of the extramural programs, particularly in Ghana and Nigeria, depended largely on two main factors: First, there were already local clubs that had been providing opportunities for their members and the general public to participate in discussions on politics and other topical issues, and therefore the extramural tradition was not entirely new to the target audience. Second, the impending independence of these colonies provided the motivation for participating in the extramural program, since the lectures offered useful information and opportunities for discussing issues of self-government. As the extramural lectures were provided all over the country, many reasonably well-educated persons had the opportunity to train for their future roles as local leaders and legislators. In Ghana, for instance, about half the members of the first National Assembly in 1951 were active participants in extramural classes. The tradition of liberal continuing education is still part of many programs of university extension divisions in Africa. In addition many institutes of adult education, extramural departments, and centers of continuing education provide a variety of vocationally oriented and professional courses for the increasing clientele in the urban areas.

In addition to the efforts of the universities, other agencies, mostly governmental (for example, Ghana's and Tanzania's Management Development and Productivity Institutes), provide vocationally oriented short courses for middle-level personnel in industry and commerce in such subjects as industrial engineering, management, sales, and accounting. There is an increasing demand for such courses from government, parastatal organizations, and private persons, which should be expected with the expanding modernization of the economies of the developing countries.

Motivation for vocationally oriented and professional courses depends largely on the individual's commitment to his life goals and ambitions and to some extent on the support employers may give, by way of incentive, such as underwriting part of course expenses and granting day release. From experience, however, it appears the availability of support from the employer along the lines indicated is not such a strong motivator as clearly stated promotional opportunities either in the adult student's place of work or elsewhere in the economic sector.

It is this need for a clearer perception of job opportunities that calls for counseling services, which are as important as the provision of the training opportunities themselves. A rural youngster of illiterate parents who has to terminate his education at the village elementary school because that is all the education available needs to be saved by good counseling from journeying to the city in a fruitless search for white-collar employment or from learning some skill that has very little market value. But more often than not counseling is not considered part of the educational process in many developing countries, and when it is available, it is usually provided for the career guidance of the few and privileged university graduates.

Since the problem of appreciating the role of education in the total national development is very great in the less-developed countries, such slogans as "Take to Agriculture" or "Go Back to the Land" do very little to persuade anybody until well-planned and properly executed counseling services are provided as part of the educational process. The schools, government manpower and labor departments, parents, and the students themselves, as soon as they are able to appreciate realities of the world, such as the consequences of unemployment, should come together to plan counseling and let the challenges of the environment guide educational content. It is only by so doing that the present dichotomy between what is taught in the schools and what life actually is in a developing country can be eliminated.

Strategies

Unreached adults are of several kinds, and their circumstances vary from country to country and even within a single country. Therefore the strategies I suggest for reaching more of the unreached focus on two major aspects: reducing illiteracy and promoting vocational and recurrent education.

Reducing Illiteracy. Despite my firm belief in the power of the written word as the most reliable and liberating tool of communication, illiteracy is a problem that will have to be fought systematic-ally. In modern times wherever illiteracy has been significantly reduced in record time, such as in Eastern Europe and Cuba, it has required considerable persuasion, almost bordering on coercion, of the populace. Illiteracy should be eliminated, but voluntarily, and any government that embarks on an illiteracy elimination pro-gram should have a high degree of commitment involving the highest authority and leadership in the land. It should demonstrate the commitment in motivating the public, providing materials and incentives for learners, and promoting a literacy environment, such as demanding the use of the language of literacy (if not the same as the official language) in the basic official and commercial business.

The most reliable way of ensuring a future society free of illiterates is to put all school-age children into school and to teach them effectively to acquire reasonable proficiency in literacy skills. But this is proving very expensive for many developing countries. It is impossible to achieve universal primary education in some developing countries in the foreseeable future. Indeed, at the Afri-can Ministers of Education Conference sponsored by UNESCO in 1976, this fact was acknowledged, and it was recommended that the nonformal approach of combining work with study should be made a permanent feature of education in African countries. The approach implies that study and work must go together as soon as possible, just as in traditional society work and learning were inter-woven. Admittedly, some arrangements will have to be worked out to give more attention to work during the planting and harvesting season while more sustained learning is pursued during compara-tively relaxed periods. In the Sudan, a comprehensive adult educa-tion program based upon cotton cultivation on irrigated lands of the Gezira region (the Gezira Cotton Project) and the functional literacy project of Mali in West Africa, which also involves extensive cultivation of cotton, are excellent examples of combination of work and study.

Being illiterate in a developing country is not always embar-rassing for the person concerned since illiterates are usually in the majority; therefore persuasion is needed if illiterate persons are to be made willing to learn. But a complex of factors usually militate against their efforts, leading to frustration and subsequent drop out. Among such factors are lack of basic materials like lamps and learning equipment.

In industrial countries, however, reaching the functionally illiterate requires an elaborate and well-conceived plan that will enable the illiterate adult to overcome his embarrassment in the first place. The efforts of the British Broadcasting Corporation and the British Adult Literacy Resource Agency in mobilizing learners and volunteer teachers, although expensive, seem to be paying off, judging by the increasing number of adults who have come forward to receive help. The direction of the British literacy drive seems to be toward more use of intimate groups of learners, preferably on a one-learner-to-one-teacher basis. This is possible in a country where volunteer teachers are not lacking and learners feel embarrassed by their functional illiteracy. In the United States, however, because of the long tradition of teaching English to non-English-speaking immigrants, the problem of embarrassment on the part of the learners is not as great.

Promoting Vocational and Recurrent Education. Adults will be motivated to learn new skills or accept new ideas only when they perceive such learning will benefit them. In the less-developed countries earning a livelihood is becoming increasingly precarious; the traditional peasant practices are no longer adequate in many cases to produce enough to support the increasing population and, as has been noted, there are thousands of young school leavers whose formal education did not equip them with skills for earning a livelihood. Therefore any learning activity that helps learners increase their productivity or earning power is not only socially desirable but will surely attract many learners. In other words, the survival need as described by Maslow is fundamentally relevant in programming for adults in the developing countries. This may seem obviously true, but many adult education programs in developing countries, especially those offered by many universities, have tended to cater to the minority of educated persons whose survival needs are not so pressing. What is therefore needed is a realistic program of action by providers of adult education services —government departments, universities, and other voluntary agencies—to reach all persons with programs that will enable them to increase their productivity. Increasing the economic position of individuals and thereby raising living standards is so important that adult educators should make it their prime target in programming to reach unreached adults.

Conclusion

Millions of persons, especially in the Third World countries, need to be reached with adult education programs that will assist them individually and collectively to improve their living standards. Some governments, notably Tanzania and a few others in Africa, have realized the important role adult education should play in national development. Unfortunately, this is yet to be appreciated in other countries, where individual potential to initiate and influence change is undervalued. One of the most encouraging developments has been the adoption of the Declaration on the Development of Adult Education by member states of UNESCO at their general meeting in Nairobi in 1976. This Declaration will provide needed encouragement and guidance to those countries not yet won over to the extensive use of adult education as the most reasonable way of equipping their adult population with skills and knowledge essential for personal and societal development.

Chapter Nine

Design and Development of Literacy Programs

John W. Ryan

This chapter discusses what literacy is, describes literacy education as an important and innovative area of adult education, and cites six case studies. On the basis of these case studies, the rest of the chapter treats the stages of program design and development.

Definition

The design and development of literacy programs is largely determined by the meaning assigned to *literacy* and the purposes served through such programs. Twenty years ago it would have been generally agreed that the purpose of a literacy program was to initiate learners into the world of *logos*, that is, to endow them with mastery of a written code. Training in the rudiments of reading, writing, and, usually, arithmetic was the objective of a literacy program. This is reflected in the definition of literacy established by an expert committee on standardization of educational statistics in 1951 and since applied by UNESCO. Literacy is defined for the purpose of this chapter as the ability to both read with understanding and write a simple statement on one's everyday life.

With the proclamation of the first development decade (1960–1970) by the United Nations, the meaning of literacy became inextricably bound up with the struggle to define and promote development. The 1965 Tehran Congress of Ministers of Education declared that literacy was not an end but a means for "preparing man for a social, civic, and economic role" (UNESCO, 1965, p. 89). The congress recommended that literacy be closely geared to development policies and objectives. The "functional literacy" projects of the joint UNESCO-UNDP (United Nations Development Program) Experimental World Literacy Program (EWLP) were an attempt to respond to the recommendations of the congress and the attitude, then prevalent among agencies funding development programs, that investments in education should yield measurable and immediate economic returns.

EWLP projects, conducted in eleven countries, represent a dramatic break with more traditional programs. Functional or work-oriented literacy, as it was frequently termed, combined literacy instruction with technical or occupational training. The professed purpose of the program was not only to provide basic education but also to improve the productivity of the self-employed and to prepare unskilled labor for semiskilled occupations. Certain of the programs were highly specific in both the economic objectives sought and the clienteles served. One Iranian program, for example, was intended exclusively for sugar beet growers. In other programs the concept of functionality was more broadly interpreted to mean the programs should enable learners to cope better with problems encountered in their environment. UNESCO employs this broader concept of functional literacy today. Functional literacy programs need not be oriented to economic objectives but may be designed to advance social or cultural goals as well. Literacy, for example, might be combined with instruction in health practices or family planning. In all programs literacy was viewed as a medium rather than as the primary objective.

Quite different perceptions of education and development

inspire the concept of literacy as cultural action, with which Paulo Freire, the influential Brazilian educator and philosopher, is associated. Its goal is to lead learners toward an understanding of the "realities" that impinge upon their lives and to provide them with the ability and self-confidence to act to improve their situation. Teaching illiterates to read is only a step toward the ultimate goal of enabling them "to hold history in their hands." Cultural literacy differs from functional literacy in that the former places primary emphasis upon imparting new visions of social and political realities whereas the latter seeks to provide the learner with a set of occupational or life skills. They are alike in justifying literacy in economic, social, and political rather than traditional educational terms. Literacy is not an end in itself but a means, in one case for economic development and in the other for social and cultural transformation. (See Duke's discussion of Freire's influence in Australia, Bangledesh, Burma, Indonesia, and Iran in Chapter Two.)

It is necessary to review these changing concepts of literacy because they are influential in the design of current programs. One would, indeed, be hard pressed today to locate a "traditional program" justified exclusively in educational terms. In all programs learning to read and write is instrumental to some more ultimate goal and not the final end in itself. These statements are borne out by Chapter Eight. In the comparative study of literacy programs, the similarities are strongest at the level of conception and design where an international influence is evident. At the development and implementation stages, the situational factors are dominant.

Literacy in Adult Education

I hope this chapter will interest not only literacy specialists but also the wider community of adult educators. Literacy is the single most important form of adult education in the developing nations of the world. Indeed, the terms *literacy* and *adult education* are sometimes used synonymously and interchangeably in developing countries. Comparative adult education is therefore compelled to consider literacy. This is particularly so in a decade in which the industrialized nations have "rediscovered" the illiterate within their societies and illiteracy has come to be recognized as a universal problem and not merely a plague of the poor nations. Ampene makes this point in Chapter Eight.

Nor are literacy programs, despite their deep historical roots, stagnant or mired in traditional practices. Because of the wide recognition of the importance of literacy and the support provided by UNESCO and the UNDP, extensive experimentation has been undertaken and careful study has been given to the design, development, and consequences of adult literacy training. The results of this experience should be found interesting and instructive to many adult educators in the industrialized countries, particularly those working in the fields of basic education and among the educationally and economically underprivileged.

Case Studies

This chapter is based upon six case studies prepared for the International Institute for Adult Literacy Methods. These studies cover programs in Burma, Colombia, India, Iran, Mali, and Thailand. Each case study focuses on the process of curriculum and program development, although each presents an overview of the project covered, including its origins, purposes, and major problems. The projects or programs covered and authors of these studies are

Burma: "Literacy Classes Among Peasants and Workers," by U Thang Tut

Colombia: "Functional Adult Education Pilot Program, Risaralda," prepared by the Colombian Ministry of National Education, Division of Nonformal and Adult Education

India: "Experimental Nonformal Education Project for Rural Women, Mahbubnagar District, Andhra Pradesh," by Anita Dighe

Iran: "Experimental Functional Literacy Project for Social and Economic Promotion of Rural Women, Saveh District," by Mindu Mirzadeh

Mali: "Functional Literacy Peanut and Cereal Operation," by Adama Berthe

Thailand: "Functional Literacy Program, Activities in Educational Region 8," by Sunthorn Sunanchai

The programs and projects under review differ markedly in their objectives and scope. The Indian and Iranian projects are experimental programs for women conducted in twenty-two and twenty-five villages, respectively. The Burmese program is a nationwide undertaking. In Colombia and Thailand the programs under discussion are being developed in selected districts with the expectation of expanding them to other areas. The peanut project in Mali was concentrated in those areas where climatic conditions and transport favored the production and export of that crop. All the programs, except the Burmese, are described as "functional literacy" activities. The Mali project is the most rigorous in specifying its economic objectives and is directed primarily to farmers engaged in the production of particular crops. The Burmese, Colombian, and Thai programs are open to all illiterates in the communities served.

The ecological, cultural, and economic circumstances of the countries in which these projects are sited vary enormously. The approximate literacy rates are Burma, 70 percent; Colombia, 80 percent; India, 35 percent; Iran, 35 percent; Mali, 15 percent; and Thailand, 80 percent. (These figures are rough estimations based upon the case studies and other published sources.)

The remainder of this chapter is organized into two parts. The first discusses program design. In the design stage, program concepts and ideas must be transformed into a feasible plan of action. This involves testing program ideas against the realities of a setting and situation by posing a number of critical questions. Does the concept of the program correspond to the needs perceived by the intended participants? If not, how can conflicting priorities and needs be reconciled? Are the resources, human and material, needed to carry through the program available? If not, can resources be mobilized or can the program be adapted to reduce its resource requirements? The design stage involves the making of major decisions regarding the program. In how many regions or communities is it to be implemented? How is the program to be organized and responsibility divided? How can the program be related to the culture and preferences of the learners? These and a score of other matters must be considered at the design stage before program development and implementation can begin.

The broad framework of the program is established at the design phase. In the development phase, a set of tasks must be managed in a manner consistent with the established design. Among these tasks are the following: learner recruitment, instructor and staff selection and training, curriculum development and decisions regarding methods and materials to be used, and program organization and support, including the establishment of a management and evaluation system.

There is no hard and clear line dividing the design from the development stages. To a considerable degree these are simultaneous rather than sequential operations. Different aspects of the same problems are dealt with at both stages. The choice of language, for example, is usually confronted in the design stage, but the implications of the choice made must be dealt with in developing and implementing the program. Similarly, at the design stage the planners may be concerned to explain and disseminate a set of development principles or a national ideology, whereas in the development stage the problem is to express these principles in concrete terms and to relate them to the well-being of the local community. In many cases the problems encountered in the development process will require reformulation of the program design to reconcile plans with possibilities. In successful programs there should be a very considerable overlap between the program designers and developers. Those who are expected to develop and implement a program should have a voice in designing and redesigning it. In the domain of adult education, thinking and doing are not distinct functions but merely different aspects of an educational action. This discussion of program design and development is essentially the same as the concept of *total instructional design*, which Ely develops in Chapter Seven.

Program Design

Among the factors that influence the design of a literacy program are the purposes or objectives the program is intended to serve, the ideology or principles that motivate the program planners, the relationship of the program to other educational and development activities, the resource constraints encountered, and the socioeconomic and environmental circumstances of the learners. In discussing the projects and programs introduced, I first discuss the basic purpose each program was intended to serve and the immediate background of the decision to create it. Then I examine three issues encountered in several or all of the programs: mobilization and coordination of resources, adaptation of the program to the sociocultural environment, and language choice.

Purpose and Background. The professed aim of the Burmese program is to assist in the creation of a "new socialist man." The program is rooted in the cultural and economic context of the nation, but it is directed toward the creation of a more egalitarian and productive society. As noted, it is not a "functional literacy" program in that it does not offer vocational or practical training. The goals of the program are to teach the three Rs and to inculcate basic political and social concepts. If the program stood alone, it might be considered "traditional." It is, however, merely a part of a more comprehensive program of political education and action. If judged by its goals of changing political and social perceptions and providing literacy training as a means for more effective political participation, the program more closely resembles the Freirean than either the functional or traditional models. The methods of Freire's cultural circle, however, are not employed. The Burmese reject the concept of functional literacy because it is incompatible with the design of their program and requires resources they do not possess. The functionality of their program, they contend, derives not from its content or pedagogical approach but from the prevailing conducive atmosphere for applying learning to community and social problems.

In Thailand, a neighboring Buddhist state in Southeast Asia, the basic design of literacy activities has resulted from a conscious effort to adapt a functional literacy approach to the traditional values of Thai culture. Thailand experimented with a functional literacy project combining agricultural training with literacy instruction from 1968 to 1970. This approach was recognized as superior to the less systematic literacy and training activities that had preceded it. The functional literacy model, however, presented a number of problems. The teachers experienced difficulty in handling the technical content and, in particular, the agricultural demonstrations. Also, it was felt the program did not take adequate account of the culture and mores of rural Thailand. Therefore a new program was launched in 1970. Agriculture, health, and family planning were introduced as discussion topics, but the teachers were not required to prepare demonstrations. The basic difference was that the new program was based upon the Buddhist concept of *khit pen*, or problem solving. *Khit pen* implies that an individual address a problem by considering the following factors and takes the course of action his analysis demonstrates to be most feasible: "his personal situation, including his values, feelings, capabilities, weaknesses, and resources; his environment, including his community's social, cultural, political, and physical conditions; and the best accumulated knowledge available related to the issue and its potential solutions" (Quoted from the Thai case study).

The Indian and Iranian projects were conceived as experiments. In both countries the education and status of rural women presents a major obstacle to development. Moreover, it was realized the situation of rural women is complex and approaches to reaching and assisting them would have to be tested in pilot projects before larger-scale programs could be launched with confidence. The Indian program, which was supported by UNICEF and conducted in a district of Andhra Pradesh, is intended to improve maternal and child health. The problems of early marriage (average age eleven), early first pregnancies (average age fourteen), and high infant mortality (60 percent among firstborn), prompted the development of the program, which combined literacy training with instruction in health and nutrition and the provision of health services and supplemental food to expectant and nursing mothers.

The prerevolutionary Iranian program addressed similar, although less severe problems. Early marriage, early and numerous pregnancies, and inadequate health information were identified as common problems in the villages of Saveh, where the program was conducted. In addition, the women desired ways to increase their family incomes, particularly during the long winter season. The program therefore sought to provide health and nutrition information, to teach useful skills through which additional income could be earned (for example, improved carpet weaving skills), and to provide basic literacy and numeracy instruction.

In Mali the functional literacy program sought to respond to both personal needs and a national problem. For a variety of reasons—including drought, inadequate incentives, and inefficient production techniques and sales networks—peanut production declined dramatically during the early 1960s. As the sale of peanuts is Mali's principal means of earning foreign exchange, the decline had serious implications for the financing of development activities. Similarly, the peasant cultivators found their cash incomes substantially reduced. The literacy project was designed to cope with this problem. Among the issues that had been a particular source of concern to the cultivators was the weighing of peanuts. In the past, producers had felt, they had often been cheated by the purchasers of their crop when it was weighed and priced. Special attention was therefore given to teaching weights and measures in the literacy courses. In addition the functional literacy curriculum provided systematic instruction in agriculture and information on health, family planning, and nutrition.

In Colombia the Functional Adult Education Pilot Program (*Risaralda*) is seeking to develop an approach based upon functional literacy concepts and methods that can be successfully applied. The experiment is essentially pedagogical in character, as the organization of the pilot project is similar to the team approach of the existing basic education program. Particular attention is being given to integrating agricultural, health, and other useful information into a program of literacy instruction. The pilot program also calls for closer cooperation with the Ministries of Health and Agriculture. It is assumed learning will be more rapid and application of learning more probable where instruction includes three elements: demonstrations, followed by a "conceptualization" or discussion of the underlying factors in the demonstration, and practice. If the project is considered sufficiently successful, the curricula and methods developed will be adopted by basic education teams working in other regions of the country.

Mobilization and Coordination. The need to provide resources and assure coordination must be foreseen at the design stage. If a government can afford it, financial support can be provided from public revenues. Manpower can likewise be assigned from existing organizations or directly recruited. Often, however, literacy programs are "shoestring operations" that must supplement meager governmental support with an abundance of initiative and imagination. The Burmese program, for example, is based upon voluntary action at both the central and community levels. The national officials of the programs are usually civil servants who assume direction of the literacy program as an added responsibility. At the local level the cadres of the political party assume primary responsibility. Extensive use is made of secondary and university students as literacy teachers during their vacation periods. The voluntary nature of the program results both from the practical need to conserve government revenues and from a desire, for ideological reasons, to provide future leaders with the opportunity to learn of the situation of their less-fortunate compatriots and to extend service to them. The political party is assigned the leading role in assuring the program receives coordinated support from government agencies.

The Iranian project was adequately financed by the government but chose to recruit and train instructors from the communities being served by the program. Not only was it difficult to recruit women from the urban areas who were prepared to live and teach in villages, but also it was felt that empathy for and understanding of the learner were perhaps the most important traits to seek in instructors and could be found only among women in similar situations. To provide governmental coordination and support for the project, an interagency committee was established at the project level. As the Iranian and Indian projects were small-scale experiments, they did not require full resource mobilization. Both projects did, however, provide instructive lessons in the nature of the resources that larger-scale activities would require and the problems of coordination they would present. The Colombian program was also a pilot project that used the existing educational infrastructures. It had, however, to provide closer coordination among an interdisciplinary team and more efficient "back up" by government agencies.

To have the government organize a literacy class, the Thai

community concerned must agree to support the program and follow-up activities in specified ways. Thailand has also given attention to providing interagency coordination and cooperation at the central, regional, and operating levels. Agriculture, health, and family planning workers are regularly involved in the program. The use of monks as instructors is being tried and shows promise of being economic as well as appealing to rural communities.

The project in Mali was supported by UNESCO-UNDP as well as by bilateral assistance. The need for such assistance resulted from the fact that literacy was only one aspect of a program to improve the productivity of agriculture and the quality of rural life. Thus the literacy project could not be planned as a separate operation but had to be related to comprehensive development activities. Knowledge alone will not grow peanuts. Seeds, fertilizers, erosion control, pesticides, transport facilities, and marketing arrangements have also to be provided.

All the projects confronted resource shortages of various kinds and intensities. Fortunately, many of these shortages were foreseen in the design stages and overcome through more efficient use of existing or potential resources. This was the case with the recruitment of teachers in Burma and Iran. Functional literacy projects that deal with agriculture, health, and other community problems require a higher level of support and more efficient coordination than do traditional programs. Several of the projects considered here recognized this need and established committees and other institutional arrangements for providing the needed coordination. In Burma the political party assumed the coordinating and mobilizing function. On the basis of the information at hand, it is not possible to judge the degree of success achieved in coordinating activities at the "grass-roots level," but it is an indication of progress that the need for such coordination was recognized in designing and implementing the programs under review.

Adaptation. "Begin where the learner is" is a basic premise of any educational action and is particularly sound advice where planners and learners are considerably removed from one another geographically and culturally. An essential step in following this dictum is that of "locating" the learner. For this purpose the programs under review made extensive use of surveys.

The Indian project conducted a systematic problem survey designed to determine the felt needs of the learners; the vocabulary in common use; the degree of awareness of problems related to health and nutrition as well as the taboos, attitudes, and misconceptions relating to these subjects; and the use made of existing health facilities. This information was collected from both individual respondents and groups of women. The information gained from the survey was used in deciding the curriculum content and designing the learning materials.

The Iranian project focused more upon learning interests than upon perceived problems. The results showed that the highest interest was expressed in such practical skills as sewing, cooking, knitting, and carpet weaving. Expressed interest in hygiene, health, and family planning was lower. Since the latter were, however, felt to be urgent needs of the population, the curriculum combined practical training—which attracted learners to the classes and held them—with discussion of health and related matters.

The Burmese and Thai projects used more informal methods of information gathering than did those in India and Iran. The Burmese project studied the life-styles and culture of the rural population. Farmers' interest in jovial get-togethers after work was noted. It was also observed that their interests in conversations ran toward a discussion of light and happy matters and that films with tragic endings usually did not attract audiences, as distressful stories are unpopular. It was concluded there was a need for light reading materials to attract people and to "fix" the reading habit as well as more informative and serious materials on agriculture, health, and related subjects. Other findings were the needs to cater to the special reading interests of women and to give an adult appearance to textbooks and follow-up reading materials.

The Thai project undertook a formal survey but found the results less useful than had been expected. On the points of greatest importance—the interests and felt needs of rural citizens—the survey provided only superficial information. As a result, considerable use was made of consultations with government officials who had extensive field experience.

In Mali villagers' needs were discussed with the headman and a representative sample of villagers. Among the problems identified were those concerned with agriculture, health, and taxes. A village survey in Colombia collected information on village facilities, agricultural conditions, and the practices, interests, and problems of potential participants.

On the basis of the sample of case studies examined, several tentative conclusions may be drawn. First, the more empirical and systematic approach to assessing needs and interests appears a considerable advance over approaches based on untested a priori assumptions. The methodologies used for collecting such information, however, seem insufficiently sensitive to the complexity of the matters under examination. There also appears to be an infatuation with "central tendency." The possibility of sharp differences in interests and perceptions associated with sex, social class, occupation, and other factors is not examined. Nonetheless, the information gathering and reality testing of design concepts indicated in the case studies is to be applauded. The manner in which needs perceived by planners may be combined with interests expressed by potential participants suggests fruitful compromises are possible.

Language Choice. Language choice represents a factor in the design of several of the projects under review and was a matter of fundamental importance in the Mali project, where the decision to teach literacy in the national languages rather than in French represented a major political decision with profound social and cultural implications. Indeed, this is reflected even in the title of the organization that administers the project: National Office of Functional Literacy and Applied Linguistics. All aspects of the program, including, in the initial stages, the need to work out agreed-upon and accurate transcriptions for the national languages, were influenced by this decision.

In the Indian program the choice of Telengana Telugu as the medium of instruction required the exclusion of Hindi- and Urdu-speaking villages from the experiment. Moreover, as the project developed, it was discovered that certain of the standard forms of Telugu were not used or easily understood in the project villages. The introductory discussion card, for example, contained the sentence *Kamala chulalu* (Kamala is pregnant). After this phrase was introduced, it was discovered that *nindumanisi* and not *chulalu* was the term for pregnant used in these communities.

In Iran, Azeri, a language of Turkish origin, rather than Persian (Farsi) was spoken in the villages of Saveh but not in the adjacent cities. The choice of Farsi as the medium of instruction, although desired by the participants who considered it the more useful and prestigious language to know, presented the need to select villages where spoken Farsi was understood and to give particular attention in preparing materials to word choice and presentation clarity. A related situation exists in Thailand, where the northern dialect rather than central Thai is spoken in the areas in which the program has been introduced.

In Burma the issue was not language choice but the need to develop an effective method for teaching the Burmese language in order that it might be mastered within a hundred classroom hours. The need for this was twofold. First, experience demonstrated it was difficult to hold the learners' interest for a longer period. Second, since the volunteer teachers were usually university and secondary school students on their vacation periods, it was necessary to complete the course within approximately a month and a half. This did not permit more than a hundred hours of instruction even when daily classes were organized. By adopting a syllabic method rather than the alphabetic one used in the formal schools and through devising efficient teaching aids, it proved possible to meet this goal.

The experiences reflected in the case studies confirm the need to consider carefully the language as well as the instruction methods used. Standard forms of a language are not always the forms employed in isolated rural communities. Careful selection and pretesting of vocabulary is therefore required. It is now common—as well as largely accurate—to observe that literacy is essentially a political problem. It should not be forgotten, however, that literacy is also a linguistic problem.

Program Development

I shall discuss two aspects of program development: the recruitment and training of instructors and the development of curricula and instructional materials. This selection reflects the critical importance of these two processes in literacy training. Although innovative approaches are being introduced, including instruction via television and the use of programmed materials, no replacement has yet been found at the introductory level for the presence of an instructor whose task is usually to motivate and encourage as much as to teach. Moreover, the recruitment of literacy instructors is a problematic and controversial issue and consequently an instructive one to examine. The curriculum and instructional materials embody the "message" of the program and must present it to the learner in an understandable and convincing manner. There is a widely shared awareness of the need to develop more relevant, interesting, and effective instructional materials for literacy programs. In several of the case studies under review, thoughtful attention is given to the development of such materials.

Instructor Recruitment and Training. One of the common constraints in the development of literacy programs is a shortage of instructors. One of the recurrent problems cited in the evaluation of literacy programs is the inadequacy of the instructors, who are the main point of contact between the program and its trainees. The case studies under review contain instructive lessons as to how the staffing constraint may be loosened and the instruction quality improved through selection and training.

The Burmese project had inadequate financial resources to employ professional instructors. Nor, indeed, would such instructors have been available in adequate number even had financing been provided. The program therefore depended upon volunteers. This fact imposed a number of constraints and limitations. It meant the literacy program had to be scheduled to coincide with the availability of the volunteers, often students on school holidays. Moreover, it was not worthwhile to offer extensive training to volunteers, who would serve for only a matter of weeks or months. In order to overcome these limitations, the methods and materials used were designed so as to simplify the task of instruction. The use of a "language wheel" to present vowel and consonant combinations, to cite one example, was found to be a valuable teaching aid as well as an excellent learning aid. As noted, use of a syllabic rather than an alphabetic approach to language teaching also served to expedite the teaching-learning process. The instructor's task was also lightened through the cooperation of the political party members in the community. The party usually assumed responsibility for the organization of the class and the recruitment of the learners. The instructor's task was thus primarily educational rather than organizational. The Burmese experience suggests the complex task of the instructor can be redesigned and simplified in a manner that facilitates use of inexperienced volunteers where the will exists to make such an arrangement work.

The Iranian literacy programs, like those in most other countries, had traditionally relied upon elementary school teachers, who were offered supplemental payments to organize evening classes for adults. This meant adult classes could be organized only in communities with a school. There was also debate as to the suitability of the primary school teacher as an adult instructor. Their professional conditioning, it has been contended, makes it difficult for them to adapt to teaching adults.

The Iranian Saveh Project, as has been seen, decided to recruit its instructors from among the literate women in the communities being served by its program. This decision obviously required that recruitment criteria be reconsidered. Instead of demanding a secondary certificate, only a primary certificate was asked. It also necessitated the rethinking of the training program needed to prepare instructors. Rather than being only a day or two in duration, the program had to be extended and intensified. In addition to orienting instructors to the purposes of the course, it was necessary to train them in teaching methods and group techniques as well as to provide some trainees with remedial education. In particular, systematic in-service training had to be provided, as it was found that the most effective learning occurred after the instructor had organized her group, begun the course, and then encountered unexpected difficulties. Weekly or fortnightly training sessions were therefore organized. The project evaluation confirms that inexperienced instructors with only limited education can do an excellent job if systematically trained and actively supported. Inadequacies in teaching skills and educational background are offset by their commitment to their assignments and their empathy for the participants.

In Mali over 90 percent of the instructors were from the same background as the participants and had less than a primary school education. The selection of instructors was made by the local community or production unit. A training course of only three to five days was provided. The information available does not indicate whether the training was adequate to enable the instructors to perform their assignments with confidence and efficiency.

In Colombia and India the instructors were part of an interdisciplinary education team. The Indian staff members were generally young and usually unmarried. It was felt their inexperience and unmarried status made them unconvincing advocates of family planning as well as reducing their authority in offering advice on child care. The fact that the unmarried women were required by their jobs to live apart from their families also reduced their prestige in the eyes of tradition-bound women. As the job requirements established for the project mandated a secondary education and teaching certificate, the project was unable to recruit and train more mature local women. A total of six weeks of training was provided to the staff. Approximately four weeks were used for preservice training and the balance for in-service training sessions of a day or two each.

The Thai project employs primary school teachers to instruct adults. An additional payment is made for assuming this added responsibility. A thoughtful discussion of the role of the teacher and the possibilities and limits of teacher training is contained in the case study of the Thai program:

> Observations during the past seven years indicate that, in general, a teacher who understands and is committed to the instructional process—its philosophy and goals more than the actual steps it involves—can easily overcome inadequacies in content relevance or the tendency of some lessons to impose solutions. On the other hand, teachers who do not share such an understanding or commitment can have great difficulty even where there are no structural or content flaws in a lesson. As a result, the division has in the past several years placed a high priority on its teacher training activities and approaches. Currently, a model is in use that is based on the same *khit pen* (problem-solving) instructional goals [that] teachers are to promote in their classes and [that] utilizes the same process to achieve them. . . .
>
> There is a growing recognition, however, that some of the problems encountered with teachers cannot be adequately addressed by training activities that will always be limited in duration.

. . . Since many reoccurring problems tend to fall under the general category of teacher attitude and commitment, division officials are now viewing them more as concerns for recruitment than training [Quoted from the Thai case study].

Curricula and Instructional Materials. The projects and program under review proceeded to develop curriculum and instructional materials in a variety of ways. In India the materials initially used in the project were developed in a writer's workshop attended by adult educators, writers, artists, photographers, and linguists. The results of the problem survey conducted in the project area were presented to the workshop and the objectives of the program were explained. The basic instructional materials consisted of seventeen sets of cards, each set treating a particular problem. To provoke and direct discussion, the first cards in each set consisted of photographs depicting a familiar setting or situation. Other cards contained key words and language drills. As a fundamental objective of the project was the development of effective teaching materials, careful attention was given to designing and testing such materials. This was done in a variety of ways. Instructors were required to keep a daily log of their teaching experiences and to note any problems they encountered in their use of materials. Direct testing, discussion with field staff, and observation were also useful in judging the effectiveness of materials. As previously noted, it was found the vocabulary used on the teaching cards did not in all cases correspond to local usage. Similarly, the visuals were sometimes interpreted in unanticipated ways. A good deal of attention was given by the project to the preparation of guides to assist the teacher in presenting information and leading discussions.

As has been seen, the Thai program was based upon the *khit pen* concept of problem solving. This concept required that course content be presented in a way designed to pose problems rather than to impose readymade solutions. For example, when the problem of environmental hygiene was discussed, villagers were not advised, as had previously been the case, to remove the stables from under their homes but were asked to discuss the pros and cons of keeping animals near their living quarters. It was found the villagers were well informed of the undesirability of the practice from a health viewpoint but considered the danger of cattle rustling to be a greater concern. The root of the problem was therefore not lack of knowledge but inadequate security. The problem-posing techniques used in the classes were found to be more interesting to adults than the previous form of instruction and also led to more realistic solutions to problems than could have been provided by outsiders unaware of local conditions and attitudes.

The curriculum of the Thai program was developed by a twenty-two-member team composed of representatives of several ministries and specialists in a variety of subjects. Seventy-three problem areas, which became the units of the curriculum, were identified. These dealt with health matters (thirty units), agriculture (eighteen), civics (fourteen), and economics (eleven). The instructional materials for each unit were prepared by a team consisting of six full-time members aided by specialists, where required. Each of the units was self-contained. As in the Indian project, the instructional materials included a photograph, the analysis and discussion of which would bring out the main issues to be covered in the unit. As the discussion progressed, the key words in the unit would be written on the blackboard. Subsequent literacy instruction would be based on these words. The use of irrelevant or nonsense words to illustrate vowel and consonant combinations was not employed. Instruction in arithmetic was also closely integrated with the problem-solving theme of the unit. To avoid overwhelming the learner and to facilitate revision, the instructional materials were presented on cards rather than in book form.

The curriculum of the Iranian project consisted of thirty-three sequences or units, which were covered in two courses of six months each. In determining the content of the curriculum, consideration was given to potential participants' professed interests, community needs as judged by project staff, and national and regional development plan objectives. Among the subjects covered were the social and family responsibilities of women, environmental hygiene, nutrition, agriculture, carpet weaving, sewing, and cooking. Each sequence was a carefully integrated unit combining technical information with instruction and practice in the three Rs. Discussion was the basic medium of instruction. Extensive use was also made of demonstrations and practical exercises. In addition to preparing a comprehensive set of learning materials, the project provided the instructor with classroom aides and detailed guides. All aspects of the program, including curriculum and instructional materials, were systematically evaluated.

Learning efficiency would appear to be the criterion that has determined the Burmese curriculum. The *Adult Burmese Reader*, the literacy text used throughout the country, is based upon a linguistic approach. This reader, first published in 1966 and revised six times since then, consists of twenty-six lessons and accompanying exercises. It is primarily designed to present the principal elements of the written language, although attention has also been given to introducing social, economic, and cultural information as well as readings to satisfy the "interests and curiosities" of adults. Numbers from one to ten thousand and basic arithmetic operations are also included in the curriculum. Newspaper reading is introduced in the classes, and careful attention is given to the provision of follow-up or postliteracy materials. The strategy of the Burmese program would appear to be that of concentrating on basic literacy during a short and intensive course and afterwards providing the learner with opportunities and incentives to continue and broaden his education.

The Colombian curriculum seeks to integrate instruction in agriculture, nutrition, and other subjects with the teaching of literacy and numeracy. Careful attention has been given to providing demonstrations and opportunities for discussion and practical work in each unit. The language elements of the unit are consolidated on a reading sheet that presents the basic vocabulary.

The literacy project in Mali is divided into two phases. In the first, priority is given to the acquisition of literacy and numeracy, although vocational content is also introduced. After an adequate level of literacy has been achieved, the emphasis is placed primarily upon vocational training, which is taught through written materials, discussion, and demonstration. The agricultural training materials have been developed in close cooperation with the staff of the peanut project to assure their accuracy and timeliness. One unit is devoted to an explanation of the use of the "Chinese" scales for weighing peanuts. Units on health, environmental hygiene, and civics—the citizen's duty to pay taxes—are also included in the curriculum.

Training materials are presented in card rather than book form, as it is considered this better retains the learners' interest and is easier to handle. The Mali project uses photographs to introduce and stimulate discussion. Attention has also been given to preparing materials to assist the instructor in understanding and carrying out his or her duties.

The preceding review suggests the design of curriculum and the development of instructional materials are usually done by interdisciplinary or interagency teams or by both. In India a special workshop was held to develop materials for the project. The selection of the curriculum takes into consideration the perceived problems, expressed problems, and expressed interests of participants as well as expert opinion. There is wide recognition of the need to test carefully and regularly revise instructional materials. Attention is being given in several of the projects reviewed to the development of demonstration materials and discussion guides to assist instructors with limited education in successfully fulfilling their assignments. Finally, the technique of introducing discussions with photographs is widely used, and presentation of learning materials in card rather than book form is common.

Conclusion

On the basis of the case materials reviewed, it can be said that in a number of contemporary literacy programs, learning is no longer its own justification. Literacy has become a means for achieving developmental or societal objectives rather than being an end in itself. The specificity and nature of the objectives being pursued vary considerably: from the precisely defined, if difficult to achieve, goal of growing more peanuts to the more vague and comprehensive notion of creating a new socialist man. Accompanying this change in goals is a more rigorous specification of the steps in designing, developing, implementing, and evaluating literacy activities.

Although oriented to the creation of new social and economic conditions, the programs reviewed are consciously rooted in their cultural and ecological settings and are forced to contend with prevailing financial and manpower constraints. In Thailand, for example, a new educational program has been founded upon a traditional religious concept: *khit pen*. All the projects examined have conducted surveys and studies to ascertain the interests, felt needs, desires, preferences, and language usage of potential participants and have sought to use their findings in planning the course of study and developing instructional materials. The Burmese and Iranian programs have been imaginative in overcoming manpower constraints by recruiting personnel who would not normally have been considered available or qualified for teaching posts. In Burma the timing, methods, and organization of the literacy courses have been adjusted to permit use of student volunteers as instructors. In Iran prior to the change in government, recruitment criteria had been reduced and training activities extended and intensified to enable village women with primary school certificates to serve in the program. There seemed to be a wide recognition of the need to coordinate literacy work with other development activities and with a search for means to achieve this end.

In sum, the field of action in literacy programs has expanded from the word to the world. New methods and approaches are being introduced; new sources of personnel and support are being mobilized; and in some programs old traditions and values are receiving new respect.

Chapter Ten

◆◆◆◆◆◆◆◆◆◆◆◆◆◆◆◆◆◆◆◆◆◆
◆◆◆◆◆◆◆◆◆◆◆◆◆◆◆◆◆◆◆◆◆

Research

◆◆◆◆◆◆◆◆◆◆◆◆◆◆◆◆◆◆◆◆◆◆
◆◆◆◆◆◆◆◆◆◆◆◆◆◆◆◆◆◆◆◆◆

J. R. Kidd

Comparative studies are intended to describe and analyze similarities and differences in order to understand the other cultures, institutions, and peoples and to understand one's own society and oneself. All the statistical tables, the computer printouts, and the packed files of information are so much pulp if the stage of understanding is not reached. Some comparativists want and claim much more than understanding; they aim at the ability to predict (Holmes, 1965) or claim a method that is valuable for decision making (King, 1967), and many other virtues are hoped for or expected. But the irreducible minimum is understanding, and if that is richly achieved, it may be enough for justification.

That is the purpose that prompted the application of comparing as an early and basic research method in the physical sciences. The method is simple: You find a specimen; you examine it and place it in juxtaposition with another specimen whose properties and functions are known according to such factors as weight, hardness, color, feel, taste, and smell; you draw inferences through systematic comparison of the properties of both specimens—inferences about origins, relationships, functions, uses, and so on—and then you replicate the process again and again until you are reasonably certain of your result. This is also what happens in comparative adult education, but the process is much more complex and it utilizes data that are far from complete. There are more unknowns than knowns.

The entire field of educational research is rather primitive, and adult education was the last member of the educational family to develop systematic research. Over whole sections of adult education, the nonformal as well as self-initiated studies, statistics are almost unknown, and even formal adult education statistics are incompletely collected or reported. The result of this lack is an inability to make even gross comparisons of inputs or outputs, or there may be grotesque outcomes when one tries.

The situation respecting quantitative comparison is not much inferior to the qualitative. In most countries there is a dearth of careful, ordered, descriptive materials about the systems, institutions, and personnel (learners and teachers, animateurs [moving spirits], organizers, and counselors) and other statements related to inputs or outputs of adult education. There is not even agreement about the essential factors in a system that should be reported. However, recent work by Colin Titmus (1976a) of the University of Glasgow and colleagues from Eastern Europe, meeting at the Center for Leisure and Education in Prague, are beginning to remedy this defect.

It would be wrong to conclude that this analysis of the present position suggests comparative adult education is hopeless and futile. The total number of systematic comparative research studies available for the Adult Education Association *Handbook of Adult Education* in 1960 (Knowles, 1960) would not have exceeded a handful; the amount available for the 1970 handbook (Smith, Aker, and Kidd, 1970) would not have exceeded a hundred. The first meeting on comparative adult education was not held until

1965 at Exeter, New Hampshire (Liveright and Haygood, 1968), and no systematic graduate course was offered in comparative adult education until 1967 at the Ontario Institute for Studies in Education. However, from this standing start, a whole new field is beginning to move. The *Anthology of Comparative Studies in Adult Education* (Bennett and others, 1975) reports much that is promising as well as much that is still to be done.

I shall deal with the larger field of comparative education (CE) and the subfield comparative adult education (CAE).

CAE goals have been identified several times and have been stated as follows:

> to become better informed about the educational system for adults of other countries;
>
> to become better informed about the ways in which people in other cultures have carried out certain social functions by means of education;
>
> to become better informed about the historical roots of certain activities and thus to develop criteria for assessing contemporary developments and testing possible outcomes;
>
> to understand better the educational forms and systems operating in one's own country;
>
> to satisfy an interest in how other human beings live and learn;
>
> to understand oneself better;
>
> to reveal how one's own cultural biases and personal attributes affect one's judgment about possible ways of carrying on learning transactions [Bennett and others, 1975, p. 10].

In earlier times CE was fostered with the definite purpose of "borrowing" successful forms and activities from abroad to be adopted in one's own system. In its early days comparative educationists were mainly reformers. Today "reformers" in this sense have been replaced by educational planners, and comparative studies are as much a preparation for educational planning as are studies of economics or sociology. In more recent decades comparative modes that might assist educationists in one country faced with difficult decisions about whether to welcome or resist cultural innovations from another have been sought. Comparative modes have been recommended as essential tools for educational planning and for educational assessment. One interesting objective for comparative adult education is to distinguish those characteristics or patterns of behavior that are culture-bound, related to a given society, from those that may have universal characteristics.

In other words, these goals may be considered *vocational* for a person who is going to another country or working with another culture as an educational planner. The same educational activity for other students may serve to satisfy their curiosity, and for them the study can be categorized as *liberal-humane*. For some, comparative studies are to obtain a perspective or a "mode of discourse" for research or writing. For others the search is for hypotheses or for clues for evaluation.

These are all positive goals. Some people would also include as a significant goal the capacity to withstand pressures to accept alien practices or to resist those aspects that are inimical to the host culture. Insights into cultural differences and values might be employed for making or resisting change. In any such consideration, of course, one's values are central.

Most of these are goals for instruction, concerned primarily with the improvement of educational content and method. Research in comparative studies is important as well, for policy and administrative decisions. Note two recent examples to see how learning practice and policy concerns are mixed.

Most of the writing about adult learning is found in the English language and has been derived from experiences primarily in North America and Western Europe. These books are now being translated into other languages and used frequently in other cultures. *How Adults Learn* (Kidd, 1974) is now in eight languages. To a considerable extent this has happened because the means of dissemination, such as printing presses, are found primarily in certain countries. It is also well established by now that Western institutions and styles of educational organization have often been unsuitable, sometimes seriously harmful, when adopted or applied in other countries. Perhaps this is also true about learning styles and learning skills: May these also be culture-bound? Recently, Malcolm Knowles and I were discussing our experiences in offering seminars in other countries. While we did not seriously disagree,

Knowles stressed similarity and I stressed difference, both of us drawing on our individual experience. But the matter is too important to be left to personal and independent observation. Carefully sustained, replicated research, and research that is not locked into methods and mind sets of Western social scientists, is needed before very much application is made of ideas, concepts, strategies, methods, techniques, and organizational plans devised in the West.

The success of the British Open University and of certain forms of nontraditional studies in the United States has attracted the interest of educational policy makers in many countries. It is known that to be productive, open-access learning depends on strong motivation, at least occasional human encounters with tutors and fellow students, and an infrastructure of media. What proportion and what mix of these factors will make possible the effective application of nontraditional methods in other countries?

Respecting research, comparative adult education offers insights and data for considering what kinds of experience may be unique or individual, what may be universal, and what may be culture-bound; for conveying basic information (inputs, outputs, qualities); and for developing and testing hypotheses about human capacities and human performance.

Related to these three kinds of goals there are a variety of methods. At this stage of development, people in comparative adult education have paid little attention to method. This is in part a function of newness, in part a reaction to what has seemed an overemphasis on sterile debates about methodology in comparative education, which has sometimes been likened to the futility of medieval debates about the number of angels standing on a pin. It has caused one observer, Benjamin R. Barbour (1973, p. 67), to state that comparative method is simply "what comparative scholars do when they are solving problems" and that the usefulness of any inquiry will depend "on the meaningfulness of the questions posed, rather than on the number of answers obtained."

I do not wish that anyone should fall into a slough of methodology, but it does seem necessary for comparativists concerned with adult education to become systematic about the methods they choose. Methods are related to goals, and since the goals are varied, precision concerning the selection of methods is needed. For illustration consider the utilization of a few methods, some that comprehend total systems and some that start with a component or a subsystem or a problem.

The modes to be selected should meet several criteria. They should serve the objectives of comparative adult education; lead to objective analysis (could be repeated by another observer); lead to reliable analysis (could be repeated by the same observer in subsequent studies); lead to valid analysis, that is, related to the real situation; be practicable, that is, be applicable by untrained or partially trained, efficient personnel; and be relatively inexpensive in money and effort. No modes presently available meet well all these criteria; one must work with the tools available while joining in the effort to refine present modes and discover improvements.

Since there are several different goals or purposes for comparative adult education, there is no single or best mode. Several are required. A mode that could lead to the valuing or appreciating of one's own educational system or cause one to become critical of it could result from a relatively simple comparison with another country of major premises, perhaps presented in documentary or dramatic films. One cannot witness the considerate way older people are provided for in some countries without being reflective and critical about the ways in which health, recreation, and education are provided for older citizens in one's own country. However, to provide a comparative estimate of the benefits that may be obtained by certain practices, counseling, for example, or certain expenditure on training, a much more sophisticated mode may be required. Sometimes a broad approximation is all that is needed or possible; at other times more precise data are needed.

The modes that have been developed or applied can be classified and described in different ways. Since education is part of the web and life of a culture, as well as an influence upon that culture, one must consider the interrelationships of education with the whole culture. As Sadler (1949, p. 262) said, "The things outside the schools matter even more than the things inside the schools, and govern and interpret the things inside"; and adult education is no less infused with the culture than the schools. This fact might lead one to conclude that to begin a comparison of two educational systems, one should start with a comparison in depth of the two host cultures. This would be a reasonable beginning, but the obvious difficulty is that a full understanding even of one culture may be the work of a lifetime. Some faster route must be found.

From this dilemma researchers have concluded that two basic methods of study are required: to study that part of society in which the particular educational system is rooted and to study problems pertaining to the educational system. They conclude that, because of the complexity of any educational situation, both methods of study are necessary and must be combined.

One of the reasons for argument about methodology is that pragmatists have often been pitted against theorists in respect to whether comparative education is a means to a reformist end or a scholarly end in itself. Many authors have claimed comparative education represents the heights of scholarship and learning about other systems is an important study in its own right. But others have insisted on more precise goals—foreign educational systems are seen as adding perspective in order to enable more appropriate reform or more balanced educational generalizations. As noted, the goals of comparative adult education comprehend both of these tendencies.

National Character

It is no longer fashionable to talk about "national character" except to make jokes about it. Unmistakably, however, there are attributes that can be associated, more or less, with particular nations, and the educational system has some part in the development and perpetuation of these attributes.

In an earlier period, when historians dominated the field of comparative education, a central, informing, and integrating notion was national character. Before long this approach came under criticism from those who pointed out that differences between people in varying economic and social classes within a country may be more important than similarities, and similarities between people in two or more countries may be more significant than differences between national stereotypes.

Whether you repudiate a concept such as national character or find the distinction between it and culture patterns or normative standards a distinction without a difference, it is essential to comprehend the impact of a nation and culture on an educational system. (Duke in Chapter Two, and Savićević in Chapter Three amply illustrate this point.)

Global Approach

Pedro Rossello and Leo Fernig, who worked at the International Education Bureau (UNESCO) in Geneva, collecting educational information from all over the world, have been working on the assumption that for comparison it is legitimate to start with the world as a whole with its two hundred or so different systems. Both of them have assumed international norms can be derived from observing the range and trends in various educational systems. Rossello was concerned with developing categories of data, which, for comparison, must be as identical as possible, and he maintained that the more global the data, the more valid it is. Fernig (1963, p. 214) asserts there are three elements involved in a global approach: descriptive, statistical, and lexical.

Descriptive—The most obvious way of arriving at a generalized account of education in the world and of noting the significant trends and differences is to secure factual descriptive information from each country, such as is collected in the *International Year Book of Education*. Reviewing each annual statement reveals movements, shifts, and trends.

Statistical—A certain amount of information about educational systems can be and is being expressed in quantitative form.

Lexical—Included under this term are the needs for agreement on the use of terms, concepts, definitions, and acceptable translations. For example, a folk high school in Germany is very different from a Canadian high school, and the equivalent of the French term *éducation permanente* is lifelong learning. (*Permanent education,* which is often wrongly used, has a connotation of being finished or complete.)

Functions

Some writers feel the best way to understand a society is to look not at factors but at functions, the ways citizens carry out their tasks of living. The manner in which a young man is introduced into an Indian tribe in Canada and the manner a young man is introduced into a factory group in Russia are far from identical, but the function is similar; so is the function performed by marriage in India or in Indiana, although the ceremonies may differ markedly. Educational systems have been created mainly to prepare people to take part in the central functions of society, and accordingly there are many points of convergence between functions and education.

Havighurst (1968, p. 126) says, "One good way to study education comparatively is to study the educational responses made by various societies to their social problems such as racial diversity, religious diversity, socioeconomic stratification, social revolution, and technological problems." He proposes that a useful way to begin comparison of countries is organizing information covering such basic functions as the family, the economy, religion, politics, and technology.

The functional approach has certain difficulties. Not everyone agrees about what functions are most crucial. For example, is the system of communications in both Canada and Lichtenstein a crucial or a peripheral function? Nor is it easy to obtain the data needed for comparison or to order them in ways that make comparison meaningful. Assuming the functions served by the ritual of entering a tribal group and a factory group have much in common, are the values associated with each similar? These questions are not easy to answer. However, the mode of comparing functions, along with others, adds a richness and a texture and may suggest questions and hypotheses for an understanding of adult education.

Problem-Centered Approaches

Henry (1973, p. 231), writes "The one method to consistently attract workers in comparative education is the problem-centered approach whereby answers to specific (or general) questions are required." The reasons for this preference may be obvious, but two at least are worthy of mention. The first relates to the action-oriented reform intentions of many comparative educationists, particularly in comparative adult education: They seek improvement, reform, or innovation as much as understanding. The second reason might be described as instrumental. It appears to some to be more effective to begin with a comparison of specific problems and then enlarge the inquiry to include a consideration of the societies in which these problems are encountered. This is the familiar educational practice of starting with the immediate and then generalizing; it is the reverse of starting with the whole before examining the parts. Most people engaged in CAE have found and will find it useful to adopt a problem-centered approach at least part of the time.

Alternatives to the global approach have included a concentration on explanatory factors, significant functions, or problems requiring action. Nicolas Haines, Robert Havighurst, and Brian Holmes have provided starting points in these areas. Adams and Farrell have demonstrated application of key concepts from sociology in educational planning. Edmund King puts his emphasis on educational policy and decision making. Cross-cultural and crossnational studies provide data for educational studies in limited areas. The learner's own statements about the educational process provide an invaluable source of direct information.

CAE Research and Development

No history of comparative studies in adult education has ever been undertaken. When one is completed, it will not match *War and Peace* in wordage, but the extent and range will surprise many readers, and its origins will appear many decades earlier than the Exeter Conference of 1966.

Presystematic Study. All educational fields, and adult education is no exception, have grown through a phase usually described as "traveler's tales," typified by some educationists who have journeyed or worked abroad and have returned to talk or write impressionistically about certain phenomena they have encountered in other cultures. By itself there is nothing wrong with such an effort.

Early issues of the American Association of Adult Education's *Journal of Adult Education*, U.S.A. (in the 1920s and 1930s, mentioned by Hutchinson in Chapter Five) were full of examples, some of them admirable statements for the time. However, some of these observations have been treated as authoritative, particularly when published under resounding titles such as "Adult Education in Atlantis" rather than under a much more accurate title such as "Some Random Observations and Personal Reflections About Certain Aspects of Adult Education Obtained During a Visit of Two Weeks to Atlantis." Such papers and books can be misleading if the reader fails to remember the experiences were not systematically planned and organized and does not scrutinize the pages with care. Moreover, such books have sometimes been read and used in place of more valid and valuable statements by indigenous observers. Along with the "traveler's tales" there have been uncritical comparisons that have suggested interrelationships, revealed insights, or advanced hypotheses.

Taken as a starting place for reflection, or if tested carefully, such observations and others much more elaborate may have some point. Any good utopia, such as Edward Bellamy's *Looking Backward* or Aldous Huxley's *Brave New World*, offers a basis for such a comparison. Bellamy's book had considerable influence on American adult education about a century ago and caused many to examine their own society and its associated educational and political processes in critical ways.

Instruction Method Comparisons. Some people in adult education have been extremely inventive in producing new educational methods. This has come about because they have often been obliged to report statements of improved productivity for their innovation as contrasted with more traditional methods in order to obtain a hearing. Many of us have been compelled to try our hand at this, employing varying degrees of rigor in carrying out the investigation. For example, during World War II Kurt Lewin's colleagues experimented with small group meetings as compared to auditorium meetings in teaching about nutrition and food practices. A summary of the results showed no differences in the amount of information mastered but substantial differences in favor of small groups in outcomes of commitment and changes in practice. During and following World War II there were many investigations of the productivity that resulted from the application of various methods under the auspices of the armed forces and universities.

One example of the many theses that contain a methods comparison is "A Comparative Study of Participants in Lecture Classes and Participants in Study Discussion Groups" by Buttedahl (1958). Many more could be cited.

This is useful research and much of it should now be replicated with somewhat more elaborate design. It is usually a case of a mix or combination of methods, not single methods, for good instruction. For example, take the alternative educational program organized in villages in the mountains of the Dominican Republic and several other countries in Latin America where a combination of radio, lessons by mail, visiting tutor-animateurs, and regional collections of books and journals has achieved results on national examinations equal to those of full-time elementary school students at less than one quarter of the cost of educating a child in school. However, *each* and *all* of the factors are needed, for an examination of the impact of radio alone or of correspondence lessons shows much less impressive gains.

Agricultural Extension Effect Studies. The gross impact of agricultural extension in the United States is well known. A much smaller proportion of the population now grows very much larger amounts of food and fiber than occurred seventy-five years ago. At the beginning of the century, agricultural extension agents began to analyze the results of their instruction. A typical inquiry analyzed the comparative results of employing differing methods (for example, demonstrations compared with pamphlets). Many of these studies were made over several decades and the research methods continued to be improved. Later came equally important studies of innovations and changes in practice carried out by agricultural agents and their colleagues in the universities, such as those of Burton Kreitlow and Coolie Verner. Verner's work on innovation, influence factors, and effect measures was the basis for a series of propositions that appear to be useful for comparative studies.

Proposition One—Every society has a need for continuous learning, but the nature and content of the need varies from one to another so that a specific need existing in one society is not necessarily common to others.

Proposition Two—Different societies develop unique methods to meet their need for continuous learning; consequently, a system of adult education established in one is not necessarily appropriate for another.

Proposition Three—The method developed to meet a specific need for learning in one culture is not necessarily suited to the same need in a different culture.

Proposition Four—A method developed at one place and time in one culture can be applied to the same need at other places at the same time in that culture.

Proposition Five—A method developed to meet a specific need in a culture at one time is not always suited to the same need in the same culture at a different time.

Proposition Six—A method developed to meet a specific need in a culture at one time may meet a different need in the same culture at a different time.

Proposition Seven—A method developed to meet a specific need in a culture at one time may meet a different need in a different culture at a different time.

These propositions have not been exhaustively tested, but they have been used as a guide for some research projects.

Institution Comparisons. Through the years many comparative observations have been made of institutions within a single country or of the same kind of institution operating in different countries. Most such studies are not well designed, and many of the data are hardly comparable. However, here and there are exceptions. Some of the cross-national studies of correspondence education are reasonably systematic and tend to support the view that this method of education does have possibilities for application in most cultures. Yousif (1974) compared two university extension departments.

There have also been useful comparisons of agricultural extensions by James Duncan of the University of Wisconsin. In a recent analysis of the Western system of agricultural extension as applied in Tanzania, De Vries (1978), who has been teaching on the staff of the university, claims a Western-oriented program of agricultural extension in that country exhibits very serious short-

(1973) used formulations and procedures associated with the studies of Allen Tough to appraise self-directed learning in Accra, Ghana. Denys did not find many differences between Accra and Toronto respondents, but his subjects seem to have been people with a "Western orientation," and replication of such a study with other subjects may reveal more profound differences. It is to be hoped that additional travel funds may be found to allow a greater number of able students to use comparative modes for their theses.

While these examples of comparative research and development do not begin to give a complete picture of what has been done, they do suggest the variety of the studies as well as the launching of new inquiries that will serve all of the goals cited.

Applications from CE to CAE

Seen from one perspective CAE is a subfield of CE. Unfortunately, there has not in the past been much interaction between CAE and the generic field. The reasons are several. CAE is a relatively new field, and those attracted to it did not always have a grounding in CE. Most practitioners in adult education have had little experience with comparative studies and knowledge of what has been accomplished. In the main CE was focused on formal education, most often with children and youth within the school. For example, the theme secondary education was chosen for the 1972 meeting of the World Council of Comparative Education Societies. Although obviously important, this was not a priority interest for many in CAE who might have taken part in such an international event. Whether correct or not, the research associated with CE was perceived as operating from outmoded conceptions such as "national character" or as being preoccupied with endless disputes over method or with abstract model building.

However, the reasons for closer association of CAE with CE are more significant than any real or imagined differences. It is still true that CE scholars such as G. F. Bereday, Bryon Holmes, and Edmund King have as much or more to contribute to CAE than those identified with the subfield. CAE has to catch up and has much to learn, and it appears its stance should be more of critical acceptance than ignorant rejection.

comings. Duke in Chapter Two compares adult education in several countries with that in Australasia. This is not conclusive research, but it does open up some very important possibilities.

Fields of Wide Application Comparisons. Many adult educational projects are local or very specific, making it difficult to carry out useful comparisons. But some forms of adult education are found in most countries, thus offering excellent examples for investigation. One such example is management training; another is literacy, as Ampene richly expounds in Chapter Eight. Examples of these forms of adult education are found in at least a hundred countries. Comparative investigation of the character or impact of management studies are still rather rare, and those I have seen (such as comparisons of practices in the United States and India) operate as if there are no cultural differences to the point that their validity is highly questionable. Some of them might be repeated, using a better design and more rigorous controls.

Despite the poverty of the record so far, this is a promising field of inquiry. Comparative studies of literacy have not been resoundingly successful either but are much more extensive and, on the whole, more carefully planned. The largest single effort was the evaluation of the UNESCO-UNDP (United Nations Development Program) sponsored Experimental World Literacy Program that operated over several years in eleven countries, with similar efforts in several additional countries (UNESCO-UNDP, 1975). Reports were prepared by evaluation teams sent to each of the eleven countries, and observations became the data for analysis by an international commission composed of persons from five continents. This commission in turn requested a comparative review by Gillette and Spaulding (1976).

The whole investigation displayed many of the difficulties to be expected. The data from each country had been collected on quite different bases. One brilliantly conceived plan by a group of French social scientists at the Sorbonne to use multivariate analysis failed, or rather was never carried out, because the data were so mixed and so poorly grounded in reality. Moreover, certain political factors had influenced most of the country reports, and the two sponsoring agencies (UNESCO and UNDP) had substantially different views about the goals of the literacy program as well as the goals of the evaluation. Despite all these difficulties and the inevitable losses and compromises, one result has been the identification of many significant factors, which in turn has led to a growing consensus about the political frames and the organizational requirements for literacy programs.

Sustained Approaches. Comparative studies require sustained collection and reporting of phenomena, but much of what has happened has been ad hoc, usually about a single episode. However, the situation is beginning to change. Efforts are being made at the International Bureau of Education, Geneva (UNESCO), and by the statistical division of UNESCO, Paris, to reach agreement upon definitions and the kinds of statistical reporting most needed.

At the UNESCO Institute in Hamburg, there has been a program sustained over at least three years of building concepts about *éducation permanente* and systematically comparing the views, opinions, hypotheses, and experiences from many countries. Some of this work has been reported by Dave (1976) of the UNESCO Institute for Education, Hamburg.

Perhaps the most important sustained effort to date in comparative adult education, starting at least six years ago, has been the product of a cooperative inquiry at the Center for Leisure and Education at Prague under the general direction of Premsyl Maydl. Each Eastern European country has developed a country description or profile and position papers based on the use of a series of prime factors identified as significant. Colin Titmus (1976a) of the University of Glasgow was asked to design a "theoretical model for the comparative study of national adult education systems in Europe." While Titmus disclaims that what he has constructed is a genuine "model," his ordering of the prime factors does constitute a useful framework. His paper was discussed, criticized, and amended at a conference in Prague in 1976, and the program will continue to provide more refined concepts as well as to suggest ways to collect and compare meaningful data. (Chapter Six, which Titmus and Pardoen have written on the function of adult education legislation, is a cross-national study.) On a much smaller scale Jindra Kulich (1971, 1973) of the University of British Columbia has used his mastery of many European languages in a series of monographs on training in Eastern European countries and also a series of annotated bibliographies.

Perhaps the leading example in North Ameri lar and systematic collection of all kinds of data agricultural extension. This collection can serve as other fields of adult education. Cyril O. Houle (19 completed a process of systematic comparative s forms of continuing professional education that model for this kind of study.

The journal of the International Council tion (*Convergence*) has consistently collected and ences from many countries around a series of t education of women, literacy, youth, and integr ment. These issues are not rigorously compara tion over ten years from all regions of the worl important base record.

Cross-National Studies. Cross-national st data from different countries, though the pro parative; they can prepare the way for more velop interest, and provide a vehicle for the tive educators. Interest in cross-national stud topics as youth leadership, training and une of women, and education of tribal peoples ing. The most consistent application of cr adult education has been in Eastern Europ Yugoslavia, with colleagues in Czechoslo and Canada, has completed one importa attitudes toward education, and more are

An excellent example of a rigoro that by Knoll on professionalization of a and the GDR (Chapter Four).

Theses. Examples of comparative tations are still rather rare, although th ing possibilities. One reason for the ra work is usually expensive in time an Amaratunga (1977) is an excellent Amaratunga studied changes and a lages, one in Ghana and one in Sri *modernization* adopted from the work design and the results obtained exe

Special Studies of Adult Education. CE has been preoccupied largely with the formal school system. However, there are cases of research that go beyond this limitation. Some persons studying educational systems have included a place for nonformal educational activities for all ages, including adult education. Such a practice is becoming more common, particularly in developing countries. Again, some comparative studies of policy issues have included concerns of mature and part-time students. Here and there the studies of the economics of education have focused on adult education. Two examples are Borus (1977) and Godfrey (1977).

One scholar whose work has frequently included adults is Paulston (1972). His studies in Cuba and of the Danish folk high schools as well as his bibliographical material on nonformal education should be better known and used by adult educationists.

Studies Deserving Replication. Some more traditional comparative studies should be replicated with particular reference to adults, both because of the methods employed and because of the results. In their best-known book Noah and Eckstein (1969) do not promise more than an attempt to move toward a science of the field, but they do achieve a systematic approach, using primarily quantitative data and methods that set high standards. Some critics argue that a limit has been reached in the application of quantitative modes. However, this does seem to be an approach worthy of further application and refinement, not to be ignored or abandoned. The combination of quantitative modes where possible along with many forms of qualitative analysis seems eminently desirable, at least in the formative years of CAE, when many approaches should be tried and evaluated. Another example of studies that might be replicated are those under the direction of King (1974) carried out simultaneously in five European countries. King's project goes considerably further than most cross-national studies and might become a useful prototype for investigations in many problems of adult education in various countries.

Next Five Years

The first international meeting on CAE was in 1965; the second was sponsored by UNESCO and the Danish Ministry of

Education in Nordberg, Denmark (Syracuse University, 1972). This second meeting had been preceded by an informal planning meeting at Pugwash, Nova Scotia, in 1970. A third meeting on a world scale, again under UNESCO and Danish sponsorship, was held in Kenya in 1975. At the Pugwash and Nordberg seminars considerable progress could be perceived in the definition of objectives, identification of methods and procedures, and plans for cooperative action in developing CAE as a field of study. While the 1975 meeting in Kenya was interesting and dealt with questions about national organization and infrastructure for adult education, no real progress was made in improving the foundation of CAE, and the situation respecting international cooperation in the development of a field of study was left much as it was in 1972.

Meanwhile several universities in the United States and at least three other countries have initiated new courses. One immediate target is to encourage those responsible for graduate programs to engage in some research. Another general objective is to link up those responsible for CAE with the corpus of research in CE. This might be done through much wider distribution of journals and research abstracts as well as by adult educationists beginning to take the part in national organizations of international and comparative education and through the World Council of Comparative Education Societies.

Many measures of international cooperation are needed in CAE, as in CE. Association is also possible with such agencies as UNESCO (where there is a vital interest in comparative studies), the International Labor Organization, the Organization for Economic Cooperation and Development, and certain international nongovernmental organizations, such as the International Council for Adult Education and the International Congress of University Adult Education. As Hutchinson makes clear in Chapter Five, such communication is one of the purposes of these organizations.

Specific projects are now needed, all of which can move forward if there is cooperation among institutions, countries, and international agencies. Failing such cooperation, progress will be delayed. For example, systematic monitoring of research in CE that may have application to CAE should be done at least in English, French, German, Spanish, Russian, and Japanese. This cooperative work could begin with some agreement about a "division of labor." There might be systematic sharing of all CAE research, perhaps through the International Bureau of Education (IBE) and the International Council for Adult Education. A number of cross-national studies that build on the experience and support the work of colleagues in Eastern Europe should be done. I have noted earlier the usefulness of the example of Edmund King and his associates. Efforts to develop basic statements of national systems, utilizing as a beginning the typologies developed in the Center for Education and Leisure, should be supported. The cooperation of social scientists interested in modes of participatory research should be obtained and they should be invited to engage in the problems of CAE. Educational projects of major importance, such as literacy, workers' education, and management education, should be influenced to mount or maintain significant research and evaluation components and to collect data so systematic comparison will be possible. An agreement between interested universities about "division of labor" in testing promising modes of inquiry and sharing and diffusing the results should be obtained. UNESCO and IBE efforts to improve statistical reporting of adult education—the building of glossaries and the agreements on translation of terms—should be supported.

If such a cooperative plan is to operate, there will need to be national, regional, and at least one international seminar, not for discussion only but also to reach agreement and commitment on a program of cooperative action. A successor conference planned to build on and go far beyond the Nordberg conference is required and should not be long delayed.

Conclusion

As I prepared this chapter while traveling through Europe, I read a newspaper that reported comparative data on vocational training, hours of work, wages, and the economic value of technical training for eight European countries. The base factor, to make all the complex information meaningful, was a pint or liter of beer. Answers were provided to such questions as how many minutes an Englishman must work to obtain his brew compared to citizens of other European countries and what the contribution of training is to his earning power. The report is an example of simple research, involving comparative vocational education, and people who govern policy about educational expenditure, people who take courses, and people who plan and teach courses can all understand what is involved to the point where it may help them all make decisions and take action as required. Not all of our educational or social problems can be handled in such simple fashion. Some adult education questions require very different modes of comparing and reporting, but the attempt to be so understandable would test our best efforts.

Comparative adult education has reached a significant stage. Some preliminary work has been completed, an increasing number of universities are now offering graduate courses, some modes of inquiry appropriate to adult education have been identified, and some concepts have been formulated. A considerable part of the CE experience can be applied. International cooperation can yield valuable insights and information.

For North America some of the next steps are obvious. Assistance should be given to any university that is beginning to offer courses so the wheel is not endlessly invented, but at the same time each should be encouraged to develop its own style and to engage in research as well as teaching. We should also play an appropriate part in associating ourselves in international efforts of cooperation. A continental meeting should be held as soon as possible to identify problems of teaching and research for which cooperative action is imperative.

Respecting instruction, CAE should continue to explore the differential values of different modes. Inquiries should also be undertaken that will establish which attributes or practices are culture-infused or culture-bound and which may be universal and to provide answers to an array of questions that will assist problem solving and decision making. However, the problems and decisions ought not just to be relatively simple ones, such as what proportion of the educational budget should go to elementary schools, secondary education, higher education, and adult education. Research, not just traditions of practice or educational business-as-usual attitudes, should guide such practical decisions. But

Europe, as documented by Saviċeviċ. But there are movements toward similarity, or at least toward a lessening of differences. Hutchinson and Titmus and Pardoen detail the general tendency of governments to involve themselves in adult education. Duke, Saviċeviċ, Ampene, and Ryan remark on the general tendency to link labor and education. Saviċeviċ, from Yugoslavia, and Knoll, from the Federal Republic of Germany, make comments that are strikingly similar and highly important.

One of these "convergent phenomena" is the increasing intervention of governments to use adult education as a means to achieve desired goals. Ryan observes that accompanying this change in goals is a more rigorous specification in designing, developing, implementing, and evaluating literacy activities, and he analyzes the process that is applicable to all programs in all countries. Ely describes the same process as it involves use of educational technology. I call attention to the need for the development of methods of evaluation not merely to assess the results of a program but at all steps to guide the planning and execution of programs to achieve the desired objectives. Saviċeviċ generalizes that during the last twenty years in most of the nine countries he describes attempts have been made to put adult education on a scientific basis. One aspect of that attempt is the movement to professionalization, which he analyzes, particularly in Poland, Hungary, Czechoslovakia, Yugoslavia, and the German Democratic Republic and which Knoll compares in the German Democratic Republic and the Federal Republic of Germany.

Titmus and Pardoen have emphasized the dilemma facing adult educators regarding government support for programs, that is, how can the educator's independence be maintained if government support brings with it the threat of external control. Accordingly adult educators have worked to influence adult education legislation so that support is forthcoming without intervention in program operations. In fact, government intervention in many countries is accompanied by efforts to encourage nongovernmental and voluntary participation, as Duke, Saviċeviċ, Hutchinson, Titmus and Pardoen, Ampene, and Ryan show.

However, legislative safeguards in the Western countries and governmental encouragement of voluntary participation in all

comparative education can also help with a different order of questions. For example, have the Chinese attained high standards of personal honesty? If so, why and how? Why and how do people in some countries work more effectively and willingly than in others? How do countries prepare people for participation? Why and how, in such a fascinating world, do many adults become bored, apathetic, isolated, alienated, prey to restlessness, alcoholism, or violence? Many other such questions might be considered, questions we rarely ask ourselves that are yet at the heart of the educational enterprise.

At the international conference on adult education for development held in Dar es Salaam in 1976, President Julius Nyerere said, "Development has a purpose; that purpose is the liberation of Man. But Man can only liberate himself or develop himself. He cannot be liberated or developed by another. For Man makes himself. It is his ability to act deliberately, for a self-determined purpose, which distinguishes him from the other animals. The expansion of his own consciousness, and therefore of his power over himself, his environment, and his society, must therefore ultimately be what we mean by development. So development is for Man, by Man, and of Man. The same is true of education. Its purpose is the liberation of Man from the restraints and limitations of ignorance and dependency. Education has to increase men's physical and mental freedom—to increase their control over themselves, their own lives, and the environment in which they live. The ideas imparted by education, or released in the mind through education, should therefore be liberating ideas; the skills acquired by education should be liberating skills" (Nyerere, 1978). It may be for development so conceived that instruction and research in comparative education has the most to offer.

Postscript

Alexander N. Charters

These concluding comments call attention to ways the preceding chapters complement each other, in both senses of that word—to complete and to produce an effect in concert different from that produced separately.

The reports are of several kinds. All of Charters and a part of Kidd give an overview of the field of comparative international adult education. Duke and Savićević make large comparisons of adult education in several countries, the former in five, the latter in nine. Hutchinson and Titmus and Pardoen, and Ely deal with elements of adult education as an area of activity—organizations and associations, legislation, and educational technology, respectively. Kidd and Knoll concern themselves with aspects of adult education as a discipline—the former, research in comparative international

adult education the latter, professionalization of a the two Germanies. Ampene and Ryan examine a ways of reaching them—Ampene, the "unreache to reach them and Ryan, the design and developr for literacy education. Both focus on activities in s in ways that are relevant to all countries.

These authors, who are from several count sider various aspects of adult education in sever several points of view, demonstrate that the fie adult education has become international in tha adults can communicate with each other as coll common body of ideas, concerns, and purpose common vocabulary. In their discussion of the f tion concerning adult education, Titmus and P apparently unimportant verbal distinctions a grounded on hard differences of policy and finar

Some of the general advantages that ca educators from comparative international adult ticularly apparent in three chapters. Westerners sympathetic descriptions of adult education in tries of Europe can share his informed insigh equally removed from the usual attitudes of ac hand and opposition on the other. While startin tion that most of the adults who are unreached grams are in the Third World countries, Ampe reached" and considers ways of reaching them applicable to all countries. After describing adu Asian countries, where he observed it, and in / lives, Duke comments explicitly on some of the tive studies.

Readers of the preceding chapters will be differences and similarities described. Duke rer centralized coordination, planning, and dir compared to the centralization he found in Bangladesh, and prerevolutionary Iran. The p legislation regarding adult education in many as documented by Titmus and Pardoen, is in prehensive nature of such legislation in the s

countries are not enough: These freedoms must be exercised by individuals and organizations. The key to their exercise is leadership from a relatively few individuals. From long experience Hutchinson has pointed out the challenge to adult educators in nongovernmental organizations. He called for mutually supportive actions that would retain the independent status of the nongovernmental providers of adult education. The task of the leaders is to work for these mutually supportive arrangements. Several of the authors of the chapters in this book are eminent among those who provide such leadership. One of them, Kidd, outlines next steps that should be taken—both specific types of studies and international meetings—to advance the field of comparative international adult education.

The role of individual and voluntary association in protecting and advancing the freedom of action of the educator and the range of effective choice of the individual learner goes far beyond supplementing programs governments support and filling the gaps these leave. It is at times even to oppose the goals of these programs and at all times to go beyond them.

At times and in some places, the task of liberation is to escape from the controls of government—controls that can be made all the more subtly powerful by "education." At all times and in all places, it is to rise above the limited goals individuals and governments set. As important as are the goals of individual self-fulfillment and national development, there are goals upon whose achievement the achievement of all other goals depends. One is to avoid the holocaust of nuclear war and to build the conditions of a positive peace. Another is to reverse the pollution of the planet and establish a harmonious relationship between mankind and nature.

Insofar as continuing education helps adults enlarge their private and public concerns and become more effective in their roles as participating citizens, it is making a contribution to the building of a positive peace and a healthy environment on earth. An evolution in the concepts of adult education can be seen in the very themes of the three international conferences on adult education sponsored by UNESCO. The theme of the first, in Elsinore in 1949, was simply "Adult Education." The theme of the second, in Montreal in 1960, was vaguely "Adult Education in a Changing

World." But the theme of the third, Tokyo, 1972, was specifically "Adult Education in the Context of Lifelong Learning." Lowe (1975, p. 19) has written that between the second and third UNESCO conferences adult education moved from being a "remedial backstop dealing with the omissions of the formal education system" to a position where both its content and function have widened. He gave as the first reason for its increased importance that policy makers, professional administrators, and adult educators have defined their field of concern more widely.

The international UNESCO conferences have stimulated the development of the field of comparative adult education. These in turn have improved the quality of the conferences.

I hope this first published volume of original papers on comparative international adult education will assist educators of adults in many countries to continue learning from each other and thus enhance the forward movement of adult education worldwide.

References

Adams, D., and Farrell, J. P. (Eds.). *Education and Social Development.* Syracuse, N.Y.: Syracuse University Center for Development Education, 1966.

"Adult Education in Russia." *World Association for Adult Education Bulletin*, May 1922, *12*.

Adult Education Legislation in Ten Countries of Europe—Supplement, 1976. Amersfoort, The Netherlands: European Bureau of Adult Education, 1976.

Adult Education—Scientific Research and Cultural Action. Bucharest: Committee for Culture and Arts, 1968. (In Rumanian.)

Amaratunga, C. M. "The Rural Adult Learner: A Crosscultural Analysis of Educational Delivery Systems in Ghana and Sri Lanka." Unpublished doctoral dissertation, Ontario Institute for Studies in Education, 1977.

Ananev, B. G., and Stepanova, E. I. *The Development of the Psycho-Physiological Functions of Adults.* Moscow: "Pedagogy," 1972. (In Russian.)

Answiler, O. "Vergleichende Erziehungswissenschaft." In *Das neue Lexikon der Pädagogik.* Vol. 4. Freiburg: Herder Verlag, 1971.

Armsey, J. W., and Dahl, N. C. *An Inquiry into the Uses of Instructional Technology.* New York: Ford Foundation, 1973.

245

Asian-South Pacific Bureau of Adult Education (ASPBAE), June 1977, 7.

Australian Journal of Adult Education, 1976, *16*, 1–3.

Axmacher, D. *Erwachsenenbildung im Kapitalismus*. Frankfurt: Fischer-Verlag, 1974.

Barbour, B. R. "Science, Salience, and Comparative Education: Some Reflections on Social Scientific Inquiry." In *Relevant Methods in Comparative Education*. Hamburg: UNESCO Institute for Education, 1973.

Bates, A. W., and Gallagher, M. *A Summary of the 1974 Broadcast Evaluation Programme.*

Bates, A. W., and Moss, G. D. "Multi Media Methods at the Open University." Milton Keynes, England: Institute of Educational Technology, Open University, 1975.

Beardsley, J. R. "The Free University of Iran." In *Open Learning*. Paris: UNESCO Press, 1975.

Beiträge zur Erwachsenenqualifizierung, Ein Leitfaden für nebenberufliche Lehrkrafte zur effektiven Gestaltung und Organisation des Unterrichts on Volkschochschulen und anderen Bildungseinrichtungen. Berlin: Verlag Volk und Wissen, 1971.

Bennett, C., and others (Eds.). *An Anthology of Comparative Education*. Syracuse, N.Y.: Syracuse University Publication in Continuing Education, 1975.

Bereday, G. F. "Reflections on Comparative Methodology in Education 1964–1966." *Comparative Education*, June 3, 1967, *3* (3), 169.

Bildung und Wissenschaft. Bulletin of Inter Nationes e.V. Bonn, periodically published, different issues.

Bildungsgesamtplan. (Abridged ed.) Stuttgart: Klett-Verlag, 1973.

Bischoff, D., and others. *Erwachsenenpädagogisches Projektstudium*. Hannover: Arbeitskreis universitäre Erwachsenenbildung, 1975.

Borus, M. "A Cost Effectiveness Comparison of Vocational Training for Youth in Developing Countries." *Comparative Education Review*, February 1977.

Bowers, J. *The Use and Production of Media in Non-Formal Adult Education*. Essex, Conn.: International Council for Educational Development, July 1972.

Brezinka, W. *Von der Pädagogik zur Erziehungswissenschaft*. Weinheim: Beltz-Verlag, 1972.

Bulatović, R. "The Kolorac People's University as a Form of University Extension." *Yearbook of the Faculty of Liberal Arts.* Vol. 2. Belgrade: Scientific work, 1978. (In Serbo-Croatian.)

Bullock, A. *A Language for Life.* Report of a Committee of Enquiry Appointed by the Secretary of State for Education. London: HMSO, 1975.

Bund-Länder Kommission für Bildungsplanung, Bildungsgesamtplan. Vol. 1. Stuttgart: Klett-Verlag, 1973.

Burmeister, J., and others. *Theorie und Praxis im Studiengang Erwachsenenbildung.* Hannover: Arbeitskreis universitäre Erwachsenenbildung, 1976.

Buttedahl, K. B. "A Comparative Study of Participants in Lecture Classes and Participants in Study Discussion Groups." Vancouver: University of British Columbia, 1958.

Buttler, G. *Das Studium der Erwachsenenpädagogik.* Hannover: Arbeitskreis universitäre Erwachsenenbildung, 1975.

Buttler, G. *Praktika im Diplom-studium der Erziehungswissenschaft mit der Studienrichtung Erwachsenenbildung.* Hannover: Arbeitskreis universitäre Erwachsenenbildung, 1976.

Buttler, G., and Buttler, I. *Die Ausbildung zum Diplompädagogen.* Hannover: Arbeitskreis universitäre Erwachsenenbildung, 1974.

Buttler, G., and others. *Materialien zur Studien- und Berufssituation in der Erwachsenenbildung.* Hannover: Arbeitskreis universitäre Erwachsenenbildung, 1974, 1975.

Buttler, I. *Arbeitsplätze in der Erwachsenenbildung.* Hannover: Arbeitskreis universitäre Erwachsenenbildung, 1976.

Campeau, P. L. *Selective Review of the Results of Research on the Use of Audiovisual Media to Teach Adults.* Strasborg: Council of Europe, 1971.

Chakarov, N. *The Development of People's Education in Bulgaria.* Sophia: BCP Publishing House, 1954. (In Bulgarian.)

Chakarov, N., and Atanasov, Z. *History of Education and Pedagogic Thought in Bulgaria.* Sovia: Science and Experience, 1962.

Characteristics of the Hungarian System of Education. Dar es Salaam: International Conference on Adult Education and Development, 1976.

Colle, R. *SCSC: An Experimental System for Communicating with Hard-*

to-Reach People. Ithaca, N.Y.: Department of Communication Arts, Cornell University, n.d.

Convergence, journal of the International Council for Adult Education. P.O. Box 250, Station F, Toronto, Canada M4Y2L5.

Coombs, P. H., Prosser, R. C., and Ahmed, M. *New Paths to Learning*. Essex, Conn.: International Council for Educational Development, October 1973.

Csoma, G., Fekete, J., and Hercegi, K. *Adult Education in Hungary*. Leiden: Leidsche Onderwijsinstellingen, 1967.

Curriculum Development for Literacy Programmes: Recent Case Studies. Tehran: International Institute for Adult Literacy Methods, forthcoming.

Darinski, A. V. "Lenin and General Adult Education." *Evening Secondary School*, 1970, *2*, 7–14. (In Russian.)

Darinski, A. V. "Present Day Problems of Evening School in USSR." *Society and Leisure*, 1972, *1*.

Dave, R. H. *Lifelong Education and School Curriculum*. Hamburg: UNESCO, 1976.

"Declaration of the Conference of Ministers for Culture and Education" (*Kultusminister-konferenz*), 20.3.1969. *Zeitschrift für pädagogik*, 1969, *2*, 209.

"Decree of the People's Chamber of the GDR Concerning the Basic Principles of Training and Further Education of the Working Population in the Development of the Socialist System of the GDR." 1970, *16* (9), Berlin.

Denys, L. O. J. "The Major Learning Efforts of Two Groups of Accra Adults." Unpublished doctoral dissertation, Ontario Institute for Studies in Education, 1973.

Deutscher Bildungsrat, Empfehlung der Bildungskommission, Strukturplan für das Bildungswesen. 1970, *13* (2), Bonn.

DeVries, J. "Agricultural Extension and Development." In B. L. Hall and J. R. Kidd (Eds.), *Adult Learning: A Design for Action*. Oxford, England: Pergamon, 1978.

Directory of Adult Education Organizations in Europe. (2nd ed.) Amersfoort, The Netherlands: European Bureau of Adult Education, 1974.

Directory of Documentation and Information Services in Adult Education. Paris: UNESCO, Adult Education Section, 1977.

Dräger, H. *Die Gesellschaft für Verbreitung von Volksbildung.* Stuttgart: Klett-Verlag, 1975.

Edding, F. "Educational Leave and Sources of Finding." In S. J. Mushkin (Ed.), *Recurrent Education.* Washington, D.C.: Department of Health, Education and Welfare, 1973.

Edling, J. V., and Paulson, C. A. "Understanding Instructional Media." In *The Contribution of Behavioral Science to Instructional Technology: The Cognitive Domain.* Washington, D.C.: Gryphm House, 1972.

Education in People's Poland. Warsaw: Ksiaska i wiedza, 1969. (In Russian.)

Eide, K. "Recurrent Education General Policy Options and Objectives." In S. J. Mushkin (Ed.), *Recurrent Education.* Washington, D.C.: Department of Health, Education and Welfare, 1973.

European Bureau of Adult Education. *Adult Education Legislation in Ten European Countries: Report Commissioned by the Council of Europe.* Amersfoort, The Netherlands: European Bureau of Adult Education, 1974.

Faure, E. (Ed.). *Learning to Be.* Paris: UNESCO, 1972.

Feidel-Mertz, H. *Erwachsenenbildung seit 1945.* Cologne: Kiepenheuer und Witsch, 1975.

Fernig, L. "The Collection of Educational Data." *International Review of Education,* 1963, *9,* 213–225.

Filipović, D. *Lifelong Education.* Leskovac: Our Word, 1971. (In Serbo-Croatian.)

Filipović, M. *Higher Education in Yugoslavia.* Belgrade: Yugoslav Institute for Educational Research, 1971.

Final Report—Third International Conference on Adult Education. Convened by UNESCO, Tokyo, July 25–August 7, 1972.

Fischer, H.-J. "Pädagogische Auslandsarbeit der DDR in Entwicklungsländern." In *Pädagogik und Schule in Ost und West.* Vol. 4. Paderborn: Schöningh-Verlag, 1975.

Fucasz, G., and others. *An Outline of the Structure of Adult Education in Hungary.* Prague: European Center for Leisure and Education, 1975.

Gage, G. G. "The Nordic Example." *Saturday Review,* September 20, 1975, 2.

Genkin, D. M. *Some Problems Concerning Practical Training of*

Cultural-Educational Workers in Cultural-Educational Institutes. Debrecen: Debrecen University Press, 1971. (In Russian.)

Gerlach, V. S., and Ely, D. P. *Teaching and Media: A Systematic Approach.* Englewood Cliffs, N.J.: Prentice-Hall, 1971.

Gernert, W. *Das Recht der Erwachsenenbildung.* Munich: 1975.

Ghana Government. *Five Year Development Plan.* Part I. Accra: Ghana Publishing Corp., 1977.

Ghana Ministry of Education. *The New Structure and Content of Education.* Accra: Government Printer, 1974.

Gillette, A., and Spaulding, S. *The Experimental World Literacy Programme,* Paris: UNESCO, 1976.

Godfrey, M. "Education, Productivity and Income, a Kenyan Case Study." *Comparative Education Review,* February 1977.

Good, C. V. *Dictionary of Education.* (3rd ed.) New York: McGraw-Hill, 1973.

Grandstaff, M. *Non-Formal Education and an Expanded Conception of Development.* East Lansing, Mich.: Program of Studies in Non-Formal Education, 1973.

Havighurst, R. *Comparative Perspectives in Education.* Boston: Little, Brown, 1968.

Hawkridge, D. G., and Coryer, J. C. C. *A Bibliography of Published and Unpublished Work by Members of the Institute.* Milton Keynes, England: Institute of Educational Technology, Open University, 1975.

Henry, M. "Methodology in Comparative Education." *Comparative Education Review,* June 1973.

Higher Education in Hungary. Budapest: Tankonyvkiado, 1973.

History of Rumania. Moscow: Science, 1971. (In Russian.)

Holmes, B. *Problems in Education: A Comparative Approach.* London: Routledge, 1965.

Houghton, V., and Richardson, K. (Eds.). *A Plea for Life-Long Learning.* London: World Lock Educational in conjunction with U.K. Association for Recurrent Education, 1974.

Houle, C. O. *Continuing Learning in the Professions.* San Francisco: Jossey-Bass, 1980.

Hutchinson, E. M. "Editorial." *Convergence,* 1970, *3* (2), 52.

Hutchinson, E. M. "Editorial." *Convergence,* 1973, *6* (3), 2.

Institute for Adult Education. *Contemporary Problems of Adult Education in Czechoslovakia Socialist Republic.* Prague: Grafia Jihlava, 1966.

"Integration of Higher Education with Production and Research in Rumania." *Higher Education in Europe*, 1976, *1*, (2).

International Handbook of Adult Education. London: World Association of Adult Education, 1929.

International Institute for Adult Literacy Methods. *Literacy Work* (Teheran), April 1975, No. 4.

Jinga, J. *Mass Culture.* Bucharest: Scientific Encyclopedia, 1975. (In Rumanian.)

Kandel, I. L. "A New Addition to Comparative Methodology." *Comparative Education Review*, 1961.

Kemner, U., and Kurze, W. "Tätigkeitsprofil der in der Weiterbildung nebenamtlich Tätigen." In *International Yearbook of Adult Education.* Cologne: Böhlau-Verlag, 1979.

Kepplinger, H. M., and Vohl, J. "Professionalisierung des Journalismus." *Rundfunk und Fernesehen*, 1976, *4*, 309.

Khokhlov, R. V. *Higher Education in the USSR at the Approach of the XXI Century.* Moscow: Moscow University Publishing House, 1975.

Kidd, J. R. *How Adults Learn.* New York: Association Press, 1974.

King, E. "Comparative Studies and Policy Decisions." *Comparative Education*, 1967, *4*.

King, E. P. *Other Schools and Ours.* London: Holt, Rinehart and Winston, 1973.

King, E. P. *Compulsory Education: A New Analysis in Western Europe.* London: Sage Publications, 1974.

Klement, T. *Some Actual Problems in Hungarian Higher Education in the 70's.* Budapest: Technical University Press, 1975.

Knoll, J. H. "Erziehungswissenschaft und Erwachsenenbildung, Gedanken zur Methodologie des Vergleichs in der BRD." In *International Yearbook of Adult Education 1973.* Düsseldorf: Bertelsmann-Universitätsverlag, 1973.

Knoll, J. H. (Ed.). *Internationale Erwachsenenbildung im Uberlick.* Düsseldorf: Bertelsmann Universitätsverlag, 1974.

Knoll, J. H. "Internationale Perspektive in der deutschen Erwachsenenbildung, Organisatorische Kontakte und Erwachsenen-pädagogische Auslandskunde." *Bildung und Erziehung*, 1976, *1*. 22.

Knoll, J. H. *Bildung und Wissenschaft un der Bundesrepublic Deutchland*. Munich: 1977.

Knoll, J. H., and Siebert, H. *Erwachsenenbildung-Erwachsenenqualifizierung*. Heidelberg: Verlag Quelle und Meyer, 1968.

Knoll, J. H., and others. *Erwachsenenbildung am Wendepunkt*. Heidelberg: Verlag Quelle und Meyer, 1967.

Knowles, M. (Ed.). *Handbook of Adult Education*. Chicago: Adult Education Association of the USA, 1960.

Kolići, H. "The System of Adult Education in Albania Today." Unpublished manuscript, 1976. (In Serbo-Croatian.)

Kranjc, A. "The Identification of Educational Values as a Basic Factor in Adult Education." Toronto: Ontario Institute for Studies in Education, 1971.

Kuhlenkamp, D. *Plan zur Fortbildung nebenberuflicher Kursleiter in der Bremischen Weiterbildung*. Hannover: Arbeitskreis universitäre Erwachsenenbildung, S 15, 1976.

Kulich, J. *The Role and Training of Adult Educators in Czechoslovakia*. Vancouver: University of British Columbia, 1967.

Kulich, J. *The Role and Training of Adult Educators in Poland*. Occasional Papers in Continuing Education, No. 6. Vancouver: Center for Continuing Education, University of British Columbia, 1971.

Kulich, J. (Comp.). *World Survey of Research in Comparative Adult Education—A Directory of Institutions and Personnel, 1972*. Vancouver: Center for Continuing Education, University of British Columbia, 1972.

Kulich, J. *Training of Adult Educators and Adult Education Research in Hungary*. Occasional Papers in Continuing Education, No. 7. Vancouver: Center for Continuing Education, University of British Columbia, 1973.

Kulich, J. (Ed.). *Training of Adult Educators in East Europe*. Vancouver: University of British Columbia, 1977.

Kuljutkin, J. N., and Suhobskaja, G. S. *Research on the Educational Activities of Evening School Students*. Moscow: Pedagogy, 1977. (In Russian.)

Kuzmina, M. N. (Ed.). *Schools in European Socialist Countries*. Moscow: Pedagogy, 1976. (In Russian.)

Lenzko, M. "Weiterbildung in der DDR." In *Erwachsenenbildung*. Münster: 1975.

Lifelong Education: The Curriculum and Basic Learning Needs. Final report of Regional Seminar Chaiapum, Thailand. Bangkok: UNESCO Regional Office for Education in Asia, 1976.

Liveright, A. A., and Haygood, N. (Eds.). *The Exeter Papers*. Report of the First International Conference on the Comparative Study of Adult Education. Syracuse, N.Y.: Publications in Continuing Education, 1968.

Lowe, J. *The Education of Adults: A Worldwide Perspective*. Paris: UNESCO, 1975.

Lyche, I. *Adult Education in Norway*. Oslo: Universitetsforlaget, 1964.

MacKenzie, N., Postgate, R., and Scupham, J. *Open Learning*. Paris: UNESCO Press, 1975.

Mader, W. "Erwachsenenbildung." In *Handlexikon zur Erziehungswissenschaft*. Munich: Kösel-Verlag, 1976.

Materialien zur Studien- und Berufssituation in der Erwachsenenbildung, Gesamterhebung 1975. Hannover: Arbeitskreis universitäre Erwachsenenbildung, 1975.

Ministry of Church and Education. *Adult Education in Norway in the 1960s: A Brief Survey*. Oslo: Norwegian National Commission for UNESCO, 1972.

Ministry of Reconstruction. *Adult Education Committee, Final Report*. London: Ministry of Reconstruction, 1919.

Minovski, J. "Adult Education in Bulgaria." Unpublished manuscript, 1974. (In Serbo-Croatian.)

National Organization for Cooperation in Adult Education—Report of a Conference at Wansfell College, Theydon Bois, Essex, England. September 9–13, 1975. Toronto: International Council for Adult Education, 1975.

Niehuls, E. *Analyse der Erwachsenenbildung in der BRD und DDR*. Heidelberg: Verlag Quelle und Meyer, 1973.

Noah, H. J., and Eckstein, M. A. *Towards a Science of Comparative Education*. New York: Macmillan, 1969.

Nonformal Education in Bangladesh: A Strategy for Development. Dacca: Committee on Nonformal Education, 1975.

"The Norwegian Adult Education Act." Oslo: Governmental Printing Office, 1977.

Notes and Studies. No. 2. Amersfoort, The Netherlands: European Bureau of Adult Education, 1976.

Nyerere, J. "Development Is for Man, by Man, and of Man." In B. L. Hall and J. R. Kidd (Eds.), *Adult Learning: A Design for Action.* Oxford, England: Pergamon, 1978.

Ogrizović, M. *Educational and Cultural Activity with Adults in Croatia in the People's Liberation Struggle.* Zagreb: Union of People's Universities of Croatia, 1960. (In Serbo-Croatian.)

Ogrizović, M. *The Problems of Andragogy.* Zagreb: Union of People's Universities of Croatia, 1963. (In Serbo-Croatian.)

Pachocinski, R., and Polturzycki, J. *Adult Education in People's Poland.* Prague: European Center for Leisure and Education, 1975.

Paulston, R. G. *Non Formal Education: An Annotated International Bibliography.* New York: Praeger, 1972.

Pedagogic Encyclopedia. Vol. 1. Moscow: Soviet Encyclopedia, 1964. (In Russian.)

Pickles, D. *The Fifth French Republic.* Appendix: "The French Constitution of October 4th, 1958, Title V, Article 34." (2nd ed.) London: Methuen, 1962.

Popesku, T. *Adult Education.* Bucharest: Poligrafica "Banat," 1974. (In Rumanian.)

Report on the Case Studies of the Non-Formal Education Program. Jakarta: Directorate of Community Education, Department of Education and Culture, 1976.

Russell, L. *Adult Education: A Plan for Development.* Report of a Committee of Enquiry. London: HMSO, 1974.

Sadler, M. "How Far Can We Learn Anything of Practical Value from the Study of Foreign Systems of Education?" In N. Hans (Ed.), *Comparative Education.* London: Routledge & Kegan Paul, 1949.

Samolovčev, B. *Adult Education in the Past and Now.* Zagreb: Knowledge, 1963. (In Serbo-Croatian.)

Savićević, D. "Ideas about Adult Education in Thoughts and Works of Serbian Socialdemocrats." *Adult Education,* 1962, 7–8 (In Serbo-Croatian.)

Savićević, D. *Instruction at Evening Political Schools.* Novi Sad: Higher Political School, 1968. (In Serbo-Croatian.)

Savićević, D. *The System of Adult Education in Yugoslavia.* Syracuse, N.Y.: Syracuse University Press, 1969.

Savićević, D. *Recurrent Education and Transformation of the System of Education in Yugoslavia.* Paris: OECD-CERI, 1971.

Savićević, D. *Recurrent Education and Associated Labour.* Belgrade: Belgrade Graphical Publishing Institute, 1975. (In Serbo-Croatian.)

Scheffknecht, J. *La formation des formateurs en Europe.* Paris: Éducation Permanente, 1971.

Schmelzer, G., and Pagoda, G. *The System of Adult Education in GDR.* Prague: European Center for Leisure and Education, 1975. (In Russian.)

Schramm, W. "Media for Non-Formal Education." In *Big Media, Little Media.* Stanford, Calif.: Institute for Communication Research, March 1973.

Schulenberg, and others. *Zur Professionalisierung der Weiterbildung.* Braunschweig: Westermann Verlag, 1972.

Schultz, E. *Deutschunterrichts in der Erwachsenenbildung.* Grafenau: Lexika-Verlag, 1976.

Schultze, W. "Vergleichende Erziehungswissenschaft." In W. Horney (Ed.), *Pädagogisches Lexikon.* Gütersloh: Bertelsmann Verlag, 1970.

Schweiz (Ed.). "Vereiningung für Erwachsenenbildung." *Jahresbericht,* 1975, p. 11.

Scupham, J. "The Open University of the United Kingdom." In N. MacKenzie, R. Postgate, and J. Scupham (Eds.), *Open Learning.* Paris: UNESCO Press, 1975.

Siebert, H. *Bildungs-Praxis in Deutschland, BRD und DDR im Vergleich.* Düsseldorf: Bertelelsmann-Universitätsverlag, 1970a.

Siebert, H. *Erwachsenenbildung in der Erziehungsgesellschaft der DDR.* Düsseldorf: Bertelelsmann-Universitätsverlag, 1970b.

Siebert, H. *Stellenangebote in der Erwachsenenbildung.* Hannover: Arbeitskreis universitäre Erwachsenenbildung, 1974, S 4.

Siebert, H. *Kontaktstudium for hauptberufliche Erwachsenenbildner.* Hannover: Arbeitskreis universitäre Erwachsenenbildung, 1975.

Siebert, H., and Lapp, P. J. "Volkshochschulen in beider deutschen Staaten." Cologne: Deutchlandfunt, 1977. (Reproduced as MS.)

Skalka, J., and Livecka, E. *The System of Adult Education in the CSSR.* Prague: European Center for Leisure and Education, 1975.

Smith, R., Aker, G., and Kidd, J. R. (Eds.). *Handbook of Adult Education.* New York: Adult Education Association of the USA, 1970.

Stamas, S. "Instructional Models." Division of Instructional Development *Occasional Papers.* Washington, D.C.: Association for Educational Communications and Technology, 1973.

Starke, M. "Erwachsenenbildung." In J. Speck and G. Wehler (Eds.), *Handbuck Pädagogischer Grundbegriffe.* Munich: Kösel Verlag, 1970.

Statistical Data on the Publications of Yugoslavia, 1945–1964. Belgrade: Yugoslav Institute for Statistics, 1964. (In Serbo-Croatian.)

Storting Proposition No. 92 (1964–1965) on Adult Education: An Abridged Version. Oslo: Ministry of Church and Education, 1964.

Syracuse University "Agenda for Comparative Studies in Adult Education." Syracuse, N.Y.: Syracuse University Publications in Continuing Education, 1972.

Tickton, S. G. (Ed.). *To Improve Learning.* New York: Bowker, 1970.

Titmus, C. "Proposed Theoretical Model for the Comparative Study of National Adult Education Systems in Europe." *Society and Leisure,* 1976a, *8* (2).

Titmus, C. "Widening Access to University Adult Education in Europe." *ICAUE Journal,* November 1976b, *3.*

Tonkonogoj, E. P. (Ed.). *Teaching in the Evening Schools.* Moscow: Pedagogy, 1976. (In Russian.)

Turos, L. *Andragogy.* Warsaw: Panstwowe Wydawnictwi Naukowe, 1976. (In Polish.)

UNESCO. *Adult Education in Czechoslovakia.* Adult Education Division, UNESCO Documentation, Box II, n.d.

UNESCO. *World Conference of Ministers of Education on the Eradication of Illiteracy, Tehran 1965.* Final Report. Paris: UNESCO, 1965.

UNESCO. *Final Report of African Ministers of Education Conference.* Lagos, Nigeria, February 1976. Paris: UNESCO, 1976.

UNESCO. *Final Report of the Meeting of Experts of Post-Literacy in*

Africa. Dakar: Regional Office for Education in Africa, April 1977.

UNESCO-UNDP. *World Experimental Literacy Project*. Paris: UNESCO, 1975.

UNESCO-UNDP. *The Experimental World Literacy Programme (EWLP)*. A Critical Assessment. Paris: UNESCO, 1976.

Vath, R. "Die Professionalisierungstendenz in der Erwachsenenbildung." Unpublished doctoral dissertation, Regensburg, 1975.

Vollmer, H. M., and Mills, D. L. *Professionalization*. Englewood Cliffs, N.J.: Prentice-Hall, 1966.

Wehler, G. "Professionalisierung erzieherischer Berufe." Munich: Pädagogik Aktwell, 1973.

Weiss, W. W. "Zur Ausbildungssituation der Diplom-Pädagogen." *Zeitschrift für Pädagogen*, 1975, *4*, 547.

Winkler, G. *The Present State and Further Development of In-Service Training in GDR*. Leipzig: Karl Marx University of Leipzig, 1975.

World Bank. *Education* (Sector Working Paper). Washington, D.C.: World Bank, 1974.

Year Book of Adult Education. Leicester, England: National Institute of Adult Education (England and Wales).

Yousif, A. A. *The Origins and Development of University Adult Education in Ghana and Nigeria 1946–1966*. Friedrich Ebert Siftung, 1974.

Zigerell, J. J., and Chausow, H. M. *Chicago's TV College, A Fifth Report*. Chicago: City Colleges of Chicago, 1974.

"Zur Situation und Aufgabe der deutschen Erwachsenenbildung." 29.1.1960. In *Empfehlungen und Gutachten Gesamtausgabe*. Stuttgart: Klett-Verlag, 1966.

Name Index

Subject Index

Administrative coordination, 5; Asian country comparisons, 25–27. *See also* Centralization issues; Governments; Local control; Voluntary support

Adult education, 5, 20–21, 129–131; and development, 16–17, 19–20, 22–23; and literacy, 198–199; out-of-school forms of, 48–49, 51, 63; purposes of, 31–32; reform tendencies of, 97–98, 107–108; relation to educational systems of, 5–6, 9, 23–24, 32–33; socialist systems of, 39–46, 85–89; system determinants of, 39–40; terminology of, 2–3, 20–22. *See also* Comparative adult education (CAE); Development focus; Literacy programs; Professionalization; Resources and support; various countries (by name)

Adult Education, 122–123

Adult Education and Development, 122

Adult Education Association of the U.S.A., 9, 116, 121, 219

"Adult Education" conference at Elsinore, 1949, 243

"Adult Education in a Changing World" Montreal, 1960, 243–244

"Adult Education in the Context of Lifelong Learning" Tokyo, 1972, 244

Adult educators: recruitment of, 210–213; training of, 26, 141–142, 210–213; voluntary and professional, 27–28

Adult Leadership, 122–123

Adult learners, 4, 17; efforts to reach, 184–187, 192–195; functional illiterates, 178–179; illiterate, 176–179; literates without relevant skills, 179–182; motivation of, 142–144; well educated, lacking motivation and opportunity, 182–184

Adult pedagogy, Germany, 92–97

Africa, 123–124; illiteracy in, 176–177, 186; unskilled labor in, 179–182. *See also* various countries (by name)

African Adult Education Association, 110, 125–126

African Ministers of Education conference, 1976, 180, 193